The Challenge of Anti-Roma Politics

The Challenge of Anti-Roma Politics

Will Guy, editor

International Debate Education Association
New York, Brussels & Amsterdam

Published by
The International Debate Education Association
P.O. Box 922
New York, NY 10009

This book is published with the generous support of the Open Society Foundations.

Library of Congress Cataloging-in-Publication Data
The Challenge of Anti-Roma Politics / Will Guy, editor.
pages cm
ISBN 978-1-61770-096-5
1. Roma populations in European Union countries. 2. Extremism and xenophobia—Anti-Roma politics 3. European Union countries—Inclusion policies. Guy, Will, 1940–
JZ1570.D54 2014
341.242'2—dc23 2013042021

Composition by Brad Walrod/Kenoza Type, Inc.
Printed in the USA

Contents

Acknowledgments

This book would not have been possible without the support of Eleanora von Dehsen and Martin Greenwald at the Open Society Foundations. My thanks also go to my wife, Jackie West, for her patient tolerance of my work on this project over the past year.

Bristol, November 17, 2014
Will Guy

Introduction: The Challenge of Anti-Roma Politics

by Will Guy

Why a New Look at Roma Rights?

Since the 2002 publication by IDEA of *Roma Rights: Race, Justice, and Strategies for Equality*, the formal status of most European Roma has changed significantly, and yet the basic realities of their lives and the discrimination they suffer remain much the same. In fact, most commentators agree that, if anything, their situation has deteriorated in a context of widespread economic decline accompanied by a sharp upsurge of racism. This is particularly true of the region of Central and Eastern Europe, where most Roma live, and emphasizes the need for an updated picture.

European Union (EU) enlargement—with the accession as member states of eight Central and Eastern European countries in 2004 and two more in 2007—brought an estimated four million Roma into the community as EU citizens.[1] This has resulted in formidable new challenges for the EU, particularly for its executive arm—the European Commission (EC)—which, as yet, it has failed to meet.

This new anthology contains articles explaining the evolving political context of Roma policymaking and growing EU involvement, as well as essays covering the key areas of employment, education, housing, and health. Also included are contributions on the rise of anti-Gypsyism and attempts to combat this threat. The aim of IDEA is to prompt debate among concerned readers about what might be done to improve the situation of the Roma. But first it is necessary to explain something of the background to current conditions in Central and Eastern Europe.

The Paradox of the Revolutions of 1989

In 1989, the political geography of Central and Eastern Europe underwent a seismic shift. Following the end of the Second World War in 1945, the countries in this region were incorporated into the Soviet bloc, and for four decades afterward their politics were controlled by domestic Communist parties, but always under

1 Those with the largest Roma populations were the Czech Republic, Hungary, Poland, and Slovakia (2004 EU enlargement), and Bulgaria and Romania (2007 enlargement).

the watchful eye of the Soviet Union. Then, beginning in 1985, the liberalizing reforms of Soviet leader Mikhail Gorbachev precipitated economic, social, and political changes at home that helped bring about an end to both the Soviet Union and the Cold War. These reforms also included greater freedom for satellite countries, prompting their peoples to stage popular revolutions to overthrow Communist rule. These uprisings were mostly without bloodshed, apart from the violent disintegration of the former Yugoslavia.

At first, the democratic environments that emerged were greeted with widespread euphoria. The hated secret police had been abolished, and all could now express themselves freely. In place of previous austerity, Western-style prosperity was eagerly anticipated. These expectations were soon disappointed, however, as newly elected governments struggled to reorganize centralized administrations, draft fresh legislation, and restructure previous rigid command systems into flexible market economies. The often chaotic period of transition resulted in abrupt changes that dramatically affected people's everyday lives. Some—such as former Communist Party bureaucrats and managers—were able to take advantage of their cultural capital acquired during the Communist era and reinvent themselves as entrepreneurs, often amassing fortunes in the process. Meanwhile, many others—particularly unskilled workers in rust-belt industries or in agriculture—were thrown into unemployment and poverty as inefficient factories were closed and agricultural land was returned to former owners. Within a few years, the mood of optimism had been replaced by feelings of apprehension and resentment as victims of these transformations sought explanations for their thwarted hopes.

Among the biggest losers were the Roma populations of Central and Eastern Europe. Although some Roma bitterly resented spasmodic attempts to assimilate them, many felt they had made real gains during the period of Communist rule. Roma had been recruited in large numbers to the mainstream labor force for the first time in their history—although overwhelmingly as unskilled laborers. Before World War II they had mostly scraped a hand-to-mouth living as casual petty craftsmen where they lived apart from the majority population, in either all-Roma urban quarters or segregated rural villages. Although there were exceptions, the dark-skinned Roma were generally reviled as a primitive and uncultured minority, fit only to provide basic services to their white "superiors" for token rewards. While Roma were not slaves,[2] in essence their situation bore many resemblances to that of African Americans in the southern United States. During the 1930s, when fascism was spreading throughout Central and Eastern Europe, interethnic tensions could escalate into sporadic pogroms. However, such incidents were

2 However, they had formerly been slaves in part of present-day Romania (p. 11).

eclipsed by the tragic events of the Second World War. The Nazis placed Roma high on their list of undesirable groups to be eliminated, and an estimated half million perished in the concentration camps.[3]

The experience of the large Roma populations of Central and Eastern Europe under Communist rule was mixed, and commentators and Roma alike still disagree strongly about how it should be characterized. In 1979, the Czechoslovak dissident human rights group Charter 77 published a fierce condemnation of Communist policy toward Roma.[4] It accused governments of denying the ethnic identity of Roma and withholding national minority status in seeking to assimilate them, whatever their own wishes. It also criticized the intermittent sterilization of Roma women, either under pressure, bribed by cash rewards, or without their knowledge during childbirth or other operations. In the later years of these regimes, as centralized Communist Party control weakened, residential and educational segregation increased in some areas because of prejudice at the local level.

A major point of contention among Roma and commentators is the effect of Communist regime policies on Roma employment. Charter 77 charged that Communist governments had intentionally proletarianized the Roma by using them as a reserve pool of cheap, unskilled labor. While the labor-hungry industries of the Soviet bloc needed such workers, the human rights group predicted that Roma laborers would be extremely vulnerable should these economies modernize in the future. An alternative perspective saw Roma as migrant workers, moving with their families to areas with relatively better-paid jobs not requiring educational qualifications as a first step on the ladder to fuller integration—a common pattern in more advanced Western economies. Indeed, over the years, many Roma did acquire skills and seek better education for their children, but these upwardly mobile families formed only a small percentage of Roma populations. Consequently, for the vast majority of Roma, Charter 77's bleak prediction was fulfilled.

The Post-Communist World and the Roma

Some Roma leaders welcomed the end of Communist rule, proclaiming: "The day our ancestors have awaited for many years has arrived. For the first time Roma...can take their fate into their own hands."[5] Such views soon proved overoptimistic, for although Roma were now recognized as national or ethnic

3 Kenrick and Puxon, *Destiny of Europe's Gypsies*.

4 For more on the Charter 77 report, see Guy, "Czech Lands and Slovakia," 292–293.

5 Davidová, *Romano Drom/Cesty Romů*, 220.

minorities, and in places even gained some representation in parliament, the hard reality for most was a steep decline in living standards as unemployment levels swiftly rose. Racial discrimination had always been present during the Communist era, although usually officially ignored. But with freedom of speech, majority populations were now uninhibited in voicing resentment against Roma forced to subsist on welfare benefits, whom they regarded as an undeserving drain on their own resources. Neo-Nazi skinhead groups emerged to daub racist graffiti on walls, chant "Gypsies to the gas chambers," and make sporadic attacks on Roma individuals and families. In one such attack a six year-old Romany boy was strangled in a playground by a skinhead using a cable. Rather than expressing outrage at these incidents, most non-Roma remained silent in tacit acquiescence if not approval, and far-right groups were shown to have sympathizers and even members among police forces.

In a climate of pervasive dread, growing numbers of Roma decided to move to the West, adding to the Roma refugees who had fled the wars of secession in former Yugoslavia. Fear was not the only reason for Roma to leave their home countries. Communist regimes had always prevented their citizens from traveling freely outside the Soviet bloc, believing that they would not return. With regime change, these restrictions vanished, and many people traveled westward seeking better work opportunities and higher earnings. Among them were similarly motivated Roma who attracted a level of media and political controversy out of all proportion to their relatively low numbers. Untypically for migrants from the region, they traveled not singly but as entire families. More significantly, unlike their non-Roma fellow countrymen, they frequently claimed asylum as victims of racism.

EU Enlargement

The fledgling, post-Communist governments of the former Soviet bloc viewed Russia as a military and economic threat and consequently sought security in membership of both the North Atlantic Treaty Organization (NATO) and the EU. Their desire for protection matched expansionist ambitions within the EU to push its boundaries eastward. After preliminary requirements for candidate countries had been set in 1993, negotiations began in earnest from 1997 onward. Embarrassingly for some candidate countries and existing EU members, these talks coincided with waves of Czech, Slovak, and Hungarian Roma arriving as asylum seekers, notably in the United Kingdom and Canada. Roma claims of discrimination in their homelands raised awkward political questions, since respect for minorities had been set as a condition for EU accession.

Even though the numbers of Roma arriving in the United Kingdom in 1997 and 1998 were a small fraction of all those claiming refugee status, the media described them in terms such as "invasion" and "tidal wave."[6] In spite of ample evidence that Roma were vulnerable targets for racists in their homelands, they were immediately accused of immigrating solely in hope of receiving generous social support and branded as "welfare spongers" and "bogus asylum seekers." Meanwhile, the UK government took the view that its overall aim of minimizing immigration took precedence over alleged human rights abuses. Therefore, it imposed visa controls, allowing screening and refusal of unwanted visitors in advance, as in the case of potential Roma immigrants from Slovakia. Alternatively, it declared the candidate country as "safe," on the grounds that formal legal procedures existed there for dealing with complaints, as it did for Roma immigrants from the Czech Republic. This second option enabled almost automatic rejection of any claims or appeals by Roma asylum seekers. Other Western European countries adopted similar approaches to repel or return would-be Roma immigrants.[7]

Throughout the period of accession negotiations, the EU urged applicants for membership to introduce antidiscrimination legislation and take action to improve the employment, education, housing, and health of their Roma populations. Candidate countries were required to undertake specific projects that were partly funded by the EU and scrutinized by the EC's enlargement division. It was hoped that if their conditions at home could be improved, fewer Roma would travel abroad. Since freedom of movement is one of the basic principles of the EU, Roma migration could not be prevented once their home countries had gained entry.

Nevertheless, progress was slow, and although EU annual reports on the preparation of candidate states strongly criticized shortcomings in integrating Roma, the ultimate sanction of withholding membership was not applied. Evidently the overriding priority was the grand narrative of enlargement. Accordingly, the May 2004 enlargement included the Czech Republic, Hungary, Poland, and Slovakia, while Bulgaria and Romania followed in January 2007. One argument in favor of allowing EU enlargement to take place as planned, in spite of the manifest failure of applicants to meet the entry requirements with respect to their Roma

6 Guy, "'No Soft Touch,'" 64.

7 Canada was initially an exception, granting asylum to a significant proportion of Czech and Hungarian Roma despite hostile media coverage similar to that in the UK. This sympathetic stance was soon reversed as visa controls were imposed on both the Czech Republic and Hungary. For a fuller discussion of Western governments' handling of Roma asylum seekers see Guy, "'No Soft Touch,'" 63–79.

inhabitants, had been that membership would allow these countries access to greatly increased funding to improve living conditions.

Among these new EU citizens were an estimated four million Roma,[8] the great majority still marginalized, impoverished, and living in segregated, unhygienic environments. Attention was drawn to their predicament by a series of comparative surveys by international NGOs from 2000 onward.[9] These stark reports coincided with the EU giving greater priority to social inclusion following its adoption in 2000 of the Lisbon Strategy, which aimed to make a decisive impact on eradicating poverty by 2010.

In 2000 the EU Charter of Fundamental Rights also was proclaimed, and the Racial Equality Directive adopted. Enlargement, therefore, offered new opportunities to counter the deteriorating situation of Roma communities using the new antidiscrimination legislation and the substantial resources of EU structural funds under the guidance of the EC's division for employment, social affairs, and equal opportunities. Shortly afterward, a World Bank/Open Society Institute initiative—the Decade of Roma Inclusion (2005–2015)—encouraged greater commitment from Central and Eastern European governments to improve Roma socioeconomic status. At the launch, eight former Communist-ruled states[10] pledged to adopt national action plans with measurable targets and indicators and to monitor progress on a regular basis.

The Anthology

The preceding paragraphs explain the historical context to the current situation of Roma in Central and Eastern Europe and are followed by brief descriptions of the substantive articles in this anthology. Following Valeriu Nicolae's shocking account of everyday life in a Romanian ghetto, the next two parts of the anthology examine the increasingly important role of the European Union and the main areas in which it seeks to make improvements. Disturbingly, the EU's policy and practical initiatives are taking place against a backdrop of mounting intolerance and outright anti-Roma racism. Articles in part 4 chronicle both the

8 In September 2010, Council of Europe average estimates of Roma populations in Bulgaria, the Czech Republic, Hungary, Poland, Romania, and Slovakia totaled four million, two-thirds of the EU average total. See statistics at www.coe.int/t/dg3/romatravellers/default_en.asp.

9 The most influential of these were Ringold, *Roma and the Transition in Central and Eastern Europe*; Ringold, Orenstein, and Wilkens, *Roma in an Expanding Europe*; United Nations Development Programme, *Roma in Central and Eastern Europe*; and United Nations Development Programme, *Faces of Poverty, Faces of Hope*.

10 Bulgaria, Croatia, the Czech Republic, Hungary, Macedonia (FYROM), Romania, Serbia and Montenegro, and Slovakia.

hostile environment and attempts to counteract alarming developments. The final part offers encouragement by demonstrating that entrenched and institutionalized racist discrimination can be overcome by determined perseverance.

The Pivotal Role of the European Union

In "The European Union and the Roma," Peter Vermeersch presents a comprehensive overview of EU involvement, "offering a contextualised exploration of the current landscape of institutions and policies of relevance to the Roma."[11] Policy development is seen in relation not only to the dynamics of European integration but to momentous events such as intra-EU Roma migration and the ensuing reactions, as well as the upsurge of anti-Roma hate speech, populist demonstrations, and racist attacks. EU-funded initiatives are reviewed and outcomes discussed.

Vermeersch emphasizes the significant impact of Romanian and Bulgarian Roma migration to Italy and France following the 2007 accession of their countries to the EU. In Italy, Roma migration led to intercommunal clashes, the bulldozing of shantytowns on the outskirts of Italian cities, and, in March 2008, the proclamation of an emergency decree. These reactions prompted sharp criticism from the EC and led the European Council of Ministers, the EU's highest political body, to require the commission to report back within six months on progress in achieving Roma inclusion. In 2010, mass expulsion of Roma migrants from France triggered a furious row between Vice President and Justice Commissioner Viviane Reding and the then French president, Nicolas Sarkozy—an unprecedented confrontation between an EU founder state and the EC.

These high-profile clashes and the prospect of continuing migration of Roma from some of the poorest countries in the east to their more prosperous fellow member states in the west sharply increased pressure on the EC to take action. Civil society NGOs united to form the European Roma Policy Coalition (ERPC) and joined the European Parliament in demanding a more proactive EU-wide approach to inclusion.[12] Eventually the previously reluctant EC adopted the Framework for National Roma Inclusion Strategies in 2011,[13] while insisting its role was supervisory and that ultimate responsibility remained with member states.

11 Vermeersch, "European Union and the Roma," 2011, 342.

12 European Parliament, *Resolution on a European Strategy on the Roma*, §6.

13 See European Commission, *Working Together for Roma Inclusion*, for a fuller explanation of the framework.

The EU made substantial structural funds available to member states for improving the situation of their Roma inhabitants, but take-up had been and remains poor. For example, by late 2010, Romania had absorbed less than 1 percent of the nearly 4 billion euros it was eligible to draw from the European Social Fund from 2007 up to 2013. Consequently it was liable to lose this funding if it did not use it.[14] In view of the disappointing results, the ERPC concluded that the majority of strategies were weak, not implemented, and failed to deliver inclusion. Meanwhile it complained that Roma were still suffering systematic racism and discrimination within the EU.[15]

Even when such funding was used, it was often hard or even impossible to discover if Roma really were the beneficiaries or whether money had been diverted elsewhere.[16] Some activists report that remittances from Romanian migrants working in Western Europe have done far more to transform Roma communities in Romania than any EU-funded inclusion project. Lack of evident progress—even where funds have been utilized—is one reason why Roma activist Valeriu Nicolae brands EU initiatives as failures and demands a retrospective independent review of the EC's actions.[17] Another is his accusation that exclusion of Roma from decision-making processes amounts to structural racism. This failure to engage with Roma drew sharp criticism not only from the ERPC but also from a broad-based EU consultative body, the European Economic and Social Committee: "The old paternalist approach under which processes were defined by majority opinion-formers and decision-makers in society must be changed, and the Roma must be recognised and accepted as responsible members of society, able and willing to actively shape their own future."[18]

Replying to Nicolae in "The EU's Roma Role," Martin Kovats—then special adviser on Roma issues to the EU's employment commissioner—points out that the EU "lacks the moral, legal or political authority to compel a state and society that is not yet willing to take the necessary steps to ensure that their Roma citizens enjoy equality of opportunity in every respect."[19] Crucially, he identifies where the real power lies, saying "political authority lies with the Council and not the Commission, meaning that any serious criticism of a government's treatment of its Roma citizens must emanate from other member states."[20] And

14 Pignal and Bryant, "Brussels Struggles to Address Roma Issue."
15 European Roma Policy Coalition, "ERPC Welcomes New Council Recommendation on Roma."
16 United Nations Development Programme, *Uncertain Impact*.
17 Nicolae, "Systemic Reform Is Urgently Needed."
18 European Economic and Social Committee, *Opinion*, §4.11.
19 Kovats, "EU's Roma Role," 2012.
20 Ibid.

yet he qualifies this statement as he concludes: "The Commission will... need to become bolder and more sophisticated in how it deploys its legal powers."[21] This ambiguous formulation acknowledges the gulf between *realpolitik* and formal legality. The Racial Equality Directive is an EU law potentially empowering the European Commission to take action against discrimination in individual member states. In practice, the European Council—composed of heads of state—would be unwilling to see the autonomy of individual states jeopardized in this way.[22]

EU Target Areas for Action

This paradox is even more striking when the main EU target areas for action are examined. Blatant cases of inequality and anti-Roma discrimination in employment, education, housing, and health are standard, everyday practice in many countries. Yet there are also examples of good practice. Accordingly, the next section of the anthology looks at these key areas in more detail.

Employment

Ann [Morton] Hyde's article "Systemic Exclusion of Roma from Employment," based on her 2007 research report for the European Roma Rights Centre (ERRC) on Roma employment in Bulgaria, the Czech Republic, Hungary, and Slovakia,[23] demonstrates that discrimination against Roma in the labor market is widespread. She finds that this behavior is based on prejudicial views that "unemployment and worklessness is a situation that most, if not all, Roma have chosen and are happy to live with both now and in the past."[24]

Education

Education is vital, since this affects future life chances and is crucial for finding regular and adequately paid employment. A significant factor in the lower school attendance and poorer qualifications for Roma has been educational segregation of Roma children from their non-Roma peers, particularly in Central and Eastern Europe. As in the United States, the leading role in combating such discrimination has been taken not by government but by civil society. An interview with

21 Ibid.

22 See Guy, "EU Initiatives on Roma," 42–46.

23 European Roma Rights Centre (ERRC), *Glass Box*, 2007.

24 Hyde, "Systemic Exclusion of Roma," 2006.

prominent Roma activist Rumyan Russinov[25] charts the long struggle of Roma NGOs to promote educational desegregation in Bulgaria.

Housing

As in the sector of education, little progress has been made in housing over the past few decades. If anything, residential segregation has increased, especially in Central and Eastern Europe. For example, some municipal authorities in the Czech Republic have collaborated with real estate developers to gentrify desirable town center sites by removing Roma residents and relocating them to substandard accommodation in peripheral ghettos.[26] Meanwhile, migrating Romanian and Bulgarian Roma, some of whom had previously lived alongside non-Roma in their home countries, established new shantytowns in Italian and French cities.

As Will Guy reports in "Municipal Programme of Shanty Towns Eradication in Avilés," Spain has proved an exception, with central, regional, and municipal governments sometimes cooperating with NGOs to eradicate Roma ghettos by offering families new housing among the majority population.[27] In Ann [Morton] Hyde's article "Roma Inclusion: Can Cities Be the Drivers of Change?,"[28] civil society partners in the Roma-NeT consortium seek similar solutions in the cities of older and newer member states. They focus not solely on housing issues but also on employment and social support. This approach recognizes that these problem areas are interlinked and need to be tackled together. It also emphasizes that stakeholder cooperation at the local level is crucial. Working with mediators, Roma-NeT partners utilize the active participation of Roma communities.

Health

The most striking aspect of the health status of Roma is their shorter life expectancy—at least ten years less than national average levels for both women and men in Central and Eastern Europe. Likewise, infant mortality rates for Roma in this region are between two to six times higher than for the general population. Access to health care services is limited, sometimes related to the absence of health insurance. In "Health and the Roma Community,"[29] Ilona Tomova

25 Rostas et al., "Interview with Rumyan Russinov," 2012.

26 Baršová, "Housing Problems of Ethnic Minorities," 11–37.

27 Guy, "Discussion Paper," annex 3, 26–28. See also European Commission, "Peer Review—Short Report."

28 Hyde, "Roma Inclusion," 2012.

29 Tomova, "Health and the Roma Community," 2009, 97–107.

paints a bleak picture of the situation in Bulgaria, where economic decline has led to a deterioration of the health system. Low wages for health professionals have driven many to seek better-paid employment in more prosperous EU countries. Diminishing resources have most affected the impoverished Roma population, especially women, who are doubly marginalized, as Valeriu Nicolae's article points out, and the most vulnerable group of all—the children.

The Rising Tide of Anti-Gypsyism

"Anti-Gypsyism"—hostility, prejudice, or discrimination usually based on racist stereotypes and directed at the Romani people—has been present in Europe since their first arrival. Distinguishable by their darker skins, ways of making a living, and non-European language, Roma have always been seen as strange outsiders in spite of having dwelt in European countries for more than six centuries. Roma have been feared as fortune-tellers with supernatural powers, foreign spies, thieves, and child kidnappers.[30]

Over the centuries, states responded differently to Roma presence. In Western Europe, Roma were regarded as worthless irritants, and periodic attempts were made to expel them and at times to execute them. In contrast, in the less-developed economies of Central and Eastern Europe, they were viewed as a source of potential labor—as they were later by Communist regimes. The Habsburg Empire made systematic attempts to enserf them, while in the Romanian provinces of Moldavia and Wallachia they were enslaved for six centuries until the mid-nineteenth century, as the eminent Roma sociologist Nicolae Gheorghe, himself the descendant of slaves, recounts in "Choices to Be Made and Prices to Be Paid."[31]

While overt anti-Roma racism was subdued during the Communist era, populist expression of resentment soon emerged in its aftermath. Results of public opinion polls consistently showed that Roma were the most despised group, with one Hungarian survey finding that 60 percent of respondents believed that the "inclination to criminality is in the blood of gypsies."[32] In the post-Communist world, a new stereotype of Roma as an undeserving yet protected and specially privileged group has assumed a dominant role in fueling racist hatred in Central and Eastern Europe. Furthermore, ultra-right-wing political parties throughout the region are able to capitalize on such popular perceptions. They criticize the

30 See Fraser, *Gypsies*, for a comprehensive account of Roma history.

31 Gheorghe, "Choices to Be Made," 2013, 53–56.

32 Bernát et al., "Roots of Radicalism."

EU policy of funding Roma inclusion projects and build support by holding marches, often while dressed in paramilitary uniforms, "to defend non-Roma citizens" in sensitive locations where there have been incidents of interethnic clashes.

Not just extremist parties but also mainstream politicians have exploited widespread anti-Roma feeling. A Czech mayor, Jiří Čunek, was elected to the Senate with an overwhelming majority after having evicted Roma families from the town center and rehousing them in porta-cabins. He characterized the Roma as "maladjusted" and described his actions as "the removal of an ulcer."[33] He went on to become leader of the Christian Democratic Party and deputy prime minister in a coalition government but later resigned after accusations he had accepted a bribe and had fraudulently accepted government social assistance payments.[34] In 2012 he was reelected to the Senate and, implausibly, was elected chair of the Senate Subcommittee on Human Rights and Equal Opportunities.[35] In Hungary, a founder member of the ruling Fidesz Party and close friend of the prime minister wrote in a newspaper with close ties to the government that "a significant portion of the Gypsies are unfit for coexistence, not fit to live among human beings. These people are animals and behave like animals." There was no attempt to expel him from the party, and the newspaper defended his right to free speech.[36] More moderate politicians have also attempted to win votes by cynically moving into the space created by extremist discourse, decrying a culture of welfare dependency as a coded way of blaming Roma.

Meanwhile, assaults—sometimes lethal—on Roma individuals and families have increased. In Slovakia, a gunman murdered six members of a Roma family, including a twelve-year-old boy, in 2010.[37] Two years later, an off-duty Slovak policeman killed three members of a Roma family and seriously wounded two others. He was sentenced to only nine years imprisonment.[38] Later that year, a Roma man was decapitated while still alive after an argument with three Slovaks, who then threw his head and body into a cesspit.[39] In 2008 and 2009, a group of four Hungarians carried out twenty attacks in nine small towns, including the murder in their homes of six Roma. In one case, a family house was set on fire

33 Asiedu, "Are the Deputy Prime Minister's Offensive Remarks about the Roma Influencing Ordinary Citizens?"

34 Johnston, "Deputy PM Jiří Čunek Resigns"; ČTK, "Czech Deputy PM Čunek Saved Millions, but Lived on Welfare."

35 Balážová, "Czech Senator Čunek Chairing Senate Subcommittee."

36 Gall, "Hungary's Alarming Climate of Intolerance."

37 Bilefsky, "Killing Spree in Slovakia."

38 ERRC, "One Year on from Roma Deaths."

39 Romea, "Slovakia: Romani Man Decapitated."

and the Roma inhabitants, including a five-year-old child, were shot as they fled.[40] After protracted delays linked to police reluctance to investigate, the perpetrators were eventually sentenced to imprisonment in 2013.

In "Killing Time: The Lethal Force of Anti-Roma Racism,"[41] Bernard Rorke details a number of savage killings of Roma in Slovakia, the Czech Republic, and Romania that occurred within the short space of six months, while emphasizing that such crimes do not occur in a vacuum. As the former Council of Europe commissioner for human rights recognized, the prevalent anti-Roma rhetoric of prominent politicians and the media is interpreted by extremists as a direct call for radical and violent action.

The deteriorating atmosphere in Hungary prompted a new wave of asylum seekers. In 2007, twenty-four Hungarian Roma had claimed refugee status in Canada, but in 2011 their numbers had risen to forty-five hundred—more than any other group.

Roma and Pro-Roma Activism: The Options

To counter the surge of hate speech and crimes in Central and Eastern Europe, Roma and pro-Roma activists have adopted different strategies. Some, like the university-based lawyer András Pap, have sought to analyze the political and legal obstacles preventing effective action to reverse these negative trends. In "Dogmatism, Hypocrisy and the Inadequacy of Legal and Social Responses Combating Hate Crimes and Extremism: The CEE Experience,"[42] he focuses on the situation in Hungary, where previous Social Democratic Party initiatives had been among the most progressive in the region in pursuing Roma inclusion. These have since been replaced by the retrogressive, right-wing Fidesz government, with the populist, vehemently anti-Roma Jobbik Party waiting in the wings. Yet the reluctance of all governments of the region to lose support by appearing to favor their Roma populations is only too evident.

In "Options of Roma Political Participation and Representation,"[43] Márton Rövid outlines the range of political options available to Roma and their potential for effective mobilization, examining actual and potential participation and representation of Roma at both the national and international levels. He reviews the main discourses of Roma and pro-Roma activists, charting the shift from

40 See Kaltenbach and Twigg, "Spoken Today, Committed Tomorrow."

41 Rorke, "Killing Time," 2011.

42 Pap, "Dogmatism, Hypocrisy," 2012.

43 Rövid, "Options of Roma Political Participation," 2013.

claims for self-determination in the 1970s, to a focus on human rights violations in the 1990s and early 2000s, and then to an emphasis on social and economic integration of Roma from the late 2000s. Rövid argues that the current approach has developed from criticism that self-determination can risk exclusion, while prioritizing human rights can neglect economic and social issues. However, as he points out, advocating the cause of impoverished Roma can reinforce negative stereotypes while ignoring the existence of a significant minority of educated and employed Roma.

As a long-term Roma activist, Nicolae Gheorghe has pursued some of the options charted by Rövid. Like him, Gheorghe, in "Choices to Be Made and Prices to Be Paid,"[44] also identifies a specific problem in Roma political mobilization—the social gulf between the narrow stratum of educated Roma, numbers of whom are employed by NGOs, and the vast majority living in Roma communities with high rates of unemployment and impoverishment. The right of this intelligentsia to speak on behalf of grassroots Roma is frequently contested by more traditional self-proclaimed "leaders," whose support is generally drawn from kinship networks.

Gheorghe claims that the position of extremists has been strengthened by the self-censorship of his fellow activists, reluctant to acknowledge publicly certain unpleasant facts. For reasons of political correctness, they remain silent about the reprehensible behavior of some Roma, fearing to provide ammunition for racists. He argues instead that Roma themselves should openly condemn those engaged in trafficking and exploiting Roma, as well as certain practices often defended as part of "traditional Romani culture." These include the subordination of women, underage marriages, and the cheating of *gadje* (non-Roma). As a repressed minority, throughout the centuries Roma have developed protective strategies for survival, but these are now counterproductive in an era when EU and UN bodies are actively promoting Roma inclusion. Consequently, he advocates seeking ways of cooperation between Roma activists and non-Roma rather than confrontation. He even justifies entering into discussion with racists, saying that this is not the same as legitimating them.

Gwendolyn Albert dismisses this suggestion as futile. In "Is There Any Point in Dialogue with Extremists?," she maintains that the "ultra-right in Europe is not interested in dialogue with the objects of their contempt."[45]

Dismayed by evidence that the tactics of far-right groupings are gaining wider popular support, Romea—a prominent pro-Roma Czech NGO—makes

44 Gheorghe, "Choices to Be Made," 2013.

45 Albert, "Is There Any Point in Dialogue with Extremists?," 2013, 169.

an impassioned appeal in "Open Letter to the Non-Extremist Anti-Romani Demonstrators in the Czech Republic"[46] for a debate with non-extremist citizens, who have nevertheless participated in anti-Roma marches.

In the final article of Part 4, "Why I Quit,"[47] award-winning Roma activist Valeriu Nicolae explains the extreme frustration with the systemic weaknesses and bureaucratic obstacles that led him to resign from the NGO he had created. In particular, he shows how Roma organizations are forced by structural pressures to conform to the agenda and wishes of the sponsors who fund them. In an increasingly neoliberal world, this frequently turns them into outsourced and underfunded providers of services that formerly were the responsibility of local or national authorities to supply. This increases the marginality of Roma communities by differentiating their treatment from that of mainstream society and diverts these NGOs from advocating the right of Roma to be treated equally as they struggle to maintain their funding streams.

Postscript: What Is to Be Done?

This anthology has ended on a bleak note, with the EU and international organizations urging countries to take more positive action to fulfill their plans for Roma inclusion. Meanwhile, reluctant governments, fearful of losing votes by introducing unpopular measures, drag their feet in implementing what they have already agreed on paper. The resulting lack of meaningful progress leads to more urgent exhortations to little effect. Indeed, this has been the sadly familiar story both before and after EU enlargement. Nevertheless, Roma activists, often working together with sympathetic local authorities, have managed to achieve limited improvements, but invariably in isolated cases that have proved difficult to replicate and extend to programs at the national level. The slow rate of change has not been sufficient to counter the growing scale of fundamental problems—not entirely unrelated to the still relatively high birthrate among Roma populations.

There was a moment of optimism at the turn of the millennium when governments and local authorities in Spain, working with the Fundación Secretariado Gitano—a national Roma NGO supported by the Catholic Church—were the first to draw on EU structural funds and supplement these with national taxes for charitable purposes. This enabled real progress to be made in residential and educational desegregation as well as in access to health care and even in the intractable area of employment. EU enlargement enabled Spanish expertise to

46 Romea, "Open Letter," 2013.
47 Nicolae,"Why I Quit," 2013.

be made available to the new member states of Central and Eastern Europe with initiatives backed by structural funds. But now, after several years of economic recession and with xenophobia on the rise, prospects for improvement appear far less promising.

Especially in Central and Eastern Europe, many grassroots Roma have responded to their situation in two ways quite unrelated to EU or government plans for their inclusion. The first—emigration—is mentioned in several articles in this anthology. Some activists have even suggested that Roma emigration to Western Europe should be used as a weapon to force the EU to make dramatic improvements in their conditions. Many ordinary Roma have concluded that they, and particularly their children, will have much better life chances in the west. A 2010 report found that children of Czech and Slovak Roma emigrants to the United Kingdom, who in their homelands had been unjustifiably consigned to "special schools" for those with learning difficulties, had caught up with the performance of their British peers within a few years.[48] At the same time, their parents have welcomed the anonymity they enjoy in multicultural British cities compared with their conspicuousness in the overwhelmingly white populations of Central and Eastern Europe.

The other response is equally important but is not mentioned in the anthology. This is to seek refuge in religion. One means of evading an intolerable situation is to reframe it by changing one's mind-set, and various studies have noted the rapid spread of Pentecostalism among Roma throughout Europe in both East and West. For these converts, ethnic identity is irrelevant, since the crucial distinction is whether people are saved or damned, and Pentecostal church congregations can include both Roma and non-Roma. Yet while religion can comfort the faithful with future salvation, in this world, employment and living conditions remain problematic. Nevertheless, religious conversion has brought about greater solidarity in Pentecostal Roma neighborhoods, as well as striking changes in behavior, such as refraining from alcohol and gambling. Sometimes there has also been cooperation between non-Roma and Roma in community ventures such as infrastructure improvements.[49]

Yet both these responses by grassroots Roma might be seen as admissions of defeat as they evade the main issue. Why have the combined efforts of the EU and its member states—new and old—with initial pre-accession financial support and then ample structural funds at their disposal, failed to make any significant

48 Fremlová, *From Segregation to Inclusion*.

49 For a vivid account of the impact of Pentecostalism in a Romanian Roma community see Ries, "'I Must Love Them with All My Heart.'"

impact in improving conditions for most Roma over a period of fifteen years? And, put another way: How is it that their situation has actually worsened in certain crucial respects since 1989?

OSCE ambassador Janez Lenarčič saw "a lack of political will, both at national and local levels," as the main challenge.[50] Another way of explaining the apparent lack of interest of some Central and Eastern European governments is that industrializing Communist command economies needed unskilled Roma workers; emerging market economies did not.[51] Martin Kovats made a similar point, that nowadays—in a divisive neoliberal climate—the poor and unskilled are redundant and marginalized. The aim is not to invest in them but to contain them.[52] Nevertheless, the World Bank sees this neglect by CEE states as self-harm, estimating the economic costs of Roma social exclusion in terms of lost productivity and fiscal contributions as billions of euros annually in the context of declining and aging majority populations.[53]

The unanimous acceptance on December 9, 2013, by the European Council of Ministers of the *Council Recommendation on Effective Roma Integration Measures in the Member States* might represent a decisive step forward.[54] Yet, although this has been described as the first EU-level legal instrument for Roma inclusion where member states commit to taking targeted action to bridge the gaps between the Roma and the rest of the population,[55] the purpose of this recommendation is to provide guidance to member states.[56] Therefore, in spite of being seen as a legal instrument, it is "not legally binding."[57]

Cynics might say that this is just more of the same. While welcoming the council's statement, the European Roma Policy Coalition pointed out sharply: "The Commission however continues to remain inactive when it comes to implementing the legal tools (infringement proceedings) at its disposal to hold member states accountable."[58,59] Likewise, the EU's Economic and Social Committee

50 Lenarčič, *Report by Ambassador Janez Lenarčič*, 8.

51 Guy, "Romani Identity."

52 Kovats, "Roma Participation."

53 See World Bank, *Economic Costs of Roma Exclusion*. Costs are estimated for Bulgaria, the Czech Republic, Romania, and Serbia.

54 European Council, *Proposal for a Council Recommendation*.

55 EURoma, "Council Adopts Recommendation."

56 European Council, *Proposal for a Council Recommendation*, 5.

57 EURoma.

58 European Roma Policy Coalition, *ERPC Welcomes New Council Recommendation*.

59 For example a brief fact sheet issued by the EU's Fundamental Rights Agency emphasizes the obligations of member states to combat mounting levels of racially motivated crime—crime directed above all at Roma. See http://fra.europa.eu/sites/default/files/fra-factsheet_hatecrime_en_final_0.pdf.

rejected the European Council's aversion to direct intervention and proposed instead that "the Council should make use of its power to adopt legally binding acts."[60]

Though the past record of the EU and its member states hardly inspires confidence, a more realistic stance to adopt might be the "pessimism of the intellect but optimism of the will" advocated by the Italian political theorist Antonio Gramsci. In spite of a deteriorating political situation, he continued to believe that severe difficulties could be overcome by committed human endeavor. And in an age when, against all the odds, both Nelson Mandela and Barack Obama became the first black presidents of their countries, we should persevere with optimism of the will when campaigning for future advances in the treatment of Roma people. In fact, when he was introduced in 1990 to Juan de Dios Ramírez-Heredia—the first Roma member of the European Parliament in Strasbourg—Nelson Mandela was well aware of the plight of the Roma and encouraged him, saying, "Continue fighting to defend those ideals because in the end you will be victorious."[61]

As an afterword, therefore, the anthology concludes with an extract from "What Is to Be Done?" by Jack Greenberg.[62] While this extract deals exclusively with Roma school segregation, his forthright approach is applicable to every policy area concerning Roma. Jack Greenberg was part of the legal team that won *Brown v. Board of Education*, the 1954 landmark case before the Supreme Court that brought about the end of legal segregated public education in the United States, demonstrating that the seeming impossible can be possible after all.

References

Albert, Gwendolyn. "Is There Any Point in Dialogue with Extremists?" In *From Victimhood to Citizenship: The Path of Roma Integration—a Debate*, edited by Will Guy, 169. Budapest: Kossuth Publishing Corp./Pakiv European Roma Fund, 2013.

Asiedu, Dita. "Are the Deputy Prime Minister's Offensive Remarks about the Roma Influencing Ordinary Citizens?" Radio Prague, April 8, 2007. http://www.radio.cz/en/section/letter/are-the-deputy-prime-ministers-offensive-remarks-about-the-roma-influencing-ordinary-citizens.

Balážová, Jarmila. "Czech Senator Čunek Chairing Senate Subcommittee on Human Rights." Romea.cz, December 10, 2012. http://www.romea.cz/en/news/czech/czech-senator-cunek-chairing-senate-subcommittee-on-human-rights.

Baršová, Andrea. "Housing Problems of Ethnic Minorities and Trends Toward Residential Segregation in the Czech Republic." In *Romany in the Town*, edited by Gabriela Rösnerová, 11–37. Prague: Socioklub/UNHCR, 2003.

60 European Economic and Social Committee, *Opinion*, §§3.6 and 3.7.

61 Ramírez-Heredia, *The Day Nelson Mandela Inspired Us*.

62 Greenberg, "Report on Roma Education Today."

Bernát, Anikó, Attila Juhász, Péter Krekó, and Csaba Molnár. "The Roots of Radicalism and Anti-Roma Attitudes on the Far Right" (based on TARKI poll, 2011). *TARKI News*, March 5, 2013. http://www.tarki.hu/en/news/2013/items/20130305_bernat_juhasz_kreko_molnar.pdf.

Bilefsky, Dan. "Killing Spree in Slovakia Taps into a Troubled Vein." *New York Times*, September 2, 2010. http://www.nytimes.com/2010/09/03/world/europe/03iht-slovakia.html?_r=0.

ČTK (Czech Press Agency). "Czech Deputy PM Čunek Saved Millions, but Lived on Welfare." Romea, October 29, 2007. http://www.romea.cz/en/news/czech/czech-deputy-pm-cunek-saved-millions-but-lived-on-welfare-ct.

Davidová, Eva. *Romano Drom/Cesty Romů 1945–1990* [Romani Roads]. Olomouc: Univerzita Palackého, 1995.

European Roma Rights Centre. *The Glass Box: Exclusion of Roma from Employment*. Budapest: European Roma Rights Centre, 2007. http://www.errc.org/article/the-glass-box-exclusion-of-roma-from-employment/2727.

———. "One Year on from Roma Deaths, ERRC Highlights Low Sentence for Mass Murderer in Slovakia." ERRC News. Budapest: ERRC, June 17, 2013. http://www.errc.org/article/one-year-on-from-roma-deaths-errc-highlights-low-sentence-for-mass-murderer-in-slovakia/4150.

EURoma. *The Council Adopts Recommendation to Step Up the Economic and Social Integration of Roma Communities*. EURoma, December 9, 2013. http://www.euromanet.eu/newsroom/archive/the_council_adopts_recommendation_to_step_up_the_economic_and_social_integration_of_roma_communities.html.

European Commission. "Peer Review—Short Report." *Municipal Programme of Shanty Towns Eradication in Avilés (Principality of Asturias)*. Brussels: European Commission, 2006. http://ec.europa.eu/employment_social/social_inclusion/docs/2006/pr_sp_en.pdf.

———. *Working Together for Roma Inclusion: The EU Framework Explained*. Brussels: Publications Office of the European Union, 2011. http://ec.europa.eu/justice/discrimination/files/working_together_for_roma_inclusion_en.pdf.

European Council. *Proposal for a Council Recommendation on Effective Roma Integration Measures in the Member States*. Brussels: Council of the European Union, December 9–10, 2013. http://www.consilium.europa.eu/uedocs/cms_data/docs/pressdata/en/lsa/139979.pdf.

European Economic and Social Committee. *Opinion of the European Economic and Social Committee on the Proposal for a Council Recommendation on Effective Roma Integration Measures in the Member States*. Brussels: European Economic and Social Committee, October 17, 2013.

European Parliament. *Resolution on a European Strategy on the Roma*, adopted January 31, 2008. P6_TA(2008)0035. §6. Strasbourg: European Parliament, 2008. http://www.europarl.europa.eu/sides/getDoc.do?pubRef=-//EP//TEXT+TA+P6-TA-2008-0035+0+DOC+XML+V0//EN.

European Roma Policy Coalition. *ERPC Welcomes New Council Recommendation on Roma*. News release, December 10, 2013. http://romapolicy.eu/erpc-welcomes-new-council-recommendation-on-roma/.

FRA (European Union Agency for Fundamental Rights). *Hate Crime in the European Union*. Fact sheet. Vienna: FRA, 2013. http://fra.europa.eu/sites/default/files/fra-factsheet_hatecrime_en_final_0.pdf.

Fraser, Angus. *The Gypsies*. Oxford: Blackwell, 1992.

Fremlová, Lucie. *From Segregation to Inclusion: Roma Pupils in the United Kingdom—a Pilot Research Project*. Budapest: Equality/Roma Education Fund, 2011. http://equality.uk.com/Education_files/From%20segregation%20to%20integration.pdf.

FXB Center for Health and Human Rights/Harvard. *Accelerating Patterns of Anti-Roma Violence in Hungary*. Boston: François-Xavier Bagnoud Center for Health and Human Rights/Harvard School of Public Health/Harvard University, 2014. http://fxb.harvard.edu/wp-content/uploads/sites/5/2014/02/FXB-Hungary-Report_Released-February-4-2014.pdf.

Gall, Lydia. "Hungary's Alarming Climate of Intolerance." *CNN World*, January 18, 2013. http://globalpublicsquare.blogs.cnn.com/2013/01/18/hungarys-alarming-climate-of-intolerance/.

Gheorghe, Nicolae, in collaboration with Gergő Pulay. "Choices to Be Made and Prices to Be Paid: Potential Roles and Consequences in Roma Activism and Policy-Making." In *From Victimhood to Citizenship: The Path of Roma Integration—a Debate*, edited by Will Guy, 41–99. Budapest: Kossuth Publishing Corp./Pakiv European Roma Fund, 2013.

Greenberg, Jack. "Report on Roma Education Today: From Slavery to Segregation and Beyond." *Columbia Law Review* 110, no. 4 (May 2010): 999–1001.

Guy, Will. "The Czech Lands and Slovakia: Another False Dawn?" In *Between Past and Future: The Roma of Central and Eastern Europe*, edited by Will Guy, 285–323. Hatfield, UK: University of Hertfordshire Press, 2001.

———. "Discussion Paper." In *Integrated Programme for the Social Inclusion of Roma (Greece)*, Greek Peer Review, annex 3, 26–28. Brussels: European Commission, 2009. http://ec.europa.eu/social/main.jsp?catId=89&langId=en&newsId=1431&furtherNews=yes.

———. "EU Initiatives on Roma: Limitations and Ways Forward." In *Romani Politics in Contemporary Europe: Poverty, Ethnic Mobilisation, and the Neo-liberal Order*, edited by Nando Sigona and Nidhi Trehan, 23–50. Basingstoke, UK: Palgrave Macmillan, 2009.

———. "'No Soft Touch': Romani Migration to the UK at the Turn of the 21st Century." *Nationalities Papers* 31, no. 1 (March 2003): 63–79.

———. "Romani Identity and Post-Communist Policy." In *Between Past and Future: The Roma of Central and Eastern Europe*, edited by Will Guy, 3–32. Hatfield, UK: University of Hertfordshire Press.

Hyde, Ann Morton. "Roma Inclusion: Can Cities Be the Drivers of Change?" In *The URBACT Tribune: Can European Cities Grow Smarter, Sustainable and Inclusive?*, 21–26. Saint-Denis La Plaine, France: URBACT, 2012. http://urbact.eu/fileadmin/general_library/TRIBUNEweb.pdf.

Hyde, Ann [Morton]. "Systemic Exclusion of Roma from Employment." *Roma Rights* 1 (April 3, 2006). http://www.errc.org/article/systemic-exclusion-of-roma-from-employment/2535.

Johnston, Rosie. "Deputy PM Jiří Čunek Resigns." Radio Praha, November 1, 2007. http://www.radio.cz/en/section/news/news-2007-11-01#1.

Kaltenbach, Jenő, and Catherine Twigg. "Spoken Today, Committed Tomorrow." *Roma Rights Journal* 1(2009): 17–22. http://www.errc.org/cms/upload/media/04/12/m00000412.pdf.

Kenrick, Donald, and Grattan Puxon. *The Destiny of Europe's Gypsies*. London: Chatto Heinemann/Sussex University Press, 1972.

Kovats, Martin. "The EU's Roma Role." *openDemocracy*, May 11, 2012. https://www.opendemocracy.net/martin-kovats/eus-roma-role.

———. "Roma Participation, Empowerment and Emancipation." Contribution to conference panel discussion. Budapest: Corvinus University, May 31, 2013.

Lenarčič, Janez. *Report by Ambassador Janez Lenarčič. Warsaw: Organization for Security and Co-operation in Europe*, September 30, 2010. http://www.osce.org/home/71487.

Nicolae, Valeriu. "Systemic Reform Is Urgently Needed for Roma." *openDemocracy*, March 14, 2012. http://www.opendemocracy.net/valeriu-nicolae/systemic-reform-is-urgently-needed-for-roma.

———. "Why I Quit." Blog, February 12, 2013. http://valeriucnicolae.wordpress.com/2013/02/12/why-i-quit/12.

Pap, András L. "Dogmatism, Hypocrisy and the Inadequacy of Legal and Social Responses Combating Hate Crimes and Extremism: The CEE Experience." In *The Gypsy 'Menace': Populism and the New Anti-Gypsy Politics*, edited by Michael Stewart, 295–331. London: Hurst & Co., 2012.

Pignal, Stanley, and Chris Bryant. "Brussels Struggles to Address Roma Issue." *Financial Times*, September 17, 2010. http://www.ft.com/cms/s/0/5b7f7c66-c28a-11df-956e-00144feab49a.html#axzz38x3B6qQL.

Ramírez-Heredia, Juan de Dios. "The Day Nelson Mandela Inspired Us to Continue the Struggle for Dignity and Recognition of the Roma People." Unión Romaní, December 12, 2013. http://www.unionromani.org/notis/2013/new2013-12-09.htm.

Ries, Johannes. "'I Must Love Them with All My Heart': Pentecostal Mission and the Romani Other." In *Anthropology of East Europe Review* 25, no. 2 (2007): 132–142. http://scholarworks.iu.edu/journals/index.php/aeer/article/view/413.

Ringold, Dena. *Roma and the Transition in Central and Eastern Europe: Trends and Challenges*. Washington, DC: World Bank, 2000. http://siteresources.worldbank.org/EXTROMA/Resources/transition.pdf.

Ringold, Dena, Mitchell Alexander Orenstein, and Erika Wilkens. *Roma in an Expanding Europe: Breaking the Poverty Cycle*. Washington, DC: World Bank, 2003. http://siteresources.worldbank.org/EXTROMA/Resources/roma_in_expanding_europe.pdf.

ROMEA. "Open Letter to the Non-Extremist Anti-Romani Demonstrators in the Czech Republic." *Romea.cz*, July 9, 2013. http://www.romea.cz/en/news/czech/romea-association-s-open-letter-to-the-non-extremist-anti-romani-demonstrators-in-the-czech-republic.

———. "Slovakia: Romani Man Decapitated While Still Alive." *Romea.cz*, January 1, 2013. http://www.romea.cz/en/news/slovakia-romani-man-decapitated-while-still-alive.

Rorke, Bernard. "Killing Time: The Lethal Force of Anti-Roma Racism." *Voices* (Open Society Foundations), July 18, 2012. http://www.opensocietyfoundations.org/voices/killing-time-lethal-force-anti-roma-racism.

Rostas, Iulius, Mihai Surdu, and Marius Taba. "Interview with Rumyan Russinov from Bulgaria." In *Ten Years After: A History of Roma School Desegregation in Central and Eastern Europe*, edited by Iulius Rostas, 131–144. New York: Central European University Press, 2012.

Rövid, Márton. "Options of Roma Political Participation and Representation." In *Roma Rights 2012, Challenges of Representation: Voice on Roma Politics, Power and Participation*. Budapest: ERRC, August 22, 2013. http://www.errc.org/article/roma-rights-2012-challenges-of-representation-voice-on-roma-politics-power-and-participation/4174.

Tomova, Ilona. "Health and the Roma Community: Analysis of the Situation in Bulgaria." In *Health and the Roma Community: Analysis of the Situation in Europe: Bulgaria, Czech Republic, Greece, Portugal, Romania, Slovakia, Spain*, 97–107. Sliven, Bulgaria: Health and Romany People Foundation (THRPF), 2009. http://ec.europa.eu/justice/discrimination/files/roma_health_en.pdf.

United Nations Development Programme. *Faces of Poverty, Faces of Hope: Vulnerability Profiles for Decade of Roma Inclusion Countries*. Bratislava: UNDP, 2005. http://issuu.com/undp_in_europe_cis/docs/faces_of_poverty__faces_of_hope.

———. *Roma in Central and Eastern Europe: Avoiding the Dependency Trap*. UNDP/ILO Regional Human Development Report. Bratislava: UNDP, 2002. http://europeandcis.undp.org/home/show/62BBCD48-F203-1EE9-BC5BD7359460A968.

———. *Uncertain Impact: Have the Roma in Slovakia Benefited from the European Social Fund?* Bratislava: UNDP, 2012. http://www.romadecade.org/cms/upload/file/9466_file9_jaroslav-kling_linking-the-decade-and-eu-resources-%255Bcompatibility-mode%255D.pdf.

Vermeersch, Peter. "The European Union and the Roma: An Analysis of Recent Institutional and Policy Developments." In *European Yearbook of Minority Issues*, vol. 10 (2011), edited by the European Centre for Minority Issues and the European Academy Bozen/Bolzano, 339–358. Leiden: Koninklijke BRILL NV, 2013.

World Bank. *Economic Costs of Roma Exclusion*. Washington, DC: World Bank, n.d. http://go.worldbank.org/G1EL5HZ8S0.

Part 1:
Ghetto Life Today

In Europe's Roma Ghettoes: Lost Generations[i]

*by Valeriu Nicolae**

FOREWORD

I did hesitate a lot before deciding to write this report about Europe's contemporary Roma ghettoes.[ii] My misgivings were of two types. First of all I felt the risk of "scavenging on poverty". All too many times I have felt that TV networks and other journalists abused the subject, transforming it into a "poverty freak show", exploiting the drastic images for what are ultimately commercial purposes.

I also hesitated because I did not wish to reinforce already existing stereotypes. I was well aware that such ghettoes are not entirely representative of the complexity of Roma issues but are quite representative when it comes to the majority populations' ideas when it comes to Roma.

On the other hand, in sharp contrast to the exploitative views of some journalists and to the ubiquitous stereotypical images held by the majority, the worst Roma ghettoes do not figure too prominently in policy documents, either on national or on European level. In fact, one can almost say that they have been submerged under the cheerful clichés of inclusive strategies, bureaucratic box-ticking exercises and compilations of real (rarely) or allegedly (mostly) "good practices".

And let us be honest about it—we ourselves, the so-called human rights community, have often shied away from addressing the situation in the ghettoes. It is too extreme in "politically correct" terms. It becomes difficult to see the Roma who live there only as victims. Indeed, for many well-intentioned colleagues in the international Roma movement, the continued existence—and growth—of such ghettoes is a nuisance and an embarrassment.

And these are perhaps the main reasons why I decided to do this report after all: To bring the harsh reality of the worst Roma ghettoes into the mainstream of policy debates. To ensure that their inhabitants are no longer the ones about

---

i [Ed. note] This extract does not include the photographs contained in the original report. Another shorter version of this account of the Ferentari ghetto in Bucharest appears on Valeriu Nicolae's blog for January 20, 2014, as "The Ghettoes I," http://valeriucnicolae.wordpress.com/2014/01/.

ii [Ed. note] In Eastern Europe and the western Balkans, the term "ghetto" often refers to groups/pockets of derelict apartment buildings or houses with unclear legal status that can be found anywhere, but especially in the big cities, or else to rural shantytowns.

whom neither the Governments nor the successful Roma NGOs wish to talk. To bring home the point that if we want to speak about ghettoes from a human rights perspective we do not need "political correctness", nor do we need to label all Roma as victims and mask their failures. We need to address the Roma as rights-holders, who should have agency and who have their share of responsibility. But we must also think of extremely limited choices these Roma have in practice and the huge, almost unimaginable difficulties involved in breaking the vicious circle. And in this context, we definitely need to address the responsibilities of local, national and European authorities as duty bearers.

This is not an academic report. It presents a personal, subjective, perhaps even impressionistic snapshot of ghettoes and their problems—as seen by me, informed by my strong belief in universal human rights, by my many years of experience in Roma activism and of community work in one of the ghettoes themselves.

While growing up I spent lots of time in what I now consider a rural Roma ghetto—in Budrea. Budrea is a Roma village 15 km from the city of Ramnicul Sarat. In the 1970s and 1980s most of the houses in Budrea were half underground (the best way to keep warm during the winter and cold during summer). We brought water from a far-away well and we did not have electricity or a sewage system. Even today the village still lacks basic amenities.

My first contact with an urban Roma ghetto was in 1978 when my family moved to Craiova. Fata Luncii—a neighbourhood at the outskirts of Craiova—was inhabited by Roma. Well over 10,000 people lived in this area of the town. It was and remains a severely segregated neighbourhood where most of the Romanians in Craiova fear to go to as it is considered violent and dangerous.

Over the years, I have visited or stayed for short periods in Roma ghettoes in Romania, the Czech Republic, Serbia, Montenegro, Bosnia and Herzegovina, Italy, Poland, Macedonia, France, Spain, Slovakia, Albania, Finland, Belgium, Turkey and Germany. I also lived in the South Side ghetto in Chicago, USA. In my view, there are few if any Roma ghettoes that have been researched properly—not even the ones whose names are most familiar. But I tried to avoid the best-known places, which is why the report looks at ghettoes that are not well documented.

I am deeply worried about the situation of ghettoes as the problems I witnessed seem to be largely ignored or unknown to the policy makers. The dangers that come with the growth of ghettoes cannot be limited to unemployment, poverty and lack of education which are most often evoked. There are also huge health risks, prostitution, drugs, crime (including the gradual infiltration by organized crime), violence and an increased risk of interethnic conflicts.

Serious research of Europe's mushrooming Roma ghettoes is needed. However, even more than research we need to stimulate governments and NGOs to work at the grassroots in these ghettoes. Unfortunately, I must admit that I did not see any significant work done in any of the ghettoes which are the subject of this report. That is in itself striking: It means that although a lot of Roma-related activities are going on, at the extreme end of segregation, exclusion and absolute poverty, those who experience this suffering remain largely abandoned.

All of the ghettoes I know have their own particularities. But there are some strident similarities, too—concentration of abject poverty, higher than average percentage of children, problems related to location and accessibility, significant problems in delivery and accessing social services, significant (worse than average) health problems, much higher than average rate of drop-outs from school, difficult access to quality education.

I saw many times the same vicious cycle—children that start being used to beg, then get involved in recycling of garbage, and finally become aggressive and illiterate youth with a high risk of ending up in prison for petty theft or violence. As adults getting out of prison, their chances become even more limited and an overwhelming majority will go back to prison. Some of them will be involved in sex work either as sex workers or as pimps, some in other petty criminality. Almost miraculously, a few of them (very few indeed!) will manage to escape the ghetto cycle. But the overwhelming majority of ghetto inhabitants will end up their lives in misery living on meager welfare or recycling garbage as they started.

In the last years the situation in Roma ghettoes around Eastern Europe has become even more complicated. Drug trafficking, sex work and theft abroad (Western Europe) can bring in much more money than before. There is a new possible future for the children living in the ghetto—but, unfortunately, this future is even more damaging for themselves and threatening for society at large than what were their alternatives in the past.

A clear characteristic of all the ghettoes I visited in the last decade is that the percentages of children in these ghettoes are at least 3–4 times over the national average. In most of the cases the majority of the populations of the ghettoes (over 50%) were children.

There are many risks that come with the expansion of ghettoes all over Europe. The worst that can happen is to see these Roma ghettoes become the equivalent of Brazilian favelas, with organized crime replacing legitimate authorities as a parallel power. The current trends clearly point in that direction.

[...][iii]

Chapter 1: Starting from Ferentari, Romania

There are six children in the big garbage dumpster—and a few others playing around it. It is a sad playground. Some of them play inside it, some look for something to eat or something to sell. None of them is over 13 years old.

It is a hot day in Bucharest and the smell of rotten garbage hangs in the air between derelict former barracks. Sewage from one building leaks out in the street. Rats are common here and so are stray dogs. During the summer the rat population explodes and there are cases of children being bitten by large rats.

This is one of the worst ghettoes, at Area Livezilor, in the Bucharest quarter of Ferentari—the place where I have been involved for 6 years in a social project, offering an alternative to children and young people, through education, sports and cultural activities. It is one of the eight different but similar ghettoes in Ferentari. The largest are Amurgului, Zetari, Pangarati and Tunsu Petre. Some 18,000 people live in ghetto-like conditions here.

Right to Housing?

Most of the inhabitants of these ghettoes live in derelict apartment buildings. However, there are also around 90 people who live behind hot water pipes in shacks without any sewage or running water and with no legal electricity.

Near to apartment buildings but on the other side of the road from the pipes there are more shacks. Around 60 people live in those. Their living conditions are slightly better but still there is just an outside toilet for all of them. Some of them lived before in the sewers close to the main Railway Station—Gara de Nord—before they moved to the shacks. They are regularly threatened by eviction, but it did not happen in the last five years.

Most of the people in the ghettoes are registered as living in other places. There are sometimes 20–30 people who are registered on the same address. Without a permanent address one cannot have a permanent ID which in turn results in serious problems in accessing welfare and social services. There is even a

iii [Ed. note] A short historical section—"Introduction: Defining Ghettoes"—has been cut and replaced by the short definition in footnote ii above.

perverse advantage in not having ID papers, especially for people in the ghettoes who live on petty crime. Through the lack of ID papers, they can sometimes avoid prosecution.

In the case of urban ghettoes (in derelict apartment buildings, not shacks) most inhabitants do not pay utilities. The way they avoid paying utilities and avoiding any type of responsibilities is by repeatedly selling the same flat between members of the same family. A series of 10–15 fictitious sales makes it impossible for the local authorities to determine in time who is the owner and has the responsibility for paying the bills. Before the elections the debts are often waived as the mayors want to ensure the votes in the ghettoes—there is a much higher concentration of voters in the ghettoes than anywhere else.

In fact, the ghettoes are paradoxically profitable for the local administrations. Garbage collection, for instance, happens much less often than they are supposed to and paid for. The same is true for lots of other social services. The money thus saved can be used to win re-elections or to enrich people with the "right" political connections.

Right to Work?

No more than 10% of the adults living in Ferentari's ghettoes have regular jobs and the estimate of the inhabitants themselves is that less than 25% of adults having ever worked in a legal job.

Most of the residents recycle garbage, collect and sometimes steal iron. Numerous businesses that buy scrap metal and plastic for recycling are a sign of the presence of pockets of ghettoes. Within less than 500 meters of the shacks behind the pipes are five such businesses, and there are over 40 such centers in the one-kilometer radius of the biggest ghettoes in Ferentari.

Begging remains one of the main sources of income for many inhabitants of ghettoes. It is, of course, a desperate survival strategy—but the approach of authorities who aggressively suppress it is a truly disastrous one if it is done without measures that can offer acceptable alternatives to those begging.

Prohibition of begging cuts drastically the income of a family and forces it to find other ways to survive. Collecting and sorting garbage for recycling is an alternative for some. However, most beggars and their families who will be in the situation of being unable to beg are likely to switch to criminal activities. Thus, the overall societal costs of a crackdown on begging are actually much higher than those of begging itself. This, of course, does not mean that there would be anything positive about begging—but a purely repressive approach, without providing real alternatives, can only make matters worse.

Right to Education?

Most of the children and teenagers living in the ghettoes will end up being functionally illiterate. The overwhelming majority of these children will drop out of school before reaching their 8th grade. A significant percentage will never go to school or give up on school very early. Among those who live in shacks, very few children go to school at all.

The children who are playing now in the dumpster do not have a perspective of growing through education—they will grow at best into adults who collect garbage for a living. The cycle is simple, cynical and scarily similar to other ghettoes. The first few years of a child's life can be economically productive for the family if the child is used for begging. As soon as he/she will not be good for or able to beg they will start picking or sorting garbage.

Most of the children from the ghettoes will end up as adults with a very poor education and extremely limited chances to find employment that will pay enough to give them the opportunity to get out of the ghettoes. Moreover, involvement in criminal activities pays much better than any job they could possibly get considering their skills and formal education. It will also not require the discipline and responsibilities of a normal job.

Some of the children will be trained . . . to steal, while others will make money washing windshields or hassling people for money. Some will do all these things. A good number of them will do these "jobs" abroad (Western Europe) as the economic gains are much higher than in their much poorer countries (Eastern Europe and the Balkans).

Gender Equality?

Women who live in ghettoes are likely to be abused and struggle for most of their lives. Most of the girls get pregnant around the age of 14. The social fabric in the worst urban ghettoes is disappearing or is already inexistent as a growing number of families are mono-parental—the mothers have children with different partners with whom they tend to have rather short relationships. Fathers tend to assume little or no responsibilities towards their children.

The alternatives for women are even fewer than those for men when it comes to employment. Most will have to work in awful toxic conditions related to garbage collection and recycling, steal, prostitute themselves or sell drugs.

Many of the teenage girls are sex workers. Some of them sleep on the pipes inside a cement casing built to protect the pipes, in a space around 40 cm wide. A number of the teenage sex workers have stories of being abused and raped by the police. Their pimps are often in cohorts with corrupt policemen.

In the last two years two of these girls disappeared. One, a 14-year-old, was found in an illegal brothel 300 km away, and resented being brought back by the police. The other one was found dead, beaten to death. Her death was never properly investigated.

Domestic violence is usually not reported in these ghettoes. Reporting violence makes no sense and leads to serious economic losses. People in the ghettoes usually live there illegally and in conditions that are considered inappropriate for children. Therefore, reporting domestic violence can lead to a forced removal of children from their parents due to child protection issues. Yet children are often vital for the support of the family as they receive allocations or/and produce money by begging, stealing, selling drugs or helping their parents to collect and sort garbage.

It is very rare that the violent male will be sent to prison—it is more likely that he will receive a fine, which is entirely counterproductive. The women risk being severely beaten up when the male returns home, having to come up with the money to pay the fine and to be left alone. The children are likely to be placed in institutionalised care where their experiences tend to be similarly traumatic—poor conditions, lack of any emotional support and frequent abuse.

For those who live in ghettoes abroad there is even less incentive to report cases of domestic violence as that will bring the attention of the police to the often-irregular settlement and can lead to deportation and an abrupt end to what is most often a much better life than in their countries of origins.

Rule of Law?

Other forms of violence are also rife and rarely (if ever) reported in the ghettoes. Break-ins and fights are common occurrences. Arson and serious damage to one's property are common occurrences. As these types on incidents take place mostly among rival gang members, they remain unreported to the police. State policing and security in the ghettoes is simply non-existent—the police may act to prevent violence outside the ghetto but only extraordinarily intervene within the ghettoes. "Protection" in the ghettoes is ensured by gangs. Affiliation to a gang brings safety, jobs and sometimes power.

The links between the police, politicians and criminal gangs are rumored to be strong. I know for a fact that the illegal drug "store" near the school is protected not only by a private security guard but also by the police. I often saw people buying drugs while policemen were standing nearby.

An overwhelming majority of the informal leaders in the community in Rahova and Ferentari are criminals leading gangs that deal in shark loans, drugs, prostitution, extortion/"protection", theft, trafficking of people. Not all of them are Roma but a good number are. Some of them have close ties with top politicians and a few are regularly invited to national and international events. In the past, a few have managed to be appointed in medium- and even high-level positions within the local and national administration.

These nominations were a reward for massive vote buying in the community. The gangs control a significant number of votes in the area of Ferentari and Rahova. One of the most corrupt politicians in Romania has won his place in the Romanian Senate here. Desperate to avoid being sentenced to a long jail term, he used money, threats involving these criminal gangs and political connections and came very close to becoming the Minister of Interior and Administration. He narrowly missed his target and is now in prison.

It is usual that the drug trafficking gangs will own some legitimate businesses in order to launder the drug money. In the ghetto where I work, most of these businesses are car-washing or auto services places. Some of these car-washing places employ drug addicts to wash the cars. These drug addicts often get paid partially or totally with drugs.

The street dealers (most of them drug addicts, women or teenagers) are taking significant risks. They are threatened, abused, robbed and beaten-up by the much powerful drug lords who intimidate them into submission and try to prevent them from communicating to the police, but they are also at risk from corrupt policemen and from addicts in urgent need for their shot. Such incidents cannot be reported either.

Prison is part of everyday life in this ghetto. Most male adults have been in prison at least once. A good part of the females have served some years in prison too. Theft, drug related crimes and prostitution are the most common causes for their imprisonment. Some people have been denounced to the police by their friends and families, in a desperate but sometimes effective way to save somebody from certain death due to drug addiction.

Residents of the ghettoes tend to receive, on average, disproportionately long sentences compared to people who can afford good lawyers and steal millions.

But prison is not only a punishment for people in the ghettoes. Sometimes, in fact, it is a preferable alternative—a way to kick addiction, find shelter during cold winters, learn new skills, "toughen up" and build networks that can be very "productive" after their release.

The probability of reoffending and returning to prison is extremely high in the case of the ghettoes—around 90%, according to a Romanian expert working for the Romanian National Agency for Prisons.

Right to Health?

Abject poverty, drug abuse, prostitution, lack of education, poorly designed or discriminatory social services, poor nutrition, toxic environment, inadequate housing, violence are some of the basic characteristics of these ghettoes.

The life expectancy of people in the ghettoes is significantly less than the average. Over the years of my work in the ghettoes, I never met anyone who would be over 80 years old. I saw many persons who looked very old but most of them were in their early 60s.

It is exceptional to see that people in the ghettoes are registered with a doctor. And indeed, it is even more exceptional that they will have the money and the needed social skills to receive good medical care. Most of the times some traditional remedies (based on plants) will be used even for illnesses that would require hospitalization.

Most of the people living in the ghettoes use emergency services. For them, the advantages of using emergency health services are obvious (free transportation, free consultation, free treatment) but these services are very expensive for the state. Abuse of the emergency services by people in the ghetto happens often as people fake emergencies in order to get consultations or treatment for illnesses that do not require such services. Due to these abuses and the high costs, emergency services often try to avoid or refuse to go to the ghettoes.

Early pregnancies in the ghettoes are far over the average numbers. Lack of sexual education and child prostitution are the main causes. Sometimes teenage girls want to escape from the ghettoes and will elope with some young man. In most cases this will result in an early pregnancy and a single-parent family.

High rates of premature birth, low birth weight, drug and alcohol abuse combined with smoking, violent abuse and poor diet during pregnancy, inadequate to terrible maternal diet, toxicity of the environment, abject poverty—all these [are] significant factors that contribute to much higher rates of premature death, significantly shorter life expectancy and greater levels of disease among the people in the ghettoes compared to the majority populations.

The health situation is influenced by all the above. It will be rare that severe disabilities of children will be treated. Unfortunately, there are many cases when these children will be considered a very strong economical asset, as they will produce a lot more money (when begging) than a healthy child. Their parents or the criminal gangs that "rent" them will never consider taking the child to a doctor.

The children in the ghettoes tend to be severely underdeveloped due to poor nutrition, health issues and overall living conditions. For children between 8 to 14 years of age, the development gap is sometimes 2–3 years compared to the average children. Despite clear facts proving that children in ghettoes are at a much higher risk of getting sick, the predominant stereotype among the majority populations is that these children are much healthier and more resistant than the majority population children. The development of their central nervous system is likely to be seriously affected, resulting in lower IQs than their peers.

Addiction to drugs, alcohol or other substances that can provide an artificial escape (such as glue, paint-thinner etc.) is already high in most of the ghettoes and increasing. In some of Ferentari's ghettoes there are lots of syringes on the ground. Many parents are addicted to drugs. Sometimes they send their children to gather syringes for the periodical syringe-exchange programs. Needles prick some of them during the process. Too many of the children have hepatitis B or C and the infection is rarely detected on time.

Drug addicts are at a very high risk of HIV. Indeed, it is likely that most are HIV positive but they have never been tested. The number of overdose deaths has increased in the last years. Since the beginning of 2013 year, five of the people I knew, including a 13-year-old, have died of overdoses. His brother died of an overdose 4 years ago. The mother is left with just one child, a boy of five. The probability that he will end up the same way is high. Out of the 109 young adults (between 21 and 23 years old) that I polled, almost a half (46) were addicted.

Most of the drug addicted persons I talked to—I interviewed 52 but talked with well over 100—justify their drug addiction as the best or only way to find relief from their previous abuses (family and street violence, sexual abuse, irresponsible parents, psychological traumas, discrimination) and their hellish present (homelessness, HIV positive status, syphilis or other serious illnesses, being forced to live in dangerous situations, being forced to prostitute themselves). In a strange way, alcohol and drugs are used as self-medication to treat severe depression and escape reality for a good part of the people living in the ghettoes.

*__Valeriu Nicolae__ is a Romanian Roma activist and was founder and president of the NGO the Policy Centre for Roma and Minorities, which carries out educational and community development work in one of Bucharest's worst ghettoes. (See also biographical note to his article "Why I Quit," pp. 182–187.)

Nicolae, Valeriu. "In Europe's Roma Ghettoes: Lost Generations." Colloquium on Roma segregation in housing, Office of the UN High Commissioner for Human Rights, Madrid, January 16, 2014. http://www.europe.ohchr.org/EN/NewsEvents/Pages/MadridColloquium.aspx.

Part 2:

The Pivotal Role of the European Union

The European Union and the Roma: An Analysis of Recent Institutional and Policy Developments

*by Peter Vermeersch**

I. Introduction

Although traditionally limited in its influence over how national governments protect ethnic minorities and vulnerable social groups, the European Union (EU) has, over the last decade, significantly stepped up its efforts to bring the situation facing the Roma onto the policy agenda, both on the European level and that of the member states. In one respect, this move is the logical outcome of larger EU concerns for building better social policies across Europe, protecting minority citizens more effectively, combating poverty, and eradicating discrimination; but it also indicates a growing recognition of the specific challenges facing many Romani communities throughout the continent. This European policy attention is the type of consideration for which many Romani advocacy groups have worked. Although some authors have noted that a severe lack of data still hampers an accurate assessment of the situation,[1] continued reporting[2] by NGOs and international institutions has now at least made the issue hard to ignore: exclusion and poverty, as well as the processes of discrimination and stereotyping that exacerbate it continue to be a reality for many Roma; thus, reports stress, these persisting problems should worry policy-makers on all institutional levels.[3]

Bringing the issues facing the Roma to the attention of EU policy-makers has of course been only one of the goals set by advocacy groups. The more important ambition has been to rely on the EU's power to bring about a large-scale domestic political and socioeconomic change that would effectively improve the position of Romani communities throughout Europe and create more inclusive societies. The sorts of domestic policies that have now been put in place to achieve this goal, and the pace at which they have been implemented, vary across European states. The results are diverse as well. We have arrived at a moment in which a better insight is needed into the factors influencing these policies and determining their successes and failures. This article will neither tackle the issue of influence directly, nor assess the success of these policies. Rather, more modestly, the goal of this article is to help lay the foundations of such an analysis by offering a contextualized exploration of the current landscape of institutions and policies of relevance to the Roma on the level of the EU. I believe a comparative examination of domestic success and failure can only be performed properly on the basis of a thorough understanding of this quickly shifting landscape of institutions and policies and of the political environment in which they have been adopted.

This article analyses the recent developments on the level of the European institutions from five different, yet related perspectives. In the first section, I outline a number of key evolutions within the EU that have had particular consequences for the ways in which the situation of the Roma is addressed. These are ongoing processes of EU policy-making and institutional change that have been driven by the overall dynamics of European integration, such as the EU's pursuit to promote fundamental rights standards, the EU enlargement process, and the evolving European social inclusion agenda. In the second section, I consider a number of important events that have clearly spurred the EU's policy-making on the Roma over the last few years. I highlight in particular the recent upsurge of intra-EU migration, the troubling responses of certain states to the east-west mobility of Roma, and the rise of anti-Roma rhetoric and behaviour. In the third section, I focus on a series of recent EU initiatives and methods meant to facilitate Romani participation in EU policy-making and to stimulate the input of a variety of stakeholders in the debate about what Europe should do. In the fourth section, I explore some of the financial means that the EU has put forward in its attempt to persuade member states to increase their efforts for the inclusion of Roma. To conclude, in the fifth section, I focus on the political dynamics of the EU's growing concern for the Roma and the unintended consequences these dynamics may produce.

II. Key Evolutions within the EU and Their Implications for the Roma

A. The EU's Fundamental Rights Agenda

The first development within the EU that warrants highlighting is the growing importance of the EU's fundamental rights agenda. Fundamental rights may not have been part of the initial institutional set-up of the EEC, but, as is argued by Smismans, "several interwoven discourses on fundamental rights developed which assigned, retrospectively, such rights as inherent in the European project and based them on a common European heritage."[4] The result is mainly visible in a number of legal shifts. The Maastricht Treaty (1992) and the Treaty of Amsterdam (1997) enabled European institutions to take measures to combat discrimination based on ethnic origin, including discrimination against the Roma. In addition, in 2000, the European Council of Nice proclaimed the EU Charter of Fundamental Rights, which, even though it had no formal legal status within Union law at the time, had a profound influence on the institutions.[5] The adoption of the Racial Equality Directive 2000/43/EC in June 2000 was another significant step; it prohibits racial discrimination in the areas of employment, education, social security, healthcare and access to goods and services in all EU member states. This directive was clearly the result of a particular set of political circumstances. It was adopted in a quick manner thanks to decisive political will among the member states prompted at that time by a widespread urge to respond forcefully to the inclusion of the [extreme right-wing] Freedom Party in the Austrian government. Since 2000, the political context seems to have made such legal breakthroughs less likely: European Commission officials have pointed out that it would be harder now to find unanimous support for new legislation proposals in the field of anti-discrimination.[6] The Racial Equality Directive is of considerable importance for the Roma; it has given victims of discrimination the right of redress, and it mandates member states to designate a special independent institution that promotes equal treatment and provides independent assistance to victims of discrimination in pursuing complaints. Responding to this new context, many EU countries have improved their anti-discrimination legislation, and victims of discrimination, including Roma, now have better access to justice, and enjoy, at least in theory, increased victim protection against discrimination.[7] The legal landscape of the EU has further developed with the coming into force of the Lisbon Treaty in December 2009, which made the Charter of Fundamental Rights an integral part of EU law.

With the establishment of a stronger fundamental rights core within the EU came additional possibilities for monitoring by independent actors. NGOs could, more effectively than before, rely on the context of European institutions and legal arrangements when drawing up their reports. Moreover, some EU member states committed themselves to cooperation with non-EU member states and international NGOs in the field of inclusion of Roma in the context of the Decade for Roma Inclusion (2005–15). Additional reporting could also be performed by independent advisory bodies to the EU, in particular by the EU Agency for Fundamental Rights (FRA), which in cooperation with EU institutions, the Council of Europe and other international organisations has devoted specific attention to the case of the Roma.[8]

B. The Enlargement Process

Monitoring by independent organizations has also happened in the context of a parallel large-scale EU development that needs to be highlighted here: the enlargement process. In the context of its enlargement to Central Europe, the EU demanded from candidate member states a number of profound institutional changes and guarantees, and these requirements are still in place for current candidates in South-Eastern Europe. In response to those demands, the candidate countries have been increasingly prepared to adopt newly emerging European legal standards on minority protection and anti-discrimination.[9] The attention for the Roma in the context of the EU enlargement process dates from the 1990s. By including the requirement of minority protection in the Copenhagen criteria of 1993, the EU aspired to set the moral standard in this field and to seek compliance from its neighbours to the East. EU demands to the Central European countries regarding the Roma were primarily outlined in the Commission's 1997 Opinion on each country's application for membership and the subsequent annual Regular Reports from 1998 to 2003. In addition, Accession Partnership documents in 1999 and 2001 emphasized priority areas for attention. For Romania and Bulgaria, there was an additional Accession Partnership in 2003, an additional Regular Report in 2004, and subsequent monitoring reports in 2005 and 2006. For all countries, these documents were supplemented by periodic statements and commissioned studies of the European Commission, the European Council, and the European Parliament, which became more numerous over time.[10] As a result, pressure increased, but lack of reciprocal commitments from the EU also led to a rather inconsistent enlargement policy.[11] The EU's conditions on minority protection appeared to be open to various interpretations and created uncertainty over which commitments exactly candidate member states needed to make to safeguard their accession;[12] for this and other reasons, membership conditionality remained rather ineffective.[13] Moreover, in the case of the Roma, adopting new policies and institutions has been far easier than fixing problems on the ground, many of which turned out to be not easy to resolve and require measures that could be unpopular among the wider electorate. Moreover, while political will to improve the lives of the Roma has been present at the national level, implementation has often been confronted with impediments at the local level.[14] Empirical research shows that both in 'old' and 'new' EU member states, problems with local policy implementation persist[15] despite the pressure that was exerted during the accession phase. There are currently no strong and effective responses to the practice of some local policy-makers of portraying Romani citizens systematically as a burden on the local economy, rather than as a group that deserves economic support as equal citizens.

C. The EU's Social Inclusion Agenda

The third development that warrants highlighting is the growing importance of the EU's social inclusion agenda, which has received particular attention in recent times as the economic crisis and severe issues of inequality among and within member states seriously threaten the EU's latest grand ambitions for economic advancement, the Europe 2020 goals.[16] Since 2000, efforts to tackle poverty and social exclusion in the EU have benefitted from the Open Method of Coordination (OMC), a 'soft' process in which states and European institutions collaborate on shared concerns in a voluntary manner. Three policy themes have dominated the Social OMC: active inclusion, which covers employment activation, minimum income and access to services; child poverty and well-being; and homelessness and housing exclusion. More recently, the social inclusion of migrants and ethnic minorities (especially the Roma) and the impact of the financial and economic crisis have come more to the fore.[17] Ongoing developments in the sphere of the EU's social inclusion agenda have reinforced particular initiatives on the Roma. For example, the Belgian Presidency of the Council of the EU in the second half of 2010 chose to focus on the issue of the early childhood development of the Roma, not only because general attention to Roma was on the rise but also because the issue of 'combating child poverty' had become a leading theme for the OMC and for the European Platform against Poverty and Social Exclusion. The subsequent Belgian report emphasized that there was 'a political window of opportunity to tackle the issue of Romani poverty through the perspective of early childhood services'.[18] Underpinning this choice was the observation that the topic of the living conditions of Romani children, although clearly quite alarming (with serious concerns about nutrition, health and early development), had remained to a large extent outside the general poverty debate. Moreover, the topic fits nicely in with the broader Belgian focus on child poverty. The work that was performed in the context of this platform meeting yielded a number of important conclusions, among them the proposal to promote the use of the Europe 2020 Strategy to mainstream the issue of inclusion of Roma into the broader policies on poverty and social exclusion. In particular, member states were recommended to present National Strategies for the Inclusion of Roma as part of their National Reform Programmes or to translate the headline targets into national and regional targets that address marginalised children. The Platform against Poverty and Social Exclusion was also recommended to devote special attention to Roma.[19]

III. Key Trends and Events That Have Prompted Responses from the EU

There are two recent sociopolitical trends to which EU institutions, often in concert with other European agencies, have felt a need to respond: certain radical policies of Western European member states directed toward Romani immigrants from the Eastern and South-Eastern parts of the EU, including ethnically targeted expulsion campaigns; and the rise of anti-Roma rhetoric in mainstream politics, accompanied sometimes by rising levels of violence against Roma perpetrated by extremist groups.

A. Migration and Mobility

Regarding migration, two popular assumptions persist: that Romani migration from east to west is massive; and that Roma are culturally and inherently inclined toward mobility. The latter idea is inherited from romantic portrayals of travelling Gypsies in popular culture, or perhaps, as Lucassen, Willems and Cottaar have argued, the result of a categorization practice by authorities and academics in the eighteenth and nineteenth century who sought to unify all sorts of itinerant groups under the single label of 'Gypsy'.[20] Both popular assumptions are faulty. Especially in Central and Eastern Europe Roma are usually not nomadic; as Matras wrote, "On the whole, the extraordinary feature of Romani migration is that so many Roma are prepared to take the risks of migrating *despite their lack of nomadic traditions*."[21] In addition, the extent of Romani migration is often exaggerated, which may be caused by a number of other factors: lack of precise official numbers, for example, and arguably also the high visibility, the relatively high level of internal cohesion, and the severe poverty of the Romani communities in question.

The example of the Belgian city of Ghent is instructive. Official figures provided by the city authorities show a strong increase of registered labour-seeking citizens from Bulgaria since 2004 (from 392 in 2004 to 5630 in 2011),[22] many of whom are assumed to be Roma. The overall number of migrants from the new EU member states in early 2012 was 3.6%, of which Bulgarian citizens were about 60%. These numbers are relatively small when compared with the presence of the total number of foreign citizens and Belgian citizens of foreign descent in Ghent (about 17.5% of the total population in 2010)[23] and certainly when compared with the size of other communities of migrants, with or without Belgian citizenship, or of migrant descent, in other Belgian urban centres. The increase between 2004 and 2011 of immigrants from the new EU member states in Ghent, however, has been highly noticeable because they often concern socioeconomically vulnerable groups: they live concentrated in particular neighbourhoods, often in detrimental circumstances, have limited access to the regular job market, and are therefore often visible in the streets during regular working hours. On the level of the municipality, extra policy initiatives have been taken to address these groups (partly on the basis of assistance through designated mediators and partly through attempts to control and stem further immigration). This extra policy attention was accompanied by rather extensive media attention and public debate, but it did not often lead to sober analysis: news headlines as well as politicians commenting on this case repeatedly spoke of a 'rush,' an 'influx,' or even 'a plague'.[24]

Similar developments could be observed in other European countries. In March 2011, the Netherlands counted about 125,000 working (but not all registered) labour immigrants from Central and Eastern Europe, of which the bulk (108,000) were Polish.[25] Although the number of Roma from Bulgaria and Romania constituted only a tiny portion of that overall figure, they are consistently talked about as if they are a vast group that will 'overrun' the West. Metaphors such as these are highly problematic: rather than offering a more or less realistic idea of the size of current Romani mobility, which may subsequently be used as the basis for a clearheaded discussion about adequate policies, they construct a dramatic illusionary image which, in turn, can easily be exploited for political purposes. An ostentatious example of such politics was the initiative of the radical Dutch Freedom Party (PVV) of Geert Wilders in February 2012 to launch an internet hotline calling on people to report complaints caused by the 'massive labour migration' of citizens from Central and Eastern Europe, in particular Poles, Romanians and Bulgarians. Although the website is not explicitly aimed at Roma, it has clearly induced and mobilized anti-Roma sentiment, a development that has been highlighted by several alarmed observers.[26]

National politicians and mainstream media in the receiving member states have mostly regarded the east-west mobility of Roma within the EU as a threat to their own fragile labour markets and social security systems, not as what it arguably could also be, that is, an opportunity to resolve some of the structural problems in those markets. Even if the Roma in question are young, inventive, active and willing to seek a job, they are seldom seen as a potential resource.

In some cases, notably in Italy and in France, the government responded by introducing targeted expulsion and migration control strategies.[27] In the summer and fall of 2010, it was the French case that reached international headlines. Responding to riots after a police shooting in July 2010, President Nicolas Sarkozy called an emergency ministerial meeting at which it was decided to shut down a large number of irregular Romani dwellings and single out Bulgarian and Romanian Roma for an expulsion campaign that would bring them back to their countries of origin, even if only temporarily. The 2010 crackdown was highly conspicuous because of its emphasis on security, its focus on foreigners (which from the perspective of the Roma in question must have seemed odd: the initial incidents did not involve Bulgarian or Romanian Roma but Gens du Voyage, that is, French citizens who cannot be expelled) and its overtones of ethnic discrimination. But the fact is that it was not a policy that came out of the blue. France had been sending Romanian and Bulgarian citizens home even before 2010. In 2009, the French government had already deported about 9,000 Roma to Romania and Bulgaria, and also other Western European countries (such as, Italy, Germany, Sweden, Denmark, Finland, and the United Kingdom) have for a number of years pursued targeted return campaigns. Mobility may not have yet become the Roma's preferred escape route from marginality, but expulsion has clearly become the preferred policy response to Romani migration.

Several EU actors and institutions responded forcefully to the highly publicized campaigns. As van Baar documents in detail, in a resolution adopted on 9 September, the European Parliament condemned the French policy and urged the French authorities to stop the expulsions immediately.[28] The European Commission responded through Viviane Reding, Commissioner for Justice, Fundamental Rights and Citizenship, who was in particular alarmed by the leaked memo of the French interior ministry that was distributed to local civil servants and urged French police officials to focus their efforts on migrants of Romani background.[29] Reding first threatened to bring France before the European Court of Justice for violating anti-discrimination laws but later, after the Commission received assurance from France that it did not single out Roma, refrained from pursuing an infringement procedure.[30]

B. Anti-Roma Politics and Behaviour

EU actors and institutions are not only spurred by domestic state policies that target Romani migrants in the countries of arrival, but also, over the last few years, they have been faced with alarming statistics of hate speech and hate crime against the Roma, both in the home countries and in the countries of arrival. Clearly, the Roma have become a more explicit target—not only discursively—of rising right-wing populism and violence.[31] Although anti-Gypsyism has a long history in Europe, today, Roma are more explicitly targeted than before as adversaries of the 'national' population in various places.

In Hungary, for example, the Roma are now widely depicted as cultural deviants and seen as an identifiable and essentially 'foreign' threat to the Hungarian economy and way of life. To some extent, anti-Roma rhetoric in Hungary now seems to eclipse anti-Semitism and resonates powerfully with anti-immigrant rhetoric in Western Europe. The trope of 'Gypsy criminality' is not entirely new—under the socialist regime, it functioned for a while as an administrative category that reified ethnic differentiation and ratified social inequality—but its resurgence today is accompanied by a new politics of nationalism. The main political exponent of this radical nationalism, Jobbik Magyarországért (Movement for a better Hungary) combines old concerns with new-style campaigning. It "promotes and perpetuates the cult of Trianon (the treaty ending World War I which 'dismembered' Hungary), licking past wounds to justify future territorial claims, whilst aggressively pushing a law and order agenda at home aimed at the supposed offenders of law and order, the Roma".[32] In the April 2010 parliamentary elections, the party gained almost 17% of the vote. Moreover, the law and order rhetoric inflated public anxieties and created an atmosphere of permissiveness toward those who propagate extremist measures to assuages those fears, be they politicians who advocate zero tolerance policies against 'the ethnic other' or private 'security' forces who claim to have the right to protect 'their' people against 'the Gypsies' with violent means. The now outlawed Magyar Gárda (Hungarian Guard), Jobbik's paramilitary wing, helped establish the idea that a 'fight against Gypsy crimes' is needed to save the nation. By joining force, even if only symbolically, with the Magyar Gárda, Jobbik managed to appoint itself to the role of civic security provider in locations in which 'Hungarians' are allegedly threatened by 'Gypsy criminality.' The party has also presented itself as the sole force resisting the Roma's so-called 'systematic usurpation' of the social security system.

In September 2011, Thomas Hammarberg, the Council of Europe's Commissioner for Human Rights, argued that "The consequences of anti-Roma rhetoric by politicians should not be underestimated. Their words can be understood as encouraging violent action against the Roma, such as mob violence and pogroms".[33] Political rhetoric for power is clearly one of the elements contributing to the sad succession of incidents that have plagued Hungary over the last few years. Between January 2008 and July 2010, observers registered at least 48 violent attacks against Roma, including nine fatalities (two of them minors). Dozens of Roma have been injured, 10 of whom have suffered life-threatening harm.[34]

Particularly worrying is the fact that the trend is not limited to Hungary. In other countries too, including states with autochthonous Romani populations (such as Slovakia) and countries in which Roma are more likely to be immigrants (such as Italy), such attacks have happened. Sometimes they bear the stamp of an organized movement; at other times they appear to be individual incidents.

IV. EU Policy on Roma and Specific Initiatives on Romani Participation

EU responses to this state of affairs have come in several forms. In the European Parliament, for example, over the last few years—2005, 2006 and 2008—new resolutions were adopted that concern the Roma.[35] In the resolution of January 2008, the European Parliament urged the European Commission to take heed of the conclusions of the European Council of December 2007 and to "develop a European Framework Strategy on Roma Inclusion aimed at providing policy coherence at EU level" (point six of the resolution).

Not only have European resolutions been voted, but also new European institutions and traditions have been established. These latter initiatives show an increased willingness on the part of the EU to take the issue of Romani participation seriously (or at the very least, participation of those who try to speak on behalf of Roma). The European Council of December 2007 gave its full symbolic support to the European Commission for the organisation of a series of 'European Roma Summits,' of which the first one was held in September 2008 in Brussels and the second one in April 2010 in Córdoba. These highly visible meetings gathered approximately 400 representatives of EU institutions, national governments, regional and local public authorities and civil society organisations. Follow-up summits were organised in cooperation with the three Presidencies in office from 2010 (Spain, Belgium, and Hungary). The "Council conclusions on advancing Roma Inclusion" from June 2010 confirmed the consolidation of this new initiative.

These summits have functioned mainly as deliberative and advisory boards; they have brought together a broad range of stakeholders and have had the ambition to increase political awareness about the situation of Roma, especially among high-level national policy-makers. Yet they have also led to specific outcomes. The first Roma Summit, for example, led to the creation of a European Platform for Roma Inclusion. This is a platform for regular meetings between member state representatives, Romani activists, policy-makers and experts led by the Council presidency and aimed at the identification of best practices and the stimulation of cooperation and exchanges of experience on successful inclusion policies. The talks have led to several outcomes, one of which is a document called the "10 Common Basic Principles for Roma inclusion" (resulting from the Platform meeting in Prague on 24 April 2009, in the framework of the Czech Presidency of the EU). These principles form a guideline for policy measures and try to reach a delicate balance between, on the one hand, advocating special measures to support Roma and, on the other hand, a mainstreaming approach (the document describes it as "explicit but not exclusive targeting"). The suggestions are primarily meant to mobilize national governments, but close collaboration with the European Commission is also set as a goal. Clearly, the actors involved in this process have also tried to find another balance, one between giving responsibility to the EU for the issue of the Roma without taking responsibility away from the member states.

In April 2011, the European Commission adopted a Communication (COM(2011) 173) which confirmed this general direction. It called for an "active dialogue with the Roma", both at the national and the EU level, and it demanded a clear policy commitment from the EU member states. The latter were urged to draw up "national Roma integration strategies", a process that, in the end, must allow countries to not only compare ideas, practices and commitments, but also to create new possibilities for more robust monitoring by independent agencies and civil society actors. The European Commission has devoted a website to what has now become known as the "EU Framework for national Roma integration strategies", where the various national strategies can be consulted.[36] On 22 March 2012, the European Commission organized an Extraordinary EU Platform for Roma inclusion in Brussels, which gave all stake-holders involved an opportunity to express their views on the submitted national strategies and to discuss issues surrounding their future implementation. At the occasion, European Commissioner Reding urged the audience to be positive and to consider the achievements since 2008, which she called spectacular. Yet, she also admitted that "there is still a lot of room for improvement, in particular when it comes to securing sufficient funding for Roma inclusion and putting monitoring mechanisms in place. Fighting discrimination in education, employment, housing and health would also need to be better addressed, with a clearer focus on Roma women and children in particular. Most important: although we see many nice words in the national strategies, concrete deliverables, quantified targets and clear, ambitious deadlines for action are missing."[37]

V. EU Means to Address Local Issues

Although within different EU institutions the situation of the Roma is now clearly regarded as a significant public policy concern, such attention has not yet produced the much needed social change. While some EU-funded projects are no doubt successful (some are, for example, discussed in the 2010 report "Improving the Tools for the Social Inclusion and Non-Discrimination of the Roma in the EU", written for the European Commission),[38] on the whole, poverty, exclusion and discrimination persist; in some places the situation is even worse than ever before. Some authors have claimed that the EU institutions are themselves at least in part responsible for this lack of positive news.[39] They have argued that the financial commitments have remained too modest, the European Commission acts too formalistically, the EU strategies are much too dependent on the political will of other actors, and that the lack of an overall policy for the Roma sometimes leads to contradictory policies on the ground.[40] Yet, one should also continue to highlight the role of domestic and local political elites and authorities who are, and should remain, the main actors responsible for effectuating local social change.[41] The longer they wait to seize the institutional opportunities that have emerged at the European level to develop policies that effectively discourage discrimination and foster greater socioeconomic equality, the harder it will be for the EU to have an impact on local developments.

What have been the most recent building blocks of this European opportunity structure? The European Commission claims that a number of instruments and mechanisms that are meant to support more generally defined population groups can be of specific use for the Roma. These include, for example, the Youth in Action Programme (a financial programme aimed at inspiring active citizenship, solidarity and tolerance among young Europeans) and the Second Programme of Community Action in the Field of Health. Somewhat more specifically directed at the primary concerns of many Romani communities is the EU's PROGRESS programme, which focuses on employment and social solidarity and can also be used to finance anti-discrimination campaigns. However, the main instruments on which the EU now counts for enticing national governments and local actors to engage in addressing the problem facing Roma are the structural funds.

To reduce inequalities within the EU (between regions and between member states) and to secure the social dimension of economic growth, the EU has traditionally relied on, respectively, regional policy and social policy instruments.[42] The EU structural funds (European Social Fund and the European Regional Development Fund) and the European Agricultural Fund for Rural Development are the main EU funding mechanisms supporting the socioeconomic integration of Roma. More particularly, the European Commission has recently emphasized the potential importance of the European Social Fund (ESF; including the Community Initiative EQUAL) and the European Regional and Development Fund (ERDF).

The EU's strategy is two-pronged. On the one hand, it wants to push governments into relying on existing funding schemes to address the issues facing Roma; the Communication of the European Commission of April 2010 stressed the choice for this strategy as the Commission found out that "Member states currently do not make yet sufficient use of available EU funds to address the needs of the Roma".[43] Suggestions were made in the Communication about how exactly national states should increase their efforts to make use of these available funding mechanisms and connect them directly to their national Roma integration strategies. On the other hand, the EU's funding schemes have been adjusted in such way that they can better serve the specific purpose of Roma inclusion.[44] This is, for example, quite apparent in the case of the European Regional Development Fund (ERDF). Regulation No. 437/2010 of the European Parliament and of the Council of 19 May 2010 amended Article 7(2) of Regulation (EC) No. 1080/2006 on the ERDF as regards the eligibility of housing interventions in favour of marginalised communities. A decision of the Council of the EU now allows the extension of financial support from the ERDF for housing interventions for extremely poor and marginalised communities. Under the previously existing ERDF rules, housing interventions were only allowed in the context of integrated urban development and for the renovation of existing houses as part of an urban development plan. This meant that housing estates of the middle class could be renovated through the use of these funds, but not the housing in isolated or rural areas in which poor and marginalized populations live. This excluded many of the poorest communities. The change of regulation is not simply administrative; it builds on the underlying logic that funding regulations can have an impact on the economic integration of communities and counter processes of social exclusion. Those who have worked toward the implementation of this change hope that the ERDF has now been designed in such a way that it can serve as a community organising tool.[45]

Yet, important challenges remain. It remains open to debate whether changes such as these—the introduction of *ex ante* conditionality in the structural funds, and more generally, European measures aimed at shaping domestic and local policies—are at this point elaborated and convincing enough to persuade member states and local governments to take the matter more seriously. Moreover, sustainability continues to be a key concern: it is still rather unclear how current opportunities should lead to lasting impact. Short-term funding might seem useful in alleviating certain pressing problems, but if the newly set-up structures for solving these problems do not survive long after the project, they might cause more distress and perhaps increase opposition to the Roma. As the 2010 PROGRESS report argues, "long-term funding programmes are needed to achieve sustainable progress. Otherwise initiatives for Roma inclusion will be vulnerable to budgetary pressures."[46] Certain examples, such as the Coexistence Village in Ostrava in the Czech Republic, where since 1997 a local NGO has tried to improve housing conditions and reduce poverty by placing responsibility in the hands of the poorest residents, demonstrate how useful and important it is to build long-term non-project-based relationships across Romani and non-Romani communities.[47] There is arguably a growing need to invest in the new spaces for citizens' participation that have emerged and now operate, either formally or informally, on the local, regional, national or European level and which may serve as a means for connecting marginalised and disadvantaged communities with mainstream society or mainstream political decision-making institutions and processes.

Moreover, a narrow focus on project-based funding might unduly raise expectations about the potential of well-defined projects to change the reality of exclusion and discrimination. Something more than the projects alone is needed—a change of mindset among local power-holders and local communities. The European Council conclusions of 24 May 2011 show that there is at least a growing European awareness of the problem.[48] They include a call upon the Commission and the member states to find a way in which the various available EU funds can "work together in a more integrated and flexible manner in the future, providing an appropriate framework for integrated, long-term actions for advancing Roma inclusion". To achieve this long- term goal, some new ideas will be needed about how to develop such a framework of integration.

Apart from sustainability, there is also the concern of continuing or even rising discrimination. A broad group of civil society organizations fear that the EU's actions in the field of promoting social inclusion might not leave enough room for strengthening the fight against anti-Gypsyism. A document distributed by the European Roma Policy Coalition and the Decade of Roma Inclusion Secretariat at the occasion of the Extraordinary Meeting of the EU Platform for Roma Inclusion in Brussels on 22 March 2012 voiced the concern of about 50 Roma civil society representatives that achieving social inclusion requires sustained attention to discrimination. It argued that the National Roma Integration Strategies "cannot succeed without clear action to combat anti-Gypsyism, as this is one of the causes of exclusion that the strategies are designed to address."[49]

VI. By Way of Conclusion: The Political Dynamics of the EU's Focus on Roma

Although the current EU approach is not so much aimed at promoting the status of the Roma as a transnational European minority or constructing new European social policies targeted only at the Roma, it is clear that the EU has tried to increase its impact on domestic social policies aimed at the social inclusion of the Roma and at finding the right methods to improve their quality. In particular, it wants to promote existing financial mechanisms to persuade national governments of member states to devise and implement better social policies for their own population as a whole, including the Roma. During the course of the process, the new EU mechanisms meant to create some form of stake-holder involvement must also encourage the inclusion of the Roma's voice in domestic decision-making processes. In addition, the EU continues to rely on membership conditionality to influence policies in acceding member states.

Even if this multi-dimensional effort is today far from completed and the results are still underway, one could assume that the European Commission has, at least in theory, the power and the money to change the situation on the ground—more perhaps than any other governmental structures beyond the level of the national state in Europe. However, as I have argued before,[50] we have to be careful not to ignore the risks related to what should perhaps be called the 'Europeanisation' of inclusion policies for Roma.

First, the enlargement conditionality policy of the EU—the policy that made EU membership conditional on a better protection of minorities, including the Roma—has clearly proved to have its limits. Such conditionality may have been influential in bringing attention to the Roma and in getting programmes and reforms adopted by governments in the acceding countries, but implementation has seriously lagged behind. In the end, the Central European countries were admitted to the EU while substantial problems remained. It is important that the problems connected to the conditionality strategy are kept in mind when devising policies toward the current candidate member states.

The second problem is that Europeanisation might give domestic governments an opportunity to evade their own responsibility. If NGOs claim that the Roma are a European minority, domestic politicians and governments can easily argue—and some of them have indeed argued—that the EU or other international institutions have a special responsibility for the Roma. Even when European institutions take special initiatives aimed at the Roma, they should make clear that national governments remain ultimately responsible for the protection of their own citizens. The Roma should not solely be regarded as Europeans but also as citizens of their own states. The process of Europeanisation risks the reinforcement the harmful and stereotypical idea that the Roma belong everywhere and thus nowhere. Analysis of debates in the European Parliament, for example, demonstrates that domestic politicians, even well-intended ones, might help to reinforce the idea that national policies are of less importance for the Roma than European ones because the problems facing the Roma are, as international documents time and again emphasize, 'European' in nature and thus extend the boundaries of the nation-states.[51] A 'European' interpretation of the problems facing the Roma might be problematic if it leads to a transfer of responsibilities for Roma inclusion to the level of the EU.

Third, the Europeanisation of the Romani issue might leave us with the impression that the situation of the Roma is very similar across Europe, and that formula-like solutions can be implemented. This is not the case. For example, it is clear from reports written for the European Commission that much variation exists, even if some key common areas for policy improvement can be defined, and that variation should be taken into account by policy-makers.[52]

Finally, European initiatives meant to remedy the problems that face the Roma should be implemented carefully to avoid the reinforcement of boundaries between the Roma and other population groups. If European support is not monitored well it might easily be interpreted as support uniquely for the Roma, rather than for society as a whole. The way funding mechanisms are structured and framed will be of crucial importance. As the 2010 report by Guy, Liebich and Marushiakova shows,

> funding that comes exclusively from outside a country (be it from the EU, bilateral or private donors) can address transitory problems or concrete infrastructure needs, but is otherwise unlikely to produce sustainable results. National financial support can be important to demonstrate political will and as a way of overcoming local opposition. But local financial support is important to underpin success. Such support, even if small, can demonstrate political will at the local level and the active role of local non-Roma communities as stakeholders.[53]

Roma inclusion strategies may now find the financial and symbolic support of the EU, but they also need the active involvement of local majority populations.[54] The views of "the community as a whole" will have to be taken into account not only in the context of the evaluation of the impact of measures, but also in the context of planning those measures. Deliberative processes, such as collaborative planning (meetings during which Romani and non-Romani inhabitants have a chance to legitimize each other's contribution to municipal plans), can be useful. Although the Roma will and should remain the focus of the main policy responses to the problems affecting this population, the results of the policy responses will be more effective when they are constructed on the basis of meaningful input from all parts of a local community, including other groups. There is a need to find mechanisms of social policy and human rights protection that promote the image of policy initiatives as beneficial for the Roma and non-Roma alike. Current initiatives are too often interpreted or portrayed as bringing resources to Roma that might otherwise have gone to non-Roma, while in fact they are lose-lose policies: the resources directed to the Roma have often been insufficient to bring any significant or lasting changes to Roma's daily lives. To avoid a backlash and at the same time create tangible socioeconomic change within Romani communities, it will be crucial to move from lose-lose to win-win policies so that the full support of the local governing elites and local majority populations can be garnered. Without such support, even the most promising initiatives on paper may not lead to lasting positive results on the ground.

Endnotes

1. Christina McDonald and Katy Negrin, *No Data—No Progress. Data Collection in Countries Participating in the Decade of Roma Inclusion 2005–2015* (Open Society Institute, New York, 2010).
2. From the broad range of reports that have appeared in recent years, high-profile examples include: EU Agency for Fundamental rights (FRA), *EU-MIDIS 01. Data in Focus Report: the Roma* (FRA, Vienna, 2009), at <http://fra.europa.eu/fraWebsite/attachments/EU-MIDIS_ROMA_EN.pdf>; UNDP, *Avoiding the Dependency Trap: The Roma in Central and Eastern Europe* (Bratislava, 2004), at <http://europeandcis.undp.org/>; UNICEF, *Towards Roma Inclusion: A Review of Roma Education Initiatives in Central and South-Eastern Europe* (2009), at <http://www.unicef.org/ceecis/ROMA_PAPER_FINAL_LAST.pdf>; and José Manuel Fresno, *What Works for Roma Inclusion in the EU: Policies and Model Approaches* (Publications Office of the EU, Luxembourg, 2011). Recent reporting by internationally active Roma civil society organisations include ERGO, *The Black and White Book: Roma Inclusion in South Eastern Europe in Practice* (2009), at <http://www.ergonetwork.org/media/userfiles/media/egro/Black%20&%20White.pdf>; and Bernard Rorke, *Review of EU Framework National Roma Integration Strategies (NRIS)* (Open Society Foundations, 2012), at <http://www.romadecade.org/files/downloads/General%20Resources/roma-integration-strategies-20120221.pdf>.
3. The term "Roma" is here used in accordance with the way in which EU documents define it. So, the term is stretched to its broadest meaning so as to include communities who rely on a variety of other designations (such as Sinti, Khale, Romungre, Gypsies, Travellers, Gens de Voyage and so forth) but are yet considered to be part of the target group for the policies discussed herein.
4. Stijn Smismans, "The European Union's Fundamental Rights Myth", 48(1) *JCMS* (2010), 45–66.
5. EU Network of Independent Experts on Fundamental Rights. *Commentary of the Charter of Fundamental Rights of the EU* (Brussels, 2006), 15.
6. Melanie Ram and Peter Vermeersch, "The Roma," in Bernd Rechel (ed.), *Minority rights in Central and Eastern Europe* (Routledge, London, 2009), 61–73, at 72.
7. See, for example, the analysis Sina van den Bogaert, "Roma Segregation in Education: Direct or Indirect Discrimination: An Analysis of the Parallels between Council Directive 2000/43/EC and recent ECtHR Case Law or Roma Educational Matters", 71(4) *Heidelberg Journal of International Law* (2011), 719–753.
8. See, at <http://fra.europa.eu/fraWebsite/roma/roma_en.htm>.
9. Ram and Vermeersch, *op.cit.* note 6.
10. *Ibid.*, 68.
11. Philip Alston and Joseph H H Weiler, "An 'ever closer union' in need of a human rights policy: the European Union and human rights", 2000, p. 13, at <http://centers.law.nyu.edu/jeanmonnet/archive/papers/99/990101.html>.
12. Peter Vermeersch, "Ethnic Mobilisation and the Political Conditionality of European Union Accession: The Case of the Roma in Slovakia," 28(1) *JEMS* (2002), 83–101.
13. Bernard Steunenberg and Antoaneta Dimitrova, "Compliance in the EU Enlargement Process: The Limits of Conditionality," 11 *EiOP* (2007).
14. Ram and Vermeersch, *op.cit.* note 6.

15. Eva Sobotka and Peter Vermeersch, “Governing Human Rights and Roma Inclusion: Can the EU be a Catalyst for Local Social Change?”, 34(3) *HRQ* (2012), forthcoming.

16. See at <http://ec.europa.eu/europe2020/index_en.htm>.

17. Hugh Frazer and Eric Marlier, “Social inclusion in the European Union: Where do We Stand, Where are We Going?” *Development and Transition* (June 2010), 5–7.

18. UNICEF, OSE and the Belgian Federal Planning Service for Social Integration, “Early Childhood Development and the Inclusion of Roma Families”, discussion paper prepared on behalf of the Belgian Presidency of the Council of the European Union (2011), 5.

19. Danielle Dierckx and Peter Vermeersch, “The Social Affairs Agenda of the Belgian Presidency: High Ambitions and Mixed Achievement”, in Steven Van Hecke and Peter Bursens (eds.), *Readjusting the Council Presidency: Belgian Leadership in the EU* (Academic and Scientific Publishers, Brussels, 2011), 153–168.

20. Leo Lucassen, Wim Willems and Annemarie Cottaar, *Gypsies and Other Itinerant Groups: A Socio-historical Approach* (Macmillan, London, 1998); Huub van Baar, *The European Roma: Minority Representation, Memory and the Limits of Transnational Governmentality* (F&N Eigen Beheer, Amsterdam, 2011), 87.

21. Yaron Matras, “Romani Migrations in the Post-Communist Era: Their Historical and Political Significance,” 13(2) *Cambridge Review of International Affairs* (2000), 32. (Emphasis in the original).

22. Integratiedienst Gent, “Cijfermaterial IEM bevolking” (Gent, 2012).

23. Integratiedienst Gent, “Beleidsplan etnisch-culturele diversiteit 2012–2014—bijlage 1: onderzoek en cijfers” (Gent, 2012), at <http://www.gent.be/docs/Departement%20bevolking%20en%20Welzijn/Integratiedienst/Beleidsplannen/Onderzoek%20en%20cijfers_ECD_2012-2014.pdf>.

24. References to these types of media responses are to be found, e.g., in Pascal Debruyne, et. al, “Welterusten, meneer de burgemeester!”, *De Wereld Morgen*, 6 December 2010, at <http://www.dewereldmorgen.be/artikels/2010/12/06/welterusten-meneer-de-burgemeester>.

25. Official data are available at <http://www.cbs.nl/nl-NL/menu/themas/arbeid-sociale-zekerheid/publicaties/artikelen/archief/2011/2011-3423-wm.htm>.

26. See, for example, the remarks by Thomas Hammarberg in his position as Commissioner for Human Rights of the Council of Europe, quoted in Leonoor Kuijk, “PVV lokt Roma-klachten uit”, *Trouw*, 28 February 2012.

27. Peter Vermeersch, “Roma and Mobility in the European Union”, in Kati Pietarinen (ed.), *Roma and Traveller Inclusion in Europe*, (Green European Foundation, Brussels, 2011), 91–97.

28. Huub van Baar, “Europe’s Romaphobia: Problematization, Securitization, Nomadization”, 29(2) *Environment and Planning D: Society and Space* (2011), 203–212.

29. Kim Willsher, “Orders to Police on Roma Expulsions from France Leaked”, *The Guardian*, 13 September 2010.

30. van Baar, *op.cit.* note 28.

31. Mabel Berezin, *Illiberal Politics in Neoliberal Times: Culture, Security and Populism in the New Europe* (Cambridge University Press, Cambridge, 2009); Jon E. Fox and Peter Vermeersch, “Backdoor Nationalism,” 51(2) *European Journal of Sociology* (2010): 325–357; Michael Stewart (ed.), *“The Gypsy Menace”: Populism and the New Anti-Gypsy Politics* (Hurst & Co, London, 2012).

32. Fox and Vermeersch, *ibid.*, at 346.

33. Thomas Hammarberg, “Anti-Roma Rhetoric Underpins Obstacles to Roma Inclusion”, speech at the Summit of Mayors on Roma, *Building mutual trust at the grassroots Plenary Panel—Roma inclusion: what obstacles?* (2011), at <https://wcd.coe.int/ViewDoc.jsp?id=1835197>.

34. Stewart, *op.cit.* note 31, at xiv.

35. European Parliament resolutions P6_TA(2005)0151; P6_TA(2006)0244 (2005/2164(INI)); P6_TA(2008)0035.

36. At <http://ec.europa.eu/justice/discrimination/roma/national-strategies/index_en.htm>.

37. Viviane Reding "Are National Governments Ready to Live up their Commitments?" Extraordinary meeting of the European Platform for Roma Inclusion (Brussels, 22 March 2012), SPEECH/12/215, at <http://europa.eu/rapid/pressReleasesAction.do?reference=SPEECH/12/215>.

38. Will Guy, André Liebich and Elena Marushiakova, "Improving the Tools for the Social Inclusion and Non-Discrimination of the Roma in the EU, European Commission", (European Commission, Brussels, 2010), at <http://ec.europa.eu/justice/discrimination/files/roma_report2010_en.pdf>.

39. See, e.g., Valeriu Nicolae, "Systemic Reform Is Urgently Needed for the Roma", *Open Democracy*, 14 March 2012, at <http://www.opendemocracy.net/valeriu-nicolae/systemic-reform-is-urgently-needed-for-roma>.

40. Iskra Uzunova, "Roma Integration in Europe: Why Minority Rights are Failing", 27(1) *Arizona Journal of International and Comparative Law* (2010), 283–323.

41. Sobotka and Vermeersch, *op.cit.* note 15.

42. Mary Daly, "Assessing the EU approach to poverty and social exclusion in the last decade", in Marlier, Eric, Natali, David, and Van Dam, Rudi, (eds), *Europe 2020: Towards a More Social EU?* (Peter Lang, Brussels, 2010), 139–157; Gabriele Tondl, "EU Regional Policy", in Michael Artis and Norman Lee (eds.), *The Economics of the European Union* (Oxford University Press, Oxford, 2001), 180–211.

43. European Commission, "Communication from the Commission to the European Parliament, the Council, the European Economic and Social Committee and the Committee of the Regions: An EU Framework for National Roma Integration Strategies up to 2020", (2010) COM/2011/0173 final, at <http://eur-lex.europa.eu/LexUriServ/LexUriServ.do?uri=CELEX:52011DC0173:en:NOT>.

44. For more details see Sobotka and Vermeersch, *op.cit.* note 15.

45. Peter Vermeersch, "Improving Access to Housing for Roma: Good Local Practices, Funding, and Legislation: Conference Report" (FRA, Open Society Fund Prague, Decade for Roma Inclusion Secretariat, Prague, 2011).

46. Guy, Liebich and Marushiakova, *op.cit.* note 38, at 37.

47. For more about the NGO in question, see <http://www.ohchr.org/EN/NewsEvents/Pages/IndianHRfightstoendRomadiscrimination.aspx> and <http://www.vzajemnesouziti.estranky.cz>.

48. Council of the EU, "An EU Framework for National Roma Integration Strategies up to 2020: Council Conclusions, 10658/11" (2011), at <http://register.consilium.europa.eu/pdf/en/11/st10/st10658.en11.pdf>.

49. European Roma Policy Coalition and Decade of Roma Inclusion Secretariat, "Document prepared at the Preparatory Meeting of Civil Society Representatives" (Brussels, 21 March 2012).

50. Peter Vermeersch, "Roma Inclusion: Can International Institutions Play a Role?" 15 *Development and Transition* (2010), 7–10.

51. Peter Vermeersch, "Reframing the Roma: EU Initiatives and the Politics of Reinterpretation", 38(8) *JEMS* (2012), 1195–1212.

52. Fresno, *op.cit* note 2.

53. Guy, Liebich and Marushiakova, *op.cit* note 38, at 36.

54. For a more elaborate argumentation of this issue, see Sobotka and Vermeersch, *op.cit.* note 15.

*Peter Vermeersch is professor of political science at the University of Leuven in Belgium, where he is affiliated with the Institute for International and European Policy and the Centre for Research on Peace and Development. He is the author of *The Romani Movement: Minority Politics and Ethnic Mobilization in Contemporary Central Europe* (Berghahn Books, 2006).

Vermeersch, Peter. "The European Union and the Roma: An Analysis of Recent Institutional and Policy Developments." In *European Yearbook of Minority Issues*, vol. 10 (2011), edited by the European Centre for Minority Issues and the European Academy Bozen/Bolzano, 339–358. Leiden: Koninklijke BRILL NV, 2013.

Used by permission.

The EU's Roma Role

*by Martin Kovats**

Roma communities are facing a hostile environment in numerous European states. The European Commission needs to strike a fine balance between promoting change and allowing states to tackle this situation themselves.

Valeriu Nicolae argues in his recent piece for openDemocracy[i] that the European Commission (EC) is not serious about the 'gathering crisis' affecting Roma. He points to the lack of Roma expertise (or even experience) among senior officials and a preference for 'positive' reports and 'watered down recommendations'. He argues that the EC's approach to Roma can be classified as 'structural racism' as it excludes Roma participation at a senior level, and implies that this is a significant factor in the wider failure of Roma policy initiatives. He calls for an investigation into the Commission's Roma work, which could be carried out by the European Parliament.

Valeriu Nicolae is right to express the urgency of the need to effectively address the deteriorating political situation of Roma in Europe. It is also unarguable that people who make important decisions should understand what they are doing. However, judging the knowledge needs of the Commission begs the questions: what is the Commission doing in respect of Roma issues and what should it do? If we look at how Roma has become an EU issue, we can see that the EU in general and the EC in particular are still working on the answer. Furthermore, focusing on the shortcomings of the Commission distracts attention away from where primary political responsibility to bring about change lies, at the national level.

About the Author

In 2009 Valeriu Nicolae and I helped the Commission produce the 10 Common Basic Principles for Roma Inclusion, which are still the cornerstone of European initiatives on the subject. Since 2010, I have been the Special Adviser on Roma issues to the Commissioner for Employment, Social Affairs and Inclusion, László Andor, and have been involved in developing the EU Framework for National

i [Ed. note] Valeriu Nicolae, "Systemic Reform Is Urgently Needed for Roma," *openDemocracy*, March 14, 2012, http://www.opendemocracy.net/valeriu-nicolae/systemic-reform-is-urgently-needed-for-roma.

Roma Integration Strategies up to 2020. Nevertheless, the opinions expressed here are entirely my own, based on twenty years of studying the Roma political phenomenon. They do not reflect the views of the Commission or any member of the Commission.

Roma on the EU's Agenda

Roma is used by the EU and in wider discourse as an 'umbrella' identity replacing the (English) generic term 'gypsy'. But Roma is more than a re-branding of gypsy, it also represents a fundamental change in the centuries-old relationship between traditionally marginalised communities, the state and mainstream society. This change is nothing less than the emergence of Roma people as active participants in public life (see "The Politics of Roma Identity: Between Nationalism and Destitution," Martin Kovats, openDemocracy 29 July 2003). Of course, there have been Roma people operating at the interface between officials and society since there have been such communities. What is different now is people using Roma identity in increasing numbers to act in organised ways to represent interests on the public stage. The EU's adoption of Roma as the umbrella term puts into practice the call of the first World Romany Congress in 1971 to have Roma adopted as the primary identity, at least in public life.

Despite some small scale initiatives going back to the 1970s, the importance of Roma for the EU is fundamentally driven by conditions in Central and South East Europe. From the mid 1990s, increasing amounts of EU funds have been spent on programmes aimed at Roma people. Analysis of the situation of Roma minorities became a regular feature in the annual pre-accession reports of several candidate countries. The enlargements eastwards of 2004 and 2007 turned the majority of Europe's Roma into EU citizens.

Migration Tensions

Within weeks of Romania's entry into the EU, authorities in Italy began complaining about the arrival of thousands of impoverished Roma migrants. Rising tensions led to the declaration of a 'Nomads Emergency', which was only lifted in late 2011. A public row broke out between EU members and even torpedoed the establishment of a far right grouping in the European Parliament due to the conflicting patriotism of Italian and Romanian nationalists. In 2010 the French government responded to a clash between police and members of the country's indigenous Gens de Voyage by announcing the closure of 300 'Roma camps' and the expulsion of thousands of Romanian and Bulgarian Roma migrants. Evidence of ethnic targeting prompted the EC's Vice-President, the Commissioner for Justice, Fundamental Rights and Citizenship, Viviane Reding, to denounce the government's behaviour as a 'disgrace' and analogous with the persecution of Roma during World War II. The robust response of the French government demonstrated the sensitivity of EU governments to Commission criticism of their treatment of Roma. The Commission subsequently accepted assurances that France would implement the Free Movement Directive appropriately.

Poverty, Values and Social Cohesion

Inter-EU migration directly links Roma to one of the EU's four freedoms and has shown how the difficulties many Roma people face in their home countries can spill over into other states. However, Roma is not solely a migration issue for the EU. The mass impoverishment of Roma people in the post-communist period has depressing implications for economic development, as well as wider EU values of equal opportunities and non-discrimination. It has also contributed to the rise of far right or nationalist movements which have begun playing the populist 'Roma card' as part of a wider rejection of rights based responses to social problems. This was first successfully deployed in 2005 by the Ataka movement in Bulgaria, but has proved particularly potent in Hungary, the European state that has done the most to promote Roma as a political identity (as part of a wider minority rights agenda seeking to protect the interests of Magyar minorities in neighbouring states.)

From 2008, the pseudo-paramilitary Magyar Gárda began holding intimidating marches and demonstrations against 'gypsy crime' and in 2009 a series of racist murders spread terror among Roma communities throughout Hungary. The main beneficiaries of this aggression against Roma were the far right Jobbik party, who won 17% of the vote at the 2010 elections, entering Parliament for the first time as the third largest party (with only 12 fewer seats than the main opposition Hungarian Socialist Party).

Therefore, within a few short years of most Roma becoming EU citizens, the situation of Roma has created challenges for the EU in respect of its core values, its economic 'model' and relationships between member states. The whole EU project itself is under threat should politicised hostility towards Roma propel a far right party to power. As a result, following the public clash between the Commission and France in 2010, the Commission accepted that it needed to take the initiative, but how?

Not an EU Roma Policy…

In fact, since 2005, the Commission had been under mounting pressure to act from a range of sources. The obviously unsatisfactory situation for Roma in a number of states means that there is an inevitable tendency to look for 'solutions' in terms of greater EU intervention. In recent years, the European Parliament has adopted a variety of reports and recommendations that the Commission come up with an EU Roma policy. This call was backed by a number of eastern EU states that have long argued that Roma is a 'European issue' and which participate in the World Bank/George Soros initiated Decade of Roma Inclusion. It was also advocated by a number of international NGOs, which formed the European Roma Policy Coalition.

However, the Commission was wary of 'Europeanising' Roma policy. In its Staff Working Paper of 2008, the Commission pointed out that EU treaties keep competency for social policy to member states. Without being granted additional legal powers, the Commission cannot compel governments to adopt a prescriptive action plan with targets for improving the social situation for Roma. Instead, in 2011, the Commission launched the EU Framework for National Roma Integration Strategies.

…but a Framework for National Policies

The EU Roma Framework was endorsed by Council and requires all 27 EU states to produce either detailed national plans (running up to 2020) for reducing Roma inequality, or integrated policy measures for helping disadvantaged citizens, including Roma (the Commission is currently analysing these national strategies and will publish its assessment at the end of April). This approach solves the problem of competency by making states responsible for their commitments rather than these being imposed by the EU. It also defines the EU's role as one of supporting national governments to deliver on their commitments, but without the EU itself being responsible for the activities of states themselves. The EU 'added value' lies in the public commitments of governments, EU funding for projects and programmes and linkage with EU policy process (notably the EU's Europe 2020 growth strategy).

From its inception, the Framework has been criticised for being weak and unrealistic in requiring action from states, many of which have failed to address the needs of Roma people until now, which has led to the very problems to which the Framework is responding. However, the Framework's emphasis on the responsibility of member states is more than a bureaucratic reflection of a legal division of labour, but seeks to address challenges at the heart of the Roma policy paradigm.

National Context and Consent

The superficial symbolism of Roma as a unique transnational people, the EU's 'largest ethnic minority' with no 'mother country', promotes the (nationalist) aspiration that there should be some form of special European governance for Roma. Yet, regardless of what distinct cultural characteristics Roma people may share to a greater or lesser extent (or not at all), Roma are also citizens with the same rights and subject to the same economic, legal and political systems, part of the same national societies and cultures as their non-Roma compatriots. Integration, inclusion, equality of opportunity are concepts that must be meaningfully applied to real people in accordance with their actual circumstances. So for example, the equality of Roma in Romania is relative to that of other Romanians, not to the situation of Roma in Spain, Ireland or wherever.

Improving the situation of Roma people can only be done through local and national systems and institutions in individual states. Critics argue that public prejudice against Roma is a major obstacle to politicians and authorities embracing effective policy initiatives. However, that just underlines the necessity of winning the argument, not avoiding it. The EU can support positive policies both discursively and through EU funds, but it lacks the moral, legal or political authority to compel a state and society that is not yet willing to take the necessary steps to ensure that their Roma citizens enjoy equality of opportunity in every respect. Indeed, the wrong kind of EU intervention would probably work to the advantage of the Eurosceptic, Roma baiting far right. [...] Related to this acknowledgement that Roma equality can only be meaningful in local and national contexts is the crucial importance of accountability. Though the Romantic ethnic discourse tends towards a narrative that Roma have always been and always will be marginalised in European societies, poverty and exclusion are neither inevitable nor a 'natural disaster', but are the consequence of decisions that have directly or indirectly determined their circumstances and opportunities. Improving opportunities for Roma people can only come about by strengthening the accountability of those who make decisions that affect Roma people, from teachers to ministers.

The danger of prescriptive EU intervention is that it could actually undermine accountability. At present accountability is clear—it rests with national authorities who are responsible for applying the law and providing services to their citizens regardless of ethnicity. If the EU were to set detailed targets for Roma policy, it would become responsible for whether those targets were met, even though it would not have the tools to deliver on them. At best, this would create confusion and would allow national governments to deflect attention from their own shortcomings. It would also keep alive the idea that if some states continue to fail their Roma citizens, sooner or later the EU may be pushed to take away from states the responsibility for addressing the needs of Roma people by establishing some kind of special European governance mechanism.

The Aims of the EU Roma Framework

The EU's Roma Framework asserts the responsibility of member states for policies to promote integration and social inclusion. It requires governments to set down their commitments in respect of Roma or disadvantaged persons in general, and to monitor and report on their progress. It encourages the active participation of Roma people, NGOs and others to critically evaluate policy initiatives allowing for the greater accountability of decision-makers to develop alongside a better focused and informed public debate. The hope is that greater transparency and scrutiny of Roma integration policies will lead to activities that will be more effective than in the past and thus (in certain states) rebuild public confidence in inclusive political initiatives.

The Framework has to gain confidence in itself too. This will not be an easy task, not least as Vice-President Commissioner Reding commented on the national strategies that 'there is still a lot of room for improvement' in a speech to the extraordinary meeting of the Roma Platform in March of this year. However, the Framework should not be judged, first and foremost, by what policies member states have written themselves, but by how successful it is in improving the accountability of local and national authorities for how they treat their (Roma) citizens.

Learning to Fulfil the EU's Role

To succeed, the Commission will have to have the judgement and capacity to play its part in achieving this strategic goal. It has to be able to support key member states to enable them to use EU funds more effectively. In monitoring the Framework, the Commission will not only need to capture the right information, but also use that information to contribute to national debates and enhance governmental accountability. The Commission will also need to become bolder and more sophisticated in how it deploys its legal powers with respect to anti-discrimination.

As social policy is still intergovernmental, the Framework allows for the sharing of good practice between EU states. There is a clear distinction expressed in the national Roma strategies between wealthy western states that insist they have functional, non-discriminating public services and administrative systems, while eastern states admit their social policy infrastructure is inadequate and anti-Roma prejudice endemic. The EU Roma Framework offers the opportunity for countries to be 'good Europeans' by transferring knowledge and expertise within the EU. Furthermore, political authority lies with the Council and not the Commission, meaning that any serious criticism of a government's treatment of its Roma citizens must emanate from other member states. The European Parliament can also play an important role in promoting better national debates about Roma, explaining the EU's role and holding both the Commission and Council to account for their Roma related activities.

The Accountability of the Commission

Valeriu Nicolae is correct that the Commission needs to account for its recruitment policies and who it considers a stakeholder. However, labelling the Commission 'structurally racist' and calling for an investigation misreads the nature of the EC's emerging role in the Roma policy debate. It is understandable that the deeply unsatisfactory and deteriorating situation for Roma in some states prompts people to look for quick solutions in terms of governance arrangements—if only the EU would sort things out. However, it should be understood that the EU's role is primarily strategic, and its success or failure can only be judged in the medium and longer terms according to how much it contributes to improving the quality of debate and accountability of its member states.

The EU has a very important role to play in the Roma policy paradigm, but not a decisive one. The danger of focusing on the EU, and the Commission in particular, is that it distracts from where substantive change is required in respect of the development and implementation of policies and programmes to support Roma people—in member states. There is a very clear principle that all governments must ensure that all their citizens are treated fairly regardless of ethnicity. The EU's Roma role is directed towards the realisation of that principle. The transnational Roma discourse and demands for European governance risk compromising this principle by implying that some states simply cannot be expected to treat their Roma citizens fairly, with potentially serious consequences for the viability of fundamental rights at a time of economic crisis, increasing social tensions and a resurgent far right.

Kovats, Martin. "The EU's Roma Role." *openDemocracy*, May 11, 2012. http://www.opendemocracy.net/martin-kovats/eus-roma-role.

QUESTIONS FOR DEBATE

After the Czech Republic, Slovakia, and Hungary had been admitted as EU members in 2004 and Bulgaria and Romania in 2007, the EU continued to offer advice and financial support in the hope of improving the situation of their Roma populations. Many Romanian and Bulgarian Roma did not wait for progress at home but headed westward, especially to Italy and France. Violent expulsion of these migrants provoked heated confrontation between the European Commission and the Italian and French governments, who raised questions about the legal right to freedom of movement within the EU.

The European Council of Ministers—the EU's highest body—voiced its concern but represents the interests of member states and their autonomy in issues of social policy. The EU sees the role of the European Commission—its executive arm—as offering guidance and support but with ultimate responsibility for the situation of Roma resting with the individual member states of which they are citizens. Consequently, direct challenges to governments about their apparent lack of political will to take meaningful action are unlikely. All member states are now required to have plans to make significant progress by 2020, but take-up of available funding is disappointing.

- Do you think the EU should do more to improve Roma inclusion? Can it? Should it take more action to enforce the directive on nondiscrimination?
- Why do you think so little progress has been made in Central and Eastern Europe in spite of more than a decade of EU advice and financial aid?
- Do you agree that, where social policy is concerned, the sovereignty of individual nation states should take precedence over an EU Roma policy? What are the pros and cons of either position?
- As EU citizens, should Roma be allowed to go anywhere they want in the EU? If not, why not?

Part 3:
EU Target Areas for Action

Systemic Exclusion of Roma from Employment[1]

*by Ann [Morton] Hyde**

The majority of working age Roma in Central and Southeastern Europe do not have a job and many have been out of work for a considerable length of time. Growing numbers, especially young people, have never had a job. Recent multi-country research by the ERRC [European Roma Rights Centre] based on structured narrative interviews with a total of 402 working age individuals, documents massive systemic discrimination in the area of employment, discrimination more serious than previously suspected.

The mass-unemployment of working-age Roma is most often perceived as a labour market supply-side issue and the high level of unemployment is attributed to Roma's inability to find employment because of their low levels of education; out-of-date work skills and detachment from the labour market. Also because large segments of the Romani community lost out during the economic and industrial restructuring that occurred during the transition from Communism. Undoubtedly, these factors create very real barriers that reduce employability and exclude many Roma from work but there is another dimension—discrimination—which significantly aggravates the situation and causes systemic exclusion from employment for vast numbers of working-age Roma.

Discrimination is not widely acknowledged as a major factor behind Romani unemployment, and when the issue is raised there is often strong resistance to discuss the subject or denial that the problem is sufficiently severe to demand attention. Employment discrimination against Roma is not considered a major determinant in the employment (or more importantly the non-employment) of Roma by the key actors in the labour market.

Recent research by ERRC, based on field research in Bulgaria, Czech Republic, Hungary, Romania and Slovakia, offers new information that augments and helps to fill some of the gaps in the knowledge base about Roma in the labour market. It reveals a number of key facts about the patterns of employment and unemployment in the Romani working age population and provides evidence that refutes most of the commonly held prejudiced opinions about the attitudes and commitment of Roma to work. It shows that very real barriers to employment are intensified by prejudiced and stereotypical views such as the comment made by the director of a Labour Office in Prague, who told the ERRC:

> It's because of the Romani culture and their lifestyle; they do not fit with the discipline of work. Roma do not have the motivation to work; they are unreliable, lazy and prefer to live on social assistance than earn a living.[3]

Discrimination is exercised at more or less every junction in the labour market and the already serious barriers that prevent access to employment for many Roma are significantly aggravated by prejudiced behaviour and views that unemployment and worklessness is a situation that most, if not all, Roma have chosen and are happy to live with both now and in the past.

The Key Facts Emerging from the Research

The Gap between Employment and Unemployment

- Two out of every three working age Roma are currently unemployed, this means that only one in three currently has a job. Of those out of work, 35% fit the description of long-term unemployed as they have been out of work for a year or more and a staggering one in three working age Roma have had a period of unemployment lasting five years or more.
- Most of the working age Roma interviewed have had a period in employment. But only about one-third of working age Roma are currently in work. This employment rate is significantly lower than the figure for the working age population as a whole—in 2004 the employment rate for people aged 15–64 was 63%,[4] in the twenty-five European Union (EU) member states.
- Given the opportunity, and like the majority of the working age population, Roma will keep the same job for a considerable length of time. Almost 50% of working age Roma reported periods of continuous employment which lasted five years or more. About two-thirds have had continuous employment of periods exceeding one year. These results contradict, and go some way to dispel the negative and prejudiced view that Roma are unreliable and do not keep steady jobs.
- There is a distinct polarisation in the patterns of employment and unemployment for working age Roma. At one end there are those Roma who are, or who have been working in jobs for a significant length of time. At the other end are Roma who have been unemployed and out of work for a very long time. When a Romani individual loses their job and becomes unemployed, they run a very high risk of remaining out of work for a very long time, possibly years.

The Kind of Work That Roma Do

- Roma are very clear about their position on the labour market, and most search for work that is at the lower unskilled end of the labour market where jobs are menial and low paid. However, these are usually highly competitive positions with a rapid turnover and being filled by employers who are quick to absorb cheap and unofficial workers.
- The type of work that Roma do is very closely correlated with their low levels of education—68% of those in work confirmed that they are in employment which reflects their educational attainment levels. Unskilled and skilled labouring, which includes jobs as tailors and machine workers and the like, and cleaning are by far the most common employment categories. By far the least common is work in shops, offices, restaurants, hotels, teaching and professional managerial positions.
- One in every three Roma in our survey who consider that they are currently in a job are actually participating in some form of public works or government funded job creation scheme rather than in employment in the primary labour market.
- Only some 16% of those in employment are in "informal" employment, which in this research means casual, without a contract and not paying tax; a figure that also contradicts the popular belief that most Roma work in the informal shadow economy.
- Very small numbers of Roma work in restaurant/hotel type work or in shops, which is surprising given that these types of occupations usually offer some unqualified opportunities for people at the lower end of the labour market. The evidence provides a strong case that employment discrimination is preventing Roma from being employed in jobs which involve contact with the public or with the preparation or service delivery of food.

  > I am a qualified cook. I was made redundant when the firm I had been employed by for many years was closed down. So I applied and was hired to work as a cook in a spa resort but there was an important condition the person in charge of recruitment imposed: I would be hired as a cook and perform my duties on the basement floor where I could not be seen by doctors and patients. (ERRC interview, Czech Republic, May 2005)[5]

- The relationship between education and better employment is reinforced by the research as university educated Roma are in employment at the higher end of the labour market; working in either office work, teaching or skilled work. Conversely, not all Roma in professional or managerial positions achieved higher levels of education.

Discrimination against Roma at the Labour Market

- The most prevalent incidence of employment discrimination against Roma is at the job search stage and in the recruitment practices that companies apply. Raw, direct discrimination prevents applicants from even reaching the phase of the interview. Many companies have a total exclusion policy regarding the employment of Roma and practice across-the-board unmitigated discrimination against Romani applicants. As a result, Romani job-seekers are eliminated and excluded from the application process at the very outset; regardless of education, qualifications and competences for the job.
- Out of 402 interviewed, 257 Romani individuals of working age have experienced discrimination in employment. The situation is almost twice as bad for Roma in the five countries targeted by the research where two out of every three working age Roma are likely to experience employment discrimination, than for ethnic minorities in the 11 countries in Europe and North America, that were surveyed by the ILO and found to have discrimination rates of up to 35%.[6]
- When asked 'How do you know it was because you are Roma,' almost one in two people said they had been openly told by the employer or someone in the company and in addition 20 individuals were told by the labour office. Therefore more than half of all Roma who reported that they have experienced employment discrimination know for sure that their ethnicity, the fact they are Romani, has prohibited and reduced their chances of getting a job.

> Before setting off to attend a job interview I called the potential employer to make sure that the position was still free. I was assured that nothing had changed and that they were looking forward to seeing me. As soon as I entered the office they told me that I had wasted my time as they do not employ Roma. (ERRC interview, Slovakia, July 2005)
>
> At my local employment office I found an announcement that a factory was hiring eight unskilled workers. I went along with a friend for a job but they told us they had no jobs available. On our way back we met two Romanian friends (non-Roma) who were also going to apply having seen the same announcement. We told them

the jobs had gone. But they went to the factory anyway and they were hired. (ERRC interview, Romania, September 2005)

The incidence of discrimination in employment was not as frequently reported as the discriminatory practices that prevent access to employment. But discrimination in employment is notoriously difficult to prove and frequently goes unreported and unchallenged for fear that action will jeopardise individuals' employment status. Inequality in employment is nonetheless a serious problem for Roma, as some 1 in 4 of those who are, or have, been in employment reported that they received lesser terms and conditions of employment than non-Romani counterparts doing the same job.

The most common differential in terms and conditions of employment took place in relation to remuneration—rates of pay. Over half of respondents who reported some form of inequality in employment claimed that they either received lower rates of pay or were denied the opportunity to work overtime.

Many Roma who are in employment find that their opportunities are severely constrained by an invisible 'Glass Box'[7] which limits their opportunities to progress upwards, sideways or to obtain employment that is not connected to the delivery of services for other Romani people. For example in Slovakia, where a higher incidence of university educated Roma was reported than in other countries, nearly all are employed in Roma related work in the Social Development Fund,[8] as Roma social workers or in the office of government specialising on Roma issues. A quote from the research was that "Roma with higher education can only get work in Roma-specific areas; otherwise they would probably be unemployed like most Roma."

The Perpetrators of Discrimination

Despite existing equality legislation that prohibits discrimination on the grounds of ethnicity, many companies appear unconcerned and take no positive measures to ensure that they comply with the legislation or ensure that equality in employment is functioning in the hiring and employment. It is clear that enterprises, no matter whether they are in the private or public sector, are making very little effort to actively apply an equal opportunity or diversity policy. Even multi-national companies from Western Europe and the USA with branch offices in Central and Southeastern Europe, where the law will have required them to observe and monitor employment equality policies, seem content to hide behind national claims in Central and Southeastern Europe that it is illegal to monitor the ethnic diversity of their workforce.

Two-thirds out of 43 employers interviewed claim that they have an equal opportunities/diversity policy in place but none could provide a detailed explanation of how the procedures operate. Similarly, none of the companies could provide information about how they monitor the ethnic composition of their workforce. Most claim that they do not measure because it is illegal to monitor ethnicity.

The public sector is one of the largest employers in each country especially government ministries, but even in the public institutions there is no evidence of a proactive approach to guarantee equality of opportunity in employment.

There is no evidence that Government Ministries are reflecting the positive methods adopted by their counterparts in Government Departments in the old EU Member States. Nor are they taking steps to ensure that their recruitment and employment practices are free from direct and indirect discrimination and compliant with the EU Employment and Race Directives. At best, some make special advisory positions on Roma related issues available for qualified Roma.

There is strong evidence of institutional racism in the labour office structures in Central and Eastern Europe. During the ERRC interviews with labour offices, what emerged was a transparent display of the racism and entrenched prejudice that exists and was openly and freely expressed.[9] The entrenched negative stereotypes of those working in public institutions, at the front-line of dealing with Roma unemployment, bring into question their capacity to deliver an unbiased and professional service that is not distorted by their prejudiced views. In fact, labour offices were reported to be the least effective means of finding a job. In many instances labour office officials have reportedly condoned discrimination against Roma respecting employers' request not to offer positions to Romani job seekers.

> Emily's girlfriend works for the local labour office and she showed her on the labour office computer screen, job offers where the employer did not want Roma people had an "R" flag to signify that no Roma were employed by the company. Joseph, from the same town, also reported that the local labour office only made placements to the locations where the "R" flag was missing from the name of the company. (ERRC interview, Hungary, August 2005)
>
> An experienced cleaner was sent by the labour office to a bank that was advertising for part-time cleaning staff. She arrived on time for interview, but the bank representative on seeing her told her the jobs had been taken. Later the labour office again announced the same job

opportunity; but this time they apparently followed the bank's signal that no Roma would get the jobs. Later the woman heard the job had been given to non-Romani students. (ERRC interview, Hungary, August 2005)

The attitude and behaviour of many labour office officials compounds the problem of employment discrimination against Roma. Although many labour office officials defend their actions on the basis of efficiency and compassion, to save an individual from the humiliation of being rejected and refused the job, their passive behaviour sends the wrong message to employers. Their laissez-faire attitude and failure to challenge employers who refuse to hire Roma is making an unacceptable situation even worse.

Labour office officials argue that affirmative action is not necessary because discrimination does not exist, and the only reason that Roma do not have jobs is their lack of education and their different attitudes to employment.[10] It was not unusual for the labour office officials to imply that the current hierarchy in the jobs market, which ensures that non-Roma get selected for jobs before Roma, is the right one—the way it should be. Statements such as, "After all there are many unemployed; Czechs, Slovaks, Bulgarians, etc. who are also searching and can't find work," confirm these widely held beliefs.

Furthermore, the services that labour offices provide are not meeting the needs of Romani job seekers. The shortcoming in the services and the lack of connection between unemployed Roma and labour offices is unacceptable given the role that labour offices have in linking out of work people with job vacancies and with government, and donor-funded employment and training opportunities.

The behaviour of the labour market gatekeepers has a very real impact on the opportunities that are made available to unemployed Roma trying to re-enter the labour market. But there is no comprehensive understanding amongst labour market gatekeepers—employers, human resource personnel and labour office officials—that their behaviour is one of the major contributors resulting in systemic exclusion from employment for vast numbers of working-age Roma.

Tackling Employment Discrimination

The ERRC research provides evidence and draws on experience from other EU countries to show that a mixture of: **strong anti-discrimination legislation** when it is vigorously enforced; **equality policies** which contain very clear directives and a convincing level of compulsion; and a public equality authority that monitors enforcement of the **public duty to promote equality** can be successful to contain, constrain and reduce discriminatory behaviour of employers and their employees.

There is strong evidence, from countries with the most effective measures to combat racial discrimination in employment, that workforce monitoring, including the collection of data on ethnicity, is a key means of obtaining statistical evidence to support positive actions to address under-representation of ethnic groups in the workplaces and more generally in specific occupations and sectors of the labour market. Monitoring, recording, reporting and responding to the ethnic composition of a workplace are key factors that guarantee the effectiveness and efficiency of equal opportunities policies. For example, mandatory monitoring and compulsory reporting of workforce composition on the basis of nationality, ethnic group and any other grounds of discrimination (religion in the case of Northern Ireland) has proven to be a significant lever that motivated improved access to the employment for a victimized group.[11]

Employment discrimination is more pervasive and insidious than the basic numbers suggest, especially when it is as blatant and explicitly exercised as the cases described by Roma who took part in the ERRC research. Achieving equality in employment for Roma will take a considerable length of time; it requires widespread commitment and cooperation across all strands of the labour market. The situation is critical and the problem demands immediate attention from Governments as well as legislators, policy makers, employers and drivers of change; from the Equality Bodies charged with the responsibility of enforcing and stimulating compliance; and from employers who are in the position to guarantee recruitment practices and workplaces that are free of discrimination.

Endnotes

1. This article summarises the results of a research on discrimination against Roma in the labour market conducted by the ERRC in the period May-September, 2005 in Bulgaria, Czech Republic, Hungary, Romania and Slovakia. The full research findings will be published in April 2006. The research was part of the transnational project "Advocacy Action in Favour of the Promotion of the Integration of Roma in Education and Employment", implemented by the International Helsinki Federation for Human Rights (IHF) in partnership with the European Roma Rights Centre (ERRC) and the European Roma Information Office (ERIO). The project is funded by the European Union and is part of the EU Community Action Programme to Combat Discrimination 2001–2006. The content of this article does not necessarily reflect the views of the European Commission.

[...]

3. ERRC interview, May 2005, Prague.
4. In the countries included in the research the rates were as follows—54.2% in Bulgaria; 64.4% in Czech Republic; 56.8% in Hungary; 57.7% in Romania; and 57% in Slovakia. Source Eurostat, Labour Force Survey 2004 News Release Number 112/2005 at website http://epp.eurostat.cec.eu.int.

5. To encourage open disclosure of information, the research interviews allowed for anonymity of individual respondents. The examples cited in this article are extracts from the Country Research Reports prepared and submitted by the research team in Bulgaria, Czech Republic, Hungary, Romania and Slovakia. The lists of Roma interviewed during the course of the research and the questionnaires have been retained and are accessible from the ERRC.
6. See International Labour Organisation. "Challenging Discrimination in Employment: A Summary of Research and A Compendium of Measures", October 2000, available at: http://www.ilo.org/public/english/protection/migrant/download/disc-01-2000.pdf.
7. The "Glass Box" metaphor is an analogy to the "Glass Ceiling" used to describe the invisible factors that limited the progress of women and ethnic minorities into senior positions.
8. The Social Development Fund, is a state institution funded by the Slovak state and the European Social Fund. The aim of the SDF is to improve the inclusion of groups at risk and marginalised groups and enable access to economic opportunities and social services.
9. In all cases ERRC interviews were not with low level public employees, but with either the Director or their representative, usually accompanied by other senior labour office officials.
10. This is an amalgam of the different views expressed when labour office officials were asked their opinion about positive action to guarantee unemployed Romani people access to government training programmes and/or jobs. A similar point was made in all the labour office interviews carried out during the course of this research.
11. Experience from Northern Ireland, relating to discrimination against Catholics in the labour force in the sixties and seventies, is comparable to the systemic exclusion from employment that many Roma in Central and South Eastern Europe currently experience.

***Ann [Morton] Hyde** is a labor market and social inclusion specialist. She is an senior consultant for the European Roma Rights Center on the research project mapping out discriminatory practices against Roma in the labour market.

Hyde, Ann [Morton]. "Systemic Exclusion of Roma from Employment." *Roma Rights* 1 (April 3, 2006). http://www.errc.org/article/systemic-exclusion-of-roma-from-employment/2535.

Used by permission.

Interview with Rumyan Russinov from Bulgaria

Question:[i] Thank you very much for agreeing to an interview. We have been talking with Romani activists at the forefront of the desegregation process in this part of Europe, and you are one of them.

Rumyan Russinov: I appreciate the idea very much. In my opinion it is a very timely effort, and I believe that desegregation is one of the most important processes which have taken place in, I would say, the past 20 years in the Romani movement. I agree that we need a more systematic effort to analyze it.

Q: How would you describe Romani education during the communist period? What are the positive and the negative aspects of that period?

R.R.: Specifically in Bulgaria, we inherited the present segregated schools in Roma neighborhoods from the communist times. These schools were built in the end of the 1940s–1950s as part of the state's campaign to fight mass illiteracy. Roma were also targets of this policy which resulted in the construction of the schools in Roma-only neighborhoods in cities. Despite the separate educational facilities for Roma, however, the levels of segregation of Roma during the communist period have not been as extreme as they became after 1989. The reason is that all Roma worked together with non-Roma, there was a contact between them and the majority society. Moreover, in smaller towns and villages the schools were integrated. It is no wonder that a big percentage of the Roma intelligentsia came from these places. However, the noxious effect of what later on was known as "the Gypsy schools" became evident in the years after 1989 when a large part of the Roma population found themselves unable to compete under the new conditions because they had low education and outdated skills. Whatever the initial intentions of the state, in 40 years, the separate schools created second-class citizens.

Q: Were the educational needs different in communism and in the transition period, after the changes? Are there similarities and differences in the way Roma perceived education in these two different periods?

---

i [Ed. note] Rumyan Russinov was the deputy director of the Roma Education Fund and the director of the Open Society Foundations' Roma Participation Program. As the director of the Human Rights Project, a Sofia-based nongovernmental organization, he led the team of Roma activists that negotiated the program for Roma with the Bulgarian government after the collapse of the communism. The interviewers were Iulius Rostas, Mihai Surdu and Marius Taba.

R.R.: First of all, we should not generalize about Roma. We are different: There have always been people who despite all circumstances, despite bad educational policy, managed to educate themselves. There are others who had more unfortunate circumstances and lives. But, of course, state policies matter a lot. I have to say that nowadays, the state is less concerned with educational policies in general, and even less with the educational status of Roma. The Roma issue in Bulgaria is not the only one ignored on the list of important issues.

I have to say that during communism our status was relatively better, because as part of the working class, Roma were also part of social interaction, part of the system. They were integrated into society; few were marginalized. Today, without jobs, isolated and with almost no contact with the majority, many have become outsiders.

Q: This "better status" in communism was somehow related to the circumstance that the system treated the working class more favorably than nowadays, and Roma had jobs during that time.

R.R.: Yes, I think the most important thing was that Roma had jobs. They had a steady income and status. They thought of themselves as part of the system. When Roma lost their jobs, they lost contact with society and became outsiders, especially when their unemployment lasted for many years. When you are an outsider, you have no optimism; you think less about the children and what education they get. Such circumstances tend to change one's way of thinking. Many Roma who were insiders then, are outsiders now.

However, although they lost status, they are not marginalized because they still think of themselves as insiders. This self-perception makes the difference between those who are marginalized and those who are not. Many non-Roma perceive Roma in general as marginalized and those like us are rather an exception. For me the difference is in the way Roma perceive themselves in the social system and the attitudes they develop towards this system. From this point of view, most of the Roma are not marginalized.

Q: What similarities are there between communism and the period of transition in regard to Roma education?

R.R.: I was 22 when the communist system collapsed, so I remember well what it was like during those times. The first difference was dramatic; the state simply deserted its key responsibilities, as I said not only with respect to Roma policies. Second, Romani parents became jobless and this changed the situation dramatically. Third, generally, values started to change, not just for us, for all of society. Old values vanished, new ones did not appear. Consumerism overtook everything. There was a vacuum. What remained from the embattled educational system is not capable of guiding children in the new circumstances. For many Roma, the only accessible institutions were, and are, various evangelical churches. They offer a system of values, perhaps not an ideal one, but one that is better than nothing. One of the reasons they were so successful among Roma is that they went to the community and sought to help the people. Even if they did not solve their problems, at least there was somebody who approached them and listened to them. These churches showed Roma that they are not forgotten.

Q: Let us speak about minority education and how authorities dealt with minority education in transition. Is the mother tongue taught in Bulgarian schools?

R.R.: Very little. There have been certain attempts for the Romani language to become an optional subject, but this happened only in two towns—in Kyustendil and in Russe, in a very small number of schools.

Q: Why do you think the number is so low?

R.R.: First of all, because Roma ourselves, do not push for Romani language classes at school. Many Romani parents would say "we speak the Romani language very well. It is better to learn to speak good Bulgarian." Also, part of the Romani community speaks Turkish as a mother tongue and some of them identify as ethnic Turks. For example, in the 2001 census 370,000 identified themselves as Roma, and 320,000 marked Romani language as their mother tongue.

Q: That's quite a high percentage that could serve as a base for minority education.

R.R.: Yes, indeed. However, we have a combination of weak demand on the part of Roma and inaction on the part of the state.

Q: Do you think the relatively low interest on the part of Roma to study in the Romani language within the educational system is somehow related to this ambiguous identity?

R.R.: I think the main reason for this is the fear that the study of the Romani language may lead to isolation from the rest of society.

Q: How does the educational system deal with this complex system of Romani identity?

R.R.: The state has made some small steps to recognize the Roma identity in the educational system. For example, in primary schools, children read Romani folklore stories and sing Romani songs. I think these are steps in the right direction but they are very insufficient.

Q: When was the issue of segregation of Romani children in schools discussed for the first time publicly in Bulgaria? When did it become an issue, a problem?

R.R.: I remember reading an article written by Elena Marushiakova and Vesselin Popov entitled "The Gypsy schools," published in the magazine of the Bulgarian Helsinki Committee, *Obektiv*. This article rang the bell that segregated education is a serious problem. At the time as part of the team of the nongovernmental organization Human Rights Project, I was travelling around the country, visiting Roma neighborhoods and collecting information about various problems facing Roma, including problems in education. People told us that Romani children complete primary school in the segregated schools and they are unable to read and write their names. In 1995–1996 we started raising this issue at meetings with various government authorities.

Q: Was there research on the issue, or were there politicians or activists who raised the issue?

R.R.: Romani politicians were not publicly visible, neither did they speak about Roma issues in public. Non-Romani politicians do not care. There was NGO activism, but there was, and still is, an absence of political participation by Roma. To some extent, NGOs filled this vacuum and played a role in raising the most important issues for public discussion. We were the most active Roma rights non-governmental organization of that time. In 1997–1998, we started elaborating a framework program for equal participation. This was the first fundamental document which we, the Human Rights Project, produced in 1998. One of the chapters in this Program was dedicated to education and school desegregation. This document which was adopted by the Bulgarian government in April 1999, was the first acknowledgement by the government of the problem with the segregated schools. It was also the first political platform which promoted Roma integration and school desegregation in particular.

Q: What do you think the government's motivation for holding these negotiations with the Romani activists was? Was it a sign that the government recognized segregation as an issue?

R.R.: In the beginning, when we proposed a framework program for Roma integration the government tried to ignore us, as expected. The government at that time did not have a culture of listening to the voice of civil society. When I approached them to negotiate the document, their reaction was, "who are you, young man? You are not legitimate." To a certain extent, this was true, because I was an NGO activist, no one voted for me to be a representative of Roma in these negotiations. The way to become legitimate was to mobilize big support from Roma NGOs and activists throughout the country. We launched a massive public campaign and involved representatives of international organizations as well. All this made it impossible for the government to continue ignoring us. For example, on March 25, 1999, in my capacity of chief negotiator of the Framework

Program on behalf of Roma NGOs, I invited representatives of the Council of Europe to support Roma NGOs to persuade the Bulgarian government to adopt the proposals for government policy in the Framework Program. On that day, the spokesperson of the Prime Minister called me and said that the Government is ready to accept our proposals.

Q: What was the key word you started using when negotiating with the government?

R.R.: We started using the word *desegregation*.

Q: When was this?

R.R.: In 1998, when we, the Human Rights Project, launched the campaign for the adoption of the Framework Program for Integration of Roma by the government. I think this was the first more or less coherent concept of Roma integration which appeared after 1989. We started to have this more fundamental understanding that yes, we want to be together with non-Roma, that we are part of society and we do not want to be the losers. At the center of this program was the proposal to desegregate the "Gypsy schools."

Q: The section on Roma of the Agenda 2000 of the European Commission, released in August 1997, and intended for candidate countries for EU membership had an influence on Roma related policies in those countries. Do you think that, in that context, the Bulgarian government became a little more open in at least accepting discussions with Roma?

R.R.: I believe it played a role, indeed. I think during the entire pre-accession process, the EU pressured the governments to create political will at the national level and make the process of policy-making for Roma integration an irreversible one. However, as we all know this goal was not achieved. Governments found a way to report progress to Brussels, without actually making any progress for Roma integration. That's why it is very important that the EU should maintain its pressure. At the same time, the EU and international organizations should continue supporting Roma civil society organizations to be active participants in the making of policies on Roma integration.

Q: So, at the end of the day, is it expedient to have pressure from outside?

R.R.: Definitely, and this pressure should persist until we have political will at national level to develop and implement integration policies.

Q: Moving back to the issue of segregation of Roma in the communist times in Bulgaria, it is clear that it existed. What were the types and patterns of segregation then?

R.R.: First of all, it was geographical segregation, and second it was educational segregation. Geographical segregation was prevalent in big cities, in smaller towns and villages Roma and non-Roma lived together. Where separate Roma neighborhoods were formed, the state also established 1–2 primary schools, which I mentioned previously. Over the years, the quality of education in these schools degraded. In later years, some of these schools were labeled "schools for children with low lifestyle and culture" which indicated that the state was not willing to ensure an equal standard of education for Roma children.

Q: Was school segregation acknowledged as an issue during communism?

R.R.: No, nobody recognized this as an issue. The goal of state educational policy at the time had not been to secure equal education for Roma but to secure a minimum level of literacy and a vocation. That's why some of the schools based in the Roma neighborhoods had intensive vocational training at the expense of academic subjects. When we challenged separate education of Roma in the 1990s, this was a new paradigm. Until then, the issue was not that separate education is bad—the issue was that Roma do not want to and are not able to accommodate to the mainstream educational system. When Roma started demanding equal education in integrated schools, the government was not anymore in the position to excuse the failures of its policy with the Roma.

Q: What was the extent of segregation under communism and now? Is it better, is it worse?

R.R.: I already partially addressed this question—the level of segregation of Roma today is much higher. Before 1989, Roma had contacts with mainstream society at their workplace. Today, many of them are totally locked up in their neighborhoods.

Q: Who do you think contributes most to maintaining the status quo in segregation? Why is segregation maintained? Who are the most important players who maintain segregation?

R.R.: The main factor is that education in general is not among the priorities of the state as it emerged in the transition period. Roma education is even less interesting for the state. Another factor is that a large number of teachers and school personnel fear that they will lose their jobs. Also, during the 1990s, many donors supported programs to improve the education of Roma. Unfortunately, this money went mainly into the segregated schools. Ironically, again, segregated schools were reinforced with good intentions. Maybe some donors at some point realized that this was a wrong direction, but, many preferred this way because it requires less effort and does not involve confrontation. Breaking the status quo is a difficult process: Working with parents on a daily basis, planning the enrollment of Romani children with school authorities, monitoring the process and evaluating the results is far more demanding than buying books and sports facilities for Romani children.

Q: What is the role of the Romani parents in maintaining the status quo?

R.R.: Many parents, unfortunately, do not understand the consequences of segregation and for years no one has made an effort to explain to them.

Q: What motivated, for example, school personnel to oppose desegregation or maintain segregation?

R.R.: The personnel of segregated schools immediately turned against the process. They understood the trend and, of course, they were afraid of losing their jobs. But schools exist to provide quality education to children, not to maintain jobs for the teachers.

Q: What were the reasons why the donors and the NGOs worked with segregated schools?

R.R.: Unfortunately, some of the donors do not believe that Roma children are capable for mainstream education. The way they express this view is to emphasize the specificity of Roma culture. They have their own prejudices in understanding the issue. Also, in the context of segregated schools, the work of the donors has bigger visibility due to the fact that these schools are almost deserted by the state and even minor improvements, can be easily seen.

Q: Why do you think donors prefer to go to the poorest communities, to the most marginalized ones?

R.R.: I think this is normal. Usually, the first thing is to go to those who really need help. It is true that the percentage of marginalized Roma increased in the transition period but as a group, Roma are not marginal. Respectively, policies and measures which are designed to address the problems of marginal communities, although well-meant, deteriorate the situation of Roma and contribute to their marginalization.

Q: Still, many programs are targeting Roma, but in fact they focus on the poorest communities.

R.R.: True, the prevailing part of the donors supports the poorest. I am not against this. The question is not whether to support the poorest Roma but whether to channel all support towards these parts of the Roma communities only. Integration of the marginalized Roma is a long process; it does not give results promptly, it takes probably a generation. In the meantime, the lack of results for a long period of time may undermine the whole idea of the integration of Roma. There are also those who are tempted to explain the lack of results with the Roma themselves—that they have no aspirations or are not able to integrate. We are fortunate that there are donors like the Open Society Institute and the Roma Education Fund which support programs for the creation of a Roma elite. School desegregation and promotion of Roma in higher education are efforts in this direction.

Q: How have Romani organizations and activists reacted to the issue of segregation? Have there been Romani groups which oppose school desegregation?

R.R.: Some of them, those who had projects in the segregated schools, reacted negatively. Others had no reaction, but many reacted positively. In the beginning, they did not understand exactly what it was about, but little by little they came to understand that, in fact, this is good for Roma. It means quality education for our children and this is the first step towards real integration.

In the past 20 years, many Roma organizations have generally played a very positive role in the movement. Some Roma organizations simply followed the policy of the donors, without questioning them. This usually happens with organizations which do not have support in their communities and derive their legitimacy not from the people who appreciate their services or support their positions but from the donors who funded them. Other organizations are trying to shape their own views, but, unfortunately, the first type is prevalent. Part of the Romani organizations do not think strategically, they tend to follow instructions. It is unfortunate because the last twenty years offered us a unique opportunity which we may never have again. Donors are already moving to Central Africa, to Central Asia, etc. I am worried that the Roma movement is not prepared for this withdrawal. I observe that when donors withdraw, many organizations remain confused, they have no ideas about Roma integration.

Q: How have political parties and the government reacted to this issue? Do they understand the problem? Have there been politicians who speak against segregation?

R.R.: No, the political elite still does not understand it, and they do not care. In my view, it is best if parties include desegregation in their programs. Some do have it in their programs but from their public speeches it seems that they do not understand it. The government first denied that this is a problem. Then they acknowledged it but did not take any responsibility. They said it was inherited and the current government did not have a policy to segregate. In 2002, there was a breakthrough when the Ministry of Education issued the so-called "instruction" for school desegregation. It meant that the problem was not only acknowledged but that there were policy-makers who thought how to solve the problem.

Q: How did academic circles react to the issue of segregation? The universities, researchers?

R.R.: Most of them positively. In fact, they understood their interest in this process. They realized that, within this movement, they will be able to engage in projects, in teacher training, methodology seminars, etc. and they supported it. We worked with Sofia University, with the Dupnitza Teacher College, and they were quite open.

Q: Let's move to Vidin, where everything started. Can you give us some background about what happened there, and how the idea came about?

R.R.: I would not say that I am the author of the idea, and I do not think it is important. At some point, discussing what government policies are needed to integrate Roma, we realized that Roma-only schools produce alarming results. In 1998, we negotiated with the government the adoption of the Framework Program which I mentioned earlier. It contained a very clear statement on the elimination of segregated education. In May 2000, I took the position Director of the Roma Participation Program (RPP) at the Open Society Institute, in Budapest. In August 2000, RPP funded the first desegregation project in Vidin. Why Vidin? Because we needed a strong person to lead the project. Donka Panayotova was this person, respected both by Roma and non-Roma in the town. She was a teacher herself, she knew the situation well and she had the capacity to go there and to start the "revolution," as we called it.

In the Romani neighborhood of Vidin, called Nov Pat (New Way), between five to ten percent of Romani children did not go to school at all. We targeted the middle class of the Romani community, people who were skilled workers for enterprises before, and who lost their jobs after 1989. Donka set up the organization Drom and together we created a support model for the Romani children from the neighborhood to access mainstream schools. We approached our target group as part of the solution—that's why our first task was to talk to the parents and motivate them to send their children to schools outside the neighborhood. Next came our work with the school authorities. We had to make them open, receptive and helpful in the process. We set up a team of people whose task was ongoing communication with parents and teachers about the progress of the child at school. Based on this information, Drom proposed to parents after-school assistance for the children. This was very important because if we had left the children on their own, many would have met difficulties in the new competitive environment and would have lost motivation to go on. Vidin is one of the poorest regions in Bulgaria, and the Romani community is also very poor there. In the beginning, a group of wealthy Romani businessmen were against the process as they thought that it would undermine their position and authority among Roma, but Donka, who is very good in diplomacy, persuaded them to be supportive.

Q: How did the Vidin project eventually unfold?

R.R.: In addition to those steps which I have already described, there was a powerful information campaign on the local Roma TV. The direct dialogue with the Roma community was one of the key factors for the success of the initiative. When there is direct dialogue, you can minimize the prejudices and fears of the people. Then, when the children were enrolled in mainstream schools, we started busing them from the *mahala*[ii] to mainstream schools. Each school where Romani children were placed had one or two supervisors, who took care of the children. When there was a problem related to learning, they discussed it with the teacher. This is how the Vidin model emerged in the school year 2000–2001. In the beginning, teachers in the mainstream schools were not enthusiastic about the initiative—some of them were openly opposed. They were concerned that "the level of education may decrease... and there may be confrontation." It was very important that Donka is part of the pedagogic community in the town, and a respected one. In this capacity, she had negotiated the enrollment with the school principals. After the first semester, I spoke to some of the teachers. One of them told me, "you know, these children are like the rest of the class." You can change things only through real action. Reports and awareness-raising cannot achieve much. You can campaign about school desegregation or talk to the media, but nothing can be as effective as bringing the children physically into the mainstream schools. But the real change started only then, after the children went to the mainstream schools.

Q: What was the reaction of the Romani parents?

R.R.: In the beginning, they reacted cautiously. Some were afraid their children would be harassed. It was very important that there was a Romani NGO to take care of the children. The presence of the supervisors was a very important argument in convincing Romani parents.

Q: Did the number of Romani children enrolled in mainstream schools eventually increase?

R.R.: Yes, the number of children kept increasing. For the parents this process was also very important. Psychologically, it helped them restore their self-esteem. Many of them had a decent social status when they were younger, and after 1989 they started on a downward spiral. To see their children together with Bulgarian children gave them hope. So this was very, very difficult in the beginning.

ii [Ed. note] Romani quarter of a town.

Q: What has happened since Vidin? Has it reached the level of a state policy, or has it remained just an isolated project?

R.R.: As I said in the beginning, the government preferred to explain the problems of Roma education by referring to the Roma themselves—as a product of their lack of interest in education, early marriages, and so on. These problems indeed exist. But if there is political will to develop and implement a policy, these problems should not be used as an excuse to do nothing. The most important question is, do we treat the Roma as able to be rescued or not?

Q: You gave this example with the Vidin case. Did the government take it? Do they consider Roma now as able to be rescued, and have they elaborated a policy based on this?

R.R.: From the very first day, our goal was to persuade the government to develop a policy based on the Vidin model. In 2002 there was the first breakthrough, then in 2004, the Ministry of Education adopted a strategy for school desegregation. I am sure that without the positive examples of the school desegregation projects, already in several towns in the country, we would have no strategy today. We launched discussions in 2004 using arguments and international pressure, and, I cannot say that the government was against it. As with all governments which are lazy and bureaucratic, it was more laziness and bureaucracy than opposition. There was an understanding that, yes, this is the right way, we have to do something.

Q: Which were the most important directions of this strategy?

R.R.: First, we emphasized the process of transferring Roma children from Roma-only schools to mainstream schools. Second, this transfer should be accompanied by the respective educational and awareness-raising measures in order to create the environment in which integration is possible.

Q: Did the strategy provide financial resources for this process?

R.R.: Not the strategy, but the Roma Decade Action Plan[iii] of 2005 did. The action plan of 2005 envisages Roma inclusion measures in four main directions: education, employment, housing and health. In the section on education, number one is school desegregation, with financial support. But, unfortunately, it never happened. Apart from some financial support from municipalities, we did not receive money for desegregation from the government. Out of ten municipalities

---

iii [Ed. note] The Decade of Roma Inclusion (2005–2015) is an international commitment by European governments to eliminate discrimination against Roma involving practical action plans to increase their integration into wider society. See http://www.romadecade.org/about-the-decade-decade-in-brief.

in which the school desegregation projects are currently implemented, only six provide support for the process, including direct financial support.

Q: Were there any initiatives made by the government?

R.R.: No, it was always us, the Roma NGOs, that were active and showed initiative. The government only approved or disapproved.

Q: What has happened to the desegregation strategy?

R.R.: This strategy illustrated the government's intent, but it was never put into practice. It did not have any practical effect until 2007, when the government included it in the budget. The real practical effect came with the creation of the Center for Educational Integration of Minority Children and Pupils at the Ministry of Education. The original idea behind the Center was that it would manage a fund to support school desegregation activities. A draft law for the fund was prepared by the Ministry of Education but it was rejected in Parliament.

Q: Can we say that school desegregation is state policy in Bulgaria? If not, what are the main obstacles to it?

R.R.: The Bulgarian government has officially declared that it will pursue a policy of school desegregation, but has done little to make good on this commitment. The main obstacle is—as I mentioned earlier—that the government does not have the political will to implement school desegregation. In addition, the Bulgarian government traditionally is cautious about undertaking visible measures to help the Roma. The political elite are afraid to support measures for them, and to talk publicly about such measures in order not to antagonize the majority.

Q: In assessing the desegregation process, what results have been achieved so far?

R.R.: For me, the main achievement is broader than the quality of education. The children who left the segregated environment have a broader horizon. Some of them will be good students, others will not. But all of them will see themselves as part of society, as equally valuable persons. Before, they used to have the understanding that the ghetto is their place. Now they dream of becoming doctors and lawyers. Some of them will not become doctors, but the first thing is to dream, that is why I say their horizon has opened. Then they will not need our efforts to desegregate their children; they will do it for themselves.

Q: How far are we from that point?

R.R.: This will take a generation.

Q: What has not been achieved yet?

R.R.: Despite the progress made, there are several things which we did not manage to accomplish. First, we did not manage to move the process into the hands of the state—it still very much depends on the efforts of the Roma NGOs. Second, we did not manage to broaden the scope of donors who support the process. And third, due to limited resources, we were not able to scale up the projects to involve more children.

Q: What is the role played so far by courts, the judicial system in fighting segregation?

R.R.: When a court decision is delivered, the government will pay the fine and they will forget about it. Tomorrow another violation may lead to another court decision—if we are lucky—a favorable one, and the government will pay and again forget.

No, in my view, court decisions cannot change our situation in education. We need other actions.

Q: How have international organizations and donors reacted to the issue of segregation and desegregation?

R.R.: Some of them reacted very positively. For instance, the Open Society Institute is a major donor which started financing the project from the very beginning, and still continues. In 2005, the Roma Education Fund continued what the OSI had started. I value this support very highly, and urge them to continue providing funds for school desegregation. The governments of Sweden, the Netherlands and the United Kingdom also donated funds for school desegregation to the REF. At the EU level, there are several resolutions of the European Parliament which call on national governments to eliminate segregated education of Roma. The Vidin model of school desegregation is recognized as a good practice by the European Commission.

Nevertheless, I cannot say that there is a coherent policy at European level. Honestly, I don't know why, given that the EU is increasingly involved in promoting Roma integration.

Q: Do you see any risk that donors will abandon this area?

R.R.: Yes, there is always the risk that donors would consider something else more important. If the government is committed to pursue school desegregation as a goal, the government will actively seek support for it and will find it. The problem is how to effectively press the government. We need to change the message and make the majority aware that they need us and that they share the loss if we cannot work for society. We need to ask the majority whether they want Roma to be receivers of social aid or taxpayers. If the latter, the majority should also pressure the government to desegregate education.

Q: What is the main lesson learned from this desegregation process?

R.R.: It gives us optimism that we, as activists, can do something useful for our people, something visible, and can prove that Roma can be rescued. Because many believe that whatever you try out for the improvement of the situation of Roma, it will not work. This is not true: we have proved the opposite.

Q: What, in your view, are the next steps as regards desegregation in your country?

R.R.: I believe that we, the NGOs, have paved the way, and it is high time the government took over from us. The government always says that they need positive examples, or best practices, in order to implement them on a large scale. Here are the best practices, please go ahead. Currently, by maintaining the ghetto schools, the government is paying for segregation.

What we want is very simple: We want the same budget, for the same children, to be spent for mainstream schools, not for the ghetto schools. So, actually it does not cost money, only an effort to do it. What we need now is more political will. Overall, I am optimistic: Roma want desegregated education; the majority is not against it. So if we push a bit more, maybe we can do it.

"Interview with Rumyan Russinov from Bulgaria." In *Ten Years After: A History of Roma School Desegregation in Central and Eastern Europe*, edited by Iulius Rostas, 131–144. Budapest: Roma Education Fund/CEU Press, 2012.

Used by permission.

Municipal Programme of Shanty Towns Eradication in Avilés (Principality of Asturias)[i]

*by Will Guy**

[...]

Political concern over the growth of shantytowns in Avilés had intensified during the economic crisis of the late 1980s. Faced with the enforced closure of the vast steel complex that had been the city's main employer, the municipal administration reacted in a remarkable way. Reflecting on a post-industrial future, it decided that the town should not contain shantytowns. But instead of razing these to the ground and driving out their mainly Roma inhabitants, as has been done recently in Italy, the administration set out to integrate them. This 1989 local plan was linked with the 1988 National Programme for the Development of Roma (NPDR).

The initial plan was that, as an intermediate step, social workers would 'resocialise' these people in a separate, purpose-built development on the outskirts of town. After a few years it was recognised that to make improvements in housing conditions, while continuing to maintain residential segregation, was failing to make progress towards social inclusion. So, in spite of the considerable expense of having constructed new accommodation, this was declared redundant and progressively demolished while a programme to match individual families to suitable normal housing was implemented. In this way, to their great satisfaction, Roma families were gradually resettled among other city-dwellers. Unsurprisingly there were some objections from future, non-Roma neighbours but officials patiently explained that the Roma were citizens too and had the same rights and added that, on the basis of personal experience, they were actually nice families. 'Try it for a few months and see!' they suggested and resistance soon ceased. This firmness in the face of difficulties exemplified the resolute political will that characterised the whole project throughout its various phases.

The main strengths of this project were that the project team recognised that factors preventing social inclusion were interrelated and in response they designed an integrated and sustainable approach. As well as providing desegregated housing, they also addressed unemployment concerns—mainly through vocational

i [Ed. note] This article, from the 2009 Greek Peer Review, refers to the 2006 Spanish Peer Review of Avilés, Principality of Asturias, http://ec.europa.eu/employment_social/social_inclusion/docs/2006/pr_sp_en.pdf. EU peer reviews are an opportunity for member states to exchange information on successful and promising practices, approaches, organisational structures and tools.

training schemes, education issues—by providing desegregated kindergarten and school places with support for pupils and they also registered Roma families at health centres and initiated inoculation programmes.

The organisational structures were no less impressive for every level of government—national, regional and municipal—played an active part alongside civil partner NGOs and Roma organisations. The national Roma NGO, the *Fundación Secretariado General Gitano* (FSGG), played a prominent part, particularly through its acclaimed and ESF-supported employment programme *Acceder*. Central government provided assistance and guidance while the regional government supplied much of the funding. This was particularly important in the most decentralised country in the EU with seventeen administrative areas with varying levels of autonomy. A crucial element in the success of the project was that agreement between political parties was negotiated in advance. This prevented the scheme ever becoming a vote-catching issue or a political football in the local media. By no means least, the team worked closely with the Roma beneficiaries who were active participants in the scheme.

The problem is therefore to discover what conceptual and institutional structures will produce the best results in fostering schemes that, whatever their scope, must ultimately be local in their application. This is for the obvious reason that all Roma communities are sited in specific locations. To be successful such schemes must gain local non-Roma support—or at least tolerance, which is one of the most important lessons from many examples of good practice. Without such support, local authorities—the elected representatives—are likely to resist or sabotage instructions from central authorities. Indeed this has been the experience of all past large-scale attempts to integrate (or sometimes assimilate) Roma populations, ranging from the endeavours of Maria Theresa in the Habsburg Empire, those of Communist regimes and more recently, some policies of post-Communist CEE/SEE [Central and Eastern European and Central and South-eastern European] governments with EU financial assistance. The necessary counterpart to non-Roma support is local Roma involvement at every stage of initiatives. This has been a stated aim of various policy transformations over the years but largely remains an unfulfilled intention.

[. . .]

***Will Guy** was thematic expert for the Spanish and Greek Peer Reviews mentioned.

Guy, Will. "Discussion Paper." In *Integrated Programme for the Social Inclusion of Roma (Greece)*, Greek Peer Review, annex 3, 26–28. Brussels: European Commission, 2009. http://ec.europa.eu/social/main.jsp?catId=89&langId=en&newsId=1431&furtherNews=yes.

Roma Inclusion: Can Cities Be the Driver of Change?[i]

*by Ann Morton Hyde**

What we need is not so much a clever solution but a new culture of working together with Roma communities

In a society where we are constantly led to believe that anything is possible and that being a celebrity is a valid 'career' choice, it should be easy for our young people to aspire to greatness whatever their race or background. Shouldn't it?

But what if you are a young Roma adult? In real terms it means you most likely did not complete your education, you probably live at the wrong address, in the wrong part of town, overcrowded and undervalued. It's likely that your parents can't support the family themselves so you had to finish school early to supplement their income. But without qualifications, the only opportunities open to you are at best in the informal job market: unskilled, poorly paid just like your parents and grandparents before you. Does that make your hopes and your dreams any different, any less important, than those of any other young adult? In May 2010 in Budapest, Viktoria Farkas, a young Roma woman who has personal aspirations told the ROMA-NeT partners that 'Employers don't really offer jobs for Roma people. Only a few people may understand how life is on the Gypsy row—what it means to have and to educate a child there. What it feels to have on your skin the non-acceptance, the exclusion whether in school, on the street, from wider society, and to be excluded from the job market. How is it possible to prove our competencies when we know that we don't have much chance in life?

Confined to the Margins of Society—Because They Are Roma

In Europe today there are hundreds of thousands of ordinary young people confined to the margins of society, often surviving in poverty, in sub-standard, even deplorable living conditions—because they are Roma. Young people who grow

i [Ed. note] This article is based on an URBACT project. URBACT is a European exchange and learning program promoting sustainable urban development and is jointly funded by the European Regional Development Fund and the member states. See urbact.eu.

up knowing that much of society is closed to their ambitions, many are resigned to the situation, aware that their full potential is diminished, because they are Roma. Even today these youngsters are compelled to embark upon the same cycle of exclusion that has plagued their people for generations, because they are Roma. In a society where equal rights and respect for diversity have been championed for decades; not only is this morally indefensible it is downright wasteful and the economic justifications to change the situation are compelling.

In an increasingly aging Europe, no country, nor city can afford to ignore the untapped potential and the contributions that could be made by this already enormous and growing section of the population. Even in these days of economic downturn our nations continue to face shortages of skilled workers, employing a variety of tactics to attract much needed skills including encouraging economic migration. Yet European cities consistently fail to recognise the most shocking neglect of one of our core economic resources, the disregarded human capital that already exists in their segregated and marginalised communities. Roma are the largest minority group in Europe, but most have been written off, living and working outside the mainstream parameters of registered employment, health insurance and income tax. Contrary to the stereotypical image of Roma, their lives are neither inactive nor lazy. For many, achieving basic subsistence demands constant innovation, arbitration, determination, and ongoing resilience to survive. Imagine the growth potential if European cities could harness and maximise that kind of capacity from an additional 10 million people living in the European Union. What that could mean for economic growth and the future of our nations, let alone the moral and social justification associated with ensuring successful integration of Roma into society. Economic crisis, competing priorities and dwindling public finances create an environment where cities can easily turn away and find other, more publicly supported, actions than investing in Roma. But they should be aware that such short-term, non-controversial decisions will have long-term irreparable consequences as the cycle of decline and segregation becomes more and more deeply entrenched.

Roma Exclusion—More Than an Eastern European Issue

For a long time Roma exclusion was regarded as mainly a Central and Eastern European issue: during the pre-accession years the European Commission pushed integration of Roma as a priority for the countries of Bulgaria, the Czech Republic, Hungary, Romania and Slovakia. By 2001, reference to the Roma Minorities in the Accession Partnership documents referred to: 'fighting against discrimination (including within the public administration), fostering employment opportunities, increasing access to education, improving housing conditions; and providing adequate financial support'.

Simultaneously in 2000, the bell began to toll, for the end of blatant ethnic exclusion, or so we thought, when the EU adopted its Racial Equality Directive (Directive 2000/43/EC–RED) aimed at combating discrimination on the grounds of race or ethnic origin and prohibiting direct or indirect discrimination in employment, education, social protection, property matters and services.

With some consensus that tackling exclusion and facilitating integration of Roma would contribute significantly to the achievement of the aims of the Lisbon Strategy, came a succession of targeted Roma policy directives: The Decade of Roma Inclusion in 2003, the OSCE Action Plan on Improving the Situation of Roma and Sinti in the OSCE Area and the first EU Roma Summit in 2008 which, reassuringly, resulted in the definition of 10 Common Basic Principles to effectively address the issue of Roma inclusion in policy implementation. Yet despite this compelling evidence of gathering momentum, support for the case for Roma integration and a genuine willingness to fund the policy changes and initiatives designed to promote Roma inclusion have so far failed to deliver significant change. In fact recent Open Society Institute evidence suggests that the living conditions and economic situations for most Roma in Europe have not improved and may actually have continued to decline.

The 10 Common Basic Principles for Roma Inclusion are (EU Roma summit, 2008):

1. Constructive, pragmatic and non discriminatory policies
2. Explicit but not exclusive targeting
3. Inter-cultural approach
4. Aiming for the mainstream
5. Awareness of the gender dimension
6. Transfer of evidence-based policies
7. Use of Community instruments
8. Involvement of regional and local authorities
9. Involvement of civil society
10. Active participation of the Roma

In the last few years the complex situation of Roma exclusion is a phenomenon that is spreading and growing across Europe. EU membership in 2004[1] and 2007[2] for countries with significant Roma populations has brought about a new dynamic to the complex situation of Roma exclusion. Namely that in significant numbers Roma have begun to exercise their freedom of movement and have chosen to live and if possible work in another EU country. Even in those old member states that have well developed anti-discrimination, equality and social inclusion policies, the behaviour, living conditions and exclusion of Roma migrants is challenging the political, economic and social responses from receiving nations and cities. A recent Fundamental Rights Agency study[3] concluded that that 'Roma from other EU Member States are now part of the townscape of almost every Member State of the European Union'.

Shift Towards Cities—Drivers of Change or Not?

Until now, the Cities of Europe and their municipal authorities have not played a big part in the development of Roma inclusion policy. Municipalities have generally been passive in their approach to Roma inclusion, sometimes supporting the action of NGOs and often taking the view that the Roma population have access to the same services as the majority population. Historically, many of the core Roma inclusion policies such as education, employment, health, housing, infrastructure, the fight against poverty and increased equality have been the responsibility of National Governments with non-governmental organisations working to provide the service delivery role at local level, through collections of essential projects often constrained by insufficient resources and short-term unsustainable funding streams.

It has long been recognised that deep-rooted cultural divides, even between Roma and their own country-nationals, and systemic institutional discrimination have fuelled exclusionary practices prominent across Nations, but they are also factors that have significantly limited previous attempts at inclusion. And there has been very little genuine progress made in attempts to reach out or to engage with the Roma community. But why should this be when many cities have adequate levels of know-how to make advances on Roma inclusion? The key component that has been missing is not the know-how, the what to do, but much more the wanting, the genuine commitment to improvement, to change and to eradicate discrimination and exclusion in the Roma communities. What is still missing in many cities is a clear-cut acknowledgement of the need to respond to the levels of exclusion that exist in the Roma communities, the political commitment and the volume of resources over the long-term that will be necessary to make a discernable difference.

There has however been a recent shift in emphasis and growing expectations of greater involvement from the cities and municipalities of Europe in the issue of Roma inclusion. The European Parliament's resolution of 31 January 2008 stressed the importance of involving local authorities and promoted full participation of the Roma community at grassroots level in order to ensure their ability to fully benefit from the inclusion policies being defined. In persistently disadvantaged neighbourhoods often there are barriers to services which are beyond the ability of individuals to overcome. Reductions in vital education, child care, health services, home care support, transport, employment, training and access to financial services can have a compound effect on poverty and exclusion that can only be reversed through local authority driven interventions and community collaboration.

Yes, cities should have the necessary know-how and they are better placed to provoke involvement, maintain commitment and to bring about sustainability than the NGOs that tried to champion Roma inclusion in the past. Cities have the breadth of experience and the strength of human resources to bring together stakeholders to build common objectives that will generate synergy between services and ensure that more relevant, more accessible and more supportive services are available for young Roma people. Cities are best placed to make use of the people they have with strong community based know-how, honed over time and spanning all facets of the district, and to re-deploy their skills to address Roma issues and to capitalise on available expertise.

Thus far however the skills for developing projects and implementing interventions for Roma communities belong more to the NGO sector than with local authorities. But with the shifting emphasis on cities, local authorities need to grow the confidence and harness the skills to drive forward and deliver joint and integrated interventions that can overcome the widespread Roma exclusion from basic and essential services.

ROMA-NeT to Pioneer the Way Other Cities Can Follow

There is a strong case for sustainable inclusion via a bottom-up approach which promotes joint responsibility and places significant importance on the development of human, social and professional capital to tackle the complexity of the problems.

ROMA-NeT: a network of nine European cities, supported by URBACT, plans to pioneer a way forward. At this early stage the 9 partner Cities of ROMA-NeT clearly recognise that Roma exclusion is multi-layered, deep-rooted and complex. No one has said that this will be easy, and they are not deterred by the complexity of the issue, but rather committed to finding the right way forward for an integrated approach that puts dialogue with the Roma community at the heart of their actions.

We support an integrated, co-operative and co-ordinated approach where commitment from local authorities can create:

- opportunities for Roma to participate in training measures and to create labour market opportunities;
- locally generated social projects, varying in scope and eligibility conditions;
- real access to social welfare provisions—whether in education, health or social care, housing, etc.;
- all of which must be underpinned by Roma communities providing support, mediation, advocacy, self-representation and active participation in the supply of local service provision.

A key start for the ROMA-NeT City partners, that could be followed by other Cities was to examine—critically analyse—what and how core services, and other special initiatives, are currently being, or have been in the past, supplied to other disadvantaged groups in the key areas of education, health, housing and employment. Initially, to establish the Critical Success Factors for each initiative and then to question if and why they failed to reach, failed to attract, or simply by-passed the Roma community. Working through the process, and involving the community should provide an opportunity to adjust and realign services in a way that is more relevant and appropriate for community need. Although it is unreasonable and potentially unsustainable to expect cities to develop a whole raft of new services, what they can do is create intermediary links, pathway projects and mediators to make existing services more accessible and more appropriate for young Roma adults. Cities will have to confront the long-standing dilemma of 'Roma-specific' or 'Roma-targeted', keeping in mind that segregation may be a short-term remedy but is never the long-term answer.

Evidence from mapping studies carried out in the ROMA-Net Cities show that, as suspected, there is a vast array of untapped expertise to be drawn out from successful implementation of a wide range of community initiatives across the partner Cities. For example, a highly innovative educational initiative used to elicit the opinions of young disadvantaged children in Almería could easily be transferred to engage adults in the Roma community and provoke in them a sense of belief that the system is interested in what they have to say and what their needs are. Bologna City is well known for its success in developing and delivering innovative approaches to health services, and although these services have somehow by-passed their resident Roma community, with some additional components, they can be made more relevant and accessible going forward. Glasgow has a strong track record in area regeneration and though a new migrant Roma population is challenging these seasoned professionals, it is clear that with some concentrated efforts, they will create a community relationship and foundation for improvement and change. Udine has demonstrated significant expertise in developing realistic employment and training projects but they fail to attract unemployed Roma to their activities. Using a slightly different recruitment procedure and supportive in-work services they can however, be much more relevant for the Roma community.

Good practice experiences can be drawn from the collections of initiatives supplied by NGOs in different countries, one of the most successful has been mediation or intermediary services to link the Roma communities to vital public services. Such initiatives have been applied successfully in many sectors, the concept is explained [below] in Good Practice No. 1.

Housing, tenure of housing and land are major issues in many Roma communities. The situation is complex and is often difficult to deal with in a way that is constructive for all sides. Although an integrated approach to housing combined with community development is frequently cited as good practice for Roma communities, there are not that many such initiatives in existence.

❑ Good Practice No. 1—Sectoral Mediators Working at Community Level

1. Using mediators, in the fields of health, education and social services, to create connections between the public service and the Roma community has proven to be good practice.
2. Roma mediators as classroom assistants have been used in many cities in Hungary, Romania, Czech Republic, Slovakia and are now seen as a critical link to engage parents in school activities to ensure children attend and remain in education.
3. Mediation has been applied effectively in many countries and in different formats, for example in Hungary to provide health promotion information to elderly members of Roma communities. In Dupnitsa, Bulgaria,

mediators are used to help solve the problem of electricity being disconnected and non-payment of electricity expenses.

4. In Karviná, Czech Republic, dedicated fieldworkers provide intermediary assistance to implement all major initiatives being undertaken in the city and are involved in all aspects of the community. Their responsibilities range from assisting with housing applications, co-ordinating health forums to accompanying children to ensure their school attendance.
5. Success of mediators can largely be attributed to the fact that the majority are chosen from the Roma community, thus creating a faster build up of trust and the ability to break down barriers with formal organisations as well as providing role models for the community.
6. Another critical and positive aspect is the fact that the positions provide good quality jobs for members of the community. They show Roma undertaking responsible employment, performing in professional roles which projects a positive image and can contribute to raising aspirations of others.
7. For the foreseeable future while Roma inclusion remains an underdeveloped practice, the role of community mediators will remain crucial to support less capable members of the community to utilise the services of the main social and public sectors such as health, education, social care, social welfare, housing and general advocacy services.
8. Although the role of mediators has been widely used there are a number of areas where the potential has not been adequately applied, for example:
   - as relationship builders between fully trained work ready Roma individuals and employers in need of new workers but who have an inherent mistrust of Roma
   - to support new entrants, men and women, into the world of work either for the first time or as adult returners.
9. The important role that mediators have in the process of community empowerment has also not been fully recognised. However it is a role that can be promoted and developed through ROMA-NeT activities as they aim to generate greater community participation and to empower and strengthen the community voice. An extension of the mediator is the community or local champion and for widespread engagement and effective communication each local support group would benefit from the input of a collection of community champions.

There are a few examples where NGOs have been able to access national level EU programmes and other donor funding to support community led development and regeneration type interventions, sometimes in partnership with a municipality, but mostly driven by NGOs. Examples of integrated Urban Regeneration activities led by municipalities and focusing on Roma communities are hard to find. Good Practice No. 2 considers a situation where the local authority and an NGO worked together with positive results.

A Culture of "With Roma" Must Replace the "For Roma" Attitude

What we need then, is to overcome and break down the barriers that all too often have presented insurmountable challenges to engaging the Roma community. Cities have to dispel the notion that there can be some 'quick fix' solution, and realise that it is not so much about haste or innovation but much more about sustained actions capitalising on expertise with long-term commitment.

Through the URBACT local support groups ROMA-NeT partners will each bring together, vital service providers, the local stakeholders and crucially members of the Roma community to start the dialogue and create the basis for joint action planning. Instead of applying sweeping homogenous interventions meant for the benefit of the Roma, what is needed is a new culture to work with Roma: from inception throughout delivery.

The ROMA-NeT partnership promotes an integrated and supportive approach from the outset, providing the perfect platform from which to share the wealth of knowledge and experience that exists. By focusing on the broader context of what has been successful, we plan to capitalise on good practice, previous experience to re-model our thinking around the issues of Roma inclusion. With the support of our experienced local stakeholders, including Roma community beneficiaries themselves, we can translate good practice into meaningful interventions that are relevant, sustainable and will have longevity because they are founded on approaches that we and Roma communities know can work.

Although there is no quick-fix, no solution nor blueprint that can guarantee success there is a very real opportunity for the cities to pull resources, to capitalise on successes and to engage with the community in a way that will permeate all aspects of their lives. We aim to provide a positive and achievable vision for the future that can capture the imaginations of the young men and women in the Roma community; engendering in them the sense of ownership required to bring about the necessary change. What we need is not so much a clever

❑ Good Practice No. 2—Integrated Community Housing

The project focuses on how to involve Roma people in reconstructing their homes and help them pay their debts and obtain valid rent-contracts.

Description

Brno, the second largest city in the Czech Republic, has a Roma population of approximately 12,000—3% of the population. These Roma people live in tenement buildings which have suffered from neglect for many years. A private non-profit organisation and the local authorities are working together to renovate the buildings and help solve the debt problems of many Roma people.

Crucial Factors

- Local authority to refurbish a Roma community centre. The centre is on the ground floor of a building where many Roma families live. The centre provides education, advice and leisure time support for Roma children, youngsters and adults, involving the local authorities, police and social work institutions to improve the situation of Roma people in Brno.
- Many of the Roma families are in debt and live in run-down apartments without paying rent.
- An international non-profit organisation is involved and wants to do more for the Roma families than just reconstructing the centre.
- Idea emerges to have tenants help the authorities to reconstruct their own homes, so that they could pay back their debts and negotiate valid leases. Well attended tenants' meeting—reactions generally positive but families were afraid that once the building was refurbished the local authorities would evict because they do not hold valid lease agreements.
- The NGO and the local authorities set up a 'work-for-debt' programme. The tenants are given the opportunity to work for the local authorities. This work consisted mainly of cleaning of the unused spaces. The money earned was deducted from their debts. People who worked their debts away could sign a new and valid lease for one year.

Results

- A large number of people worked in and around the buildings and not only cleared their debts, but have also started to make regular rent payments.
- Two tenant committees have been set up: a total of forty-one people willing to be involved.
- The project is unique because many local authorities in [Central and] Eastern Europe are reluctant to allow Roma people to live in inner city areas. In this case the local authorities took a relaxed approach towards the families' illegal rent situation.
- This is the first time an integrated approach has been used to solve problems with Roma people.

Learning Experiences

- It proved difficult to achieve concrete results during tenant meetings, to which the Roma people are not accustomed. Roma tenants should be seen as active citizens instead of a problem. Both sides, local authorities and Roma families, needed time to adapt. And an attitude of apathy does not change overnight even where both sides are cooperating.
- Within the local authorities there are still people who do not agree with any non-standard approach towards solving debt problems. Also the general public is sceptical.
- After so many years of neglect, there are a whole range of problems to be addressed. It is not possible to solve one problem without addressing the others.
- It is important to keep the decision-making process as transparent and straightforward as possible and to make important decisions during meetings in which all participating organisations take part. Corruption is something that can ruin a project like this.

Key to success—'the active involvement of residents in the management and administration as well as financial support and commitment from the local authorities'. The project has a voluntary Self Administration and Management Committee. This example should be looked upon as a model of good practice relevant in all cities.

solution but a society that recognises, and is prepared to be fully committed to the concept of greater equality for all. In so doing, Europe will not only benefit from a more diverse and inclusive society; but also from a pool of viable workers who are contributing to wider society, to economic growth and in the future of their own communities.

ENDNOTES

1. Czech Republic, Hungary, Slovakia and Poland.
2. Bulgaria and Romania.
3. *The Situation of Roma EU Citizens Moving to and Settling in Other EU Member States*, 2009 http://fra.europa.eu/fraWebsite/attachments/Roma_Movement_Comparative-final_en.pdf.

*Ann Morton Hyde** is the lead expert of the ROMA-NeT Thematic Network.

Hyde, Ann Morton. "Roma Inclusion—Can Cities Be the Driver of Change?" In *The URBACT Tribune: Can European Cities Grow Smarter, Sustainable and Inclusive?*, 21–26. Saint-Denis La Plaine: URBACT. Undated. http://urbact.eu/fileadmin/general_library/TRIBUNEweb_.pdf.

Health and the Roma Community: Analysis of the Situation in Bulgaria[i]

*by Ilona Tomova**

Roma, Europe's most numerous minority, have been victims of prejudice, stigmatization and discrimination for centuries. They are especially vulnerable during times of important social transformation and crises. Mass unemployment and poverty affected between two thirds and three fourths of Roma households during the post-Communism period.

The transition from a planned state economy to a free market was extremely long and painful in Bulgaria. An entire Roma generation was virtually excluded from the mainstream labour market for almost twenty years. The community's geographical isolation increased, affecting approximately 80% of Roma (in the late 1980s fewer than 45% of Roma lived in segregated neighbourhoods). Geographical segregation had an adverse effect on Roma's ability to find jobs during times of crisis and especially affected the socialization process of young people. Many Roma neighbourhoods turned into ghettoes. Most of the institutions abandoned these *mahali*[ii] and Roma access to administrative, medical and other services became very difficult. A large number of young Roma dropped out of school. Ensuing functional illiteracy has hampered labour market integration and led to poverty extending over generations. Serious mass poverty was the plight of at least two thirds of the Bulgarian Roma population until just recently and will probably rise again due to the current global crisis. All of this has had a negative effect on Roma health and their access to medical services.

Access to health services depends on different factors that have cumulative negative effect on Roma health.

The quality of medical services depends on the macroeconomic situation and on state policies specifically targeting health. Total per capita expenditure on health is very low in Bulgaria and Romania. This means that Bulgarian and Romanian citizens have more restricted access to quality health services and that

---

i [Ed. note] This project received funding from the European Union in the framework of the Public Health Programme and was coordinated and edited by the Fundación Secretariado Gitano, Madrid. The Bulgarian section, pp. 97–107, was published by The Health of Romany People Foundation (THRPF), Sliven.

ii [Ed. note] Romani quarters of towns.

the package of health services in these countries is very meagre. Government curtailment of spending on health services has the greatest effect on the poor. Bulgaria has the highest share of out-of-pocket expenditure on health. Private medicine accounts for two fifths of the total expenditure on health in Bulgaria and 96.3% of that is paid out-of-pocket. If patients need surgery or long or permanent treatment, the share of out-of-pocket payment may increase significantly. Financial difficulties are extremely severe for the poorer social classes and are unbearable for more than two thirds of Roma people.

Bulgaria had quite a good physician, dentist, hospital bed and medical centre ratio but due to low salaries, thousands of nurses and midwives left the country and now the nurse:physician ratio is only 1.2:1. This had led to a deterioration of the quality of medical services and adversely affects care provided to the most vulnerable groups: i.e. newborns, young children, the elderly, the chronically ill and the disabled. The Roma community has the highest proportion of newborns and young children and their perinatal, neonatal, infant and under five morbidity and mortality rates are the highest in the country. The Roma infant mortality rate in 2001–2004 was 25.0 per 1000, while that of ethnic Bulgarians was 9.9. The insufficient number of nurses and midwives has an even greater negative effect on Roma because of communication difficulties between physicians and people with lower levels of education.

Another problem that hits Roma harder than the rest of the population is the uneven distribution of physicians and medical centres. The highest number of patients per physician is found in the regions with a high proportion of Turks and Roma. This means that the people in these regions, especially rural areas, endure lower quality medical services, spend longer time waiting in physician's offices and travel longer to visit specialists, medical laboratories or hospitals.

More than two thirds of adult Roma have abandoned the legal labour market and many now work at temporary, seasonal or informal jobs mainly in the grey economy. This sort of work is often associated with health problems due to lack of insurance. According to the survey *Health and the Roma Community: Analysis of the Situation in Europe*, 26% of adult Roma (18% of the entire population) have no health insurance. As a result, Roma rely more on emergency services, physician's altruism and on pharmacists' advice when purchasing medicines without a physician's prescription.

The mortality rate of those who have undergone successful surgery in hospital emergency rooms is very high because of the poor hygienic conditions in many Roma neighbourhoods or because of the lack of medical care when they return home after a short stay in the emergency unit. Those who survive often have chronic health problems or become disabled as a result of lack of proper care, diet and medication. Insufficient paediatric care may also account for part of the high infant mortality rate, especially in isolated rural settlements.

Stiff regulation of pharmacies by the Bulgarian health system, especially the most recent reform of regulations governing prescriptions for chronically ill patients, put many pharmacies out of business or prompted them to simply refuse to work with the public health system. The sale of medicines on the grey market increased and these can now be purchased in cosmetic stores or the offices of advertising firms. There is no health control regarding the storage of medicines or their quality. According to the survey *Health and the Roma Community* . . . four fifths of adult Roma consume medicines without a prescription. If the trend of bankrupt pharmacies and medicines being sold by people without proper training as pharmacists continues, the lives of thousands of Roma will be at great risk.

Another factor hindering Roma access to health services is their lack of confidence in physicians. Many Roma (especially those with lower educational levels or who are illiterate) are convinced that physicians and nurses are biased against them on ethnic and social grounds. Many of the problems between Roma patients and physicians could be described as communication problems. The majority of physicians and nurses working in Roma neighbourhoods or in settlements where many Roma reside are not prepared to deal with people with a different culture or who are severely impoverished and or who face social exclusion.

Another significant factor contributing to bad health and a high early mortality rate is poor living conditions. According to the Bulgarian National Statistical Institute [NSI], almost half of the Roma population lacked potable water in their homes in 2001 and were forced to use water from street pipes or wells. Most Roma neighbourhoods have damaged sewerage systems or none at all and this increases the risk of hepatitis and gastrointestinal disease.

Overpopulation in Roma neighbourhoods and homes is the norm. NSI data show that one fifth of Roma people live in homes where they have less than 4 sq. m. per capita. Another two fifths have between 4 and 8 sq. m. floor space at their disposal. Often more than three generations live under the same roof. Overpopulation in Roma neighbourhoods and homes fosters the spread of disease and is also a cause of everyday distress—intimately related to high morbidity.

Local governments fail to look after hygienic conditions in Roma neighbourhoods. In some cases this is the result of narrow unpaved streets but, generally speaking, there are no cleaning or garbage collection services in some parts of settlements. This lack of proper hygiene and overpopulation are the cause of infectious disease and epidemics.

A sociological survey conducted in eight large Roma neighbourhoods in city centres in 2007 showed that in most some repairs or enlargement of the sewerage system had taken place during the previous 2–3 years. The problem is that in half of these cases, engineering or technical mistakes were made and contaminated water floods houses, yards and streets. Hundreds of Euros have been wasted and hygienic conditions for many families have deteriorated.

Most municipal authorities have [abandoned] Roma neighbourhoods and now there is no control over illegal construction and use of sidewalks and streets there. In many places streets are blocked by illegal buildings or they are so narrow that cars cannot go down them. Ambulances cannot reach large sections of Roma ghettoes and physicians are unable to find the homes of their patients.

Roma have suffered the difficulties of the transition to a market economy more than anyone. For the majority of men who found themselves permanently excluded from the mainstream labour market, their only chance to gain higher social status and self-respect was illegal activity and control over women. Social exclusion has caused Rome to become increasingly closed off into micro-groups in their homes and ghettoes. This sparked a return and enforcement of the role of conservative pre-modern patriarchal forms of social and cultural life in the Roma community, especially in large Roma ghettoes. The cult of physical male strength and violence, control over women, restricted possibilities for human development, mass inclusion of young people in deviant forms of behaviour—characteristics of all poor urban ghettoes all over the world—spread among Roma. In some marginalized groups the survival of the family is always at the expense of women and children who are exploited or at the expense of long-term goals like obtaining a good education or qualification or taking good care of one's health.

The Roma community is the one which marries the earliest in Bulgaria. The Roma fertility rate from 2001–2004 was 26.7 per thousand in comparison with 6.9 per thousand among ethnic Bulgarians. Bulgaria has Europe's highest teen-age pregnancy rate and it is highest among Roma women—10–12 times higher than that of ethnic Bulgarians. Teen-age pregnancy is a risk factor due to the low birth-weight of newborns, higher neonatal, perinatal and infant mortality and morbidity and higher mortality rate for women giving birth. All of these problems have likewise been observed during this sociological survey.

The survey *Health and the Roma Community* . . . defined the major characteristics and changes in the social status and family life of rural Roma and those of them who live in large towns and cities in 2008:

- Roma with stable employment increased in 2007–2008. One third of Roma adults were employed in 2008 and received their health insurance through their job. Despite this improvement, the Roma employment rate is still extremely low.

- Roma women depend on their work and own incomes much less in comparison with Roma men and with ethnic Bulgarian women. Moreover, most employed Roma women work at seasonal or temporary jobs. This type of employment does not provide its employees with social or health insurance thus putting them in a vulnerable position in times of crises or bad weather conditions.
- 14% of children age 7–15 are early school leavers and 1.1% of them work full time to provide for the family.
- Roma men hold the main authority positions in the family and play a major role in providing for the family (thanks to their own work or through organizing the exploitation of women and children). Men were characterized as the 'head of the household' or the main provider in nine tenths of Roma households.
- In 85% of the households young couples and their children live together with the husband's parents. Most young families depend entirely on their parents' financial support during the first 10 years of their marriage as a result of early marriages and the high level of youth unemployment in the Roma community. Two thirds of Roma children age 0–9 depend on the financial support of their grandparents rather than their own parents. Only in the 10–15 year old group is the percentage of those who depend on their parents' incomes equal to those who depend on their grandparents' incomes. Dependency on the husband's parents and on the grandfathers' financial support perpetuates the patriarchal model and the authority of men and mothers-in-law.
- Sons, much more often than daughters, depend on their parents' financial support and help in raising their children.
- No less than 18% of Roma live in households where three or more generations live under the same roof.
- There are more grandmothers than grandfathers in the extended Roma family given women's longer life expectancy. They help more in raising the children but their incomes are much lower than those of men. Older women are often chronically sick or disabled and this contributes to the financial difficulties of extended Roma families.

Roma have been suffering severe and extended exclusion from the labour market and from other main social spheres. They have no political party with the power to protect their economic, social and cultural interests in Bulgaria. Neither do they have access to the social networks engaged in transforming social capital from the former regime into economic capital in the new market society. The only legitimate power resource they possess is that of male dominance over women in the family and in the community as a whole. Women are the main means of exchange and the accumulation of power in Kaldarash, Lovara, Thracian tinkers, and among some Muslim Roma groups. The honour and dignity of the *pater-familias* and all the men in the family depend on the merits and worthiness of their women, especially soon-to-be-wed daughters. That is why control over girls' and women's bodies in most Roma groups is so strong and brides' virginity is valued so high[ly]. But this exaggerated focus on pre-marital virginity is one of the reasons behind teen-age marriages in traditional Roma sub-groups: if girls marry in their early teens, the risk of casual sexual contact is extremely low. The other very important reason for early marriages is to keep young people in the community and thus "protect" them from the evils of the outside society. Elders go as far as to encourage even the best Roma students to drop out of school early in order to preserve the community.

Total male control over women is considered necessary for a wide array of reasons. Roma boys will only be considered full-fledged men when they marry and father a child. This accounts for the strong family and group pressure for early marriage and parenthood. All relatives expect the first child to come within the first year after the wedding. A good wife is one who serves her husband by fulfilling all of his desires and who shoulders a large part of the housekeeping burden from her mother-in-law. Her work and that of her children, or the social benefits she receives if she is an unemployed mother, often cover the household's expenditure for food and other goods. The family's economic survival is often secured at the expense of women's (reproductive) health (and sometimes of that of her children as well).

Young women often say they favour modern birth control methods but do not use them because of their husbands. They often blame their mothers-in-law for perpetuating an old-fashioned attitude towards sex and reproductive health.

The Roma community is the youngest one in the country. Two thirds are children and youth—almost twice as many young people as among ethnic Bulgarians. But this does not mean that theirs is the healthiest community.

As a whole, those surveyed assessed their health and that of their relatives positively: more than half of the Roma over 16 assessed their own health as good or very good. According to 70% of them their children's health is also (very) good as is that of their family members (67% gave positive answers). One third of those surveyed gave ambivalent answers concerning their own health, 12% claiming it was (very) bad. One fourth said the health of their children and/or that of other family members was not very good and 6% declared that their children or other family members were in a bad health.

The most positive self-assessments were given by Roma age 10–44. The decline occurs immediately after age 45. Less than one fourth of Roma above that age assessed their health positively, one half offering ambivalent answers and 28% claiming their health to be bad. The most frequently declared maladies diagnosed by physicians were high blood pressure, migraines or headaches, arthritis and rheumatism, asthma, chronic bronchitis, chronic obstructive lung disease, heart diseases, menopause-related problems, allergy, high cholesterol, stomach ulcers and prostate problems.

Very serious problems in Roma neighbourhoods are linked with infectious diseases. The overpopulation of Roma settlements and households makes it more difficult to isolate virus carriers and diseases frequently turn into epidemics. Some cultural peculiarities also contribute to the spread of disease. One of these is the empathy norm and commitment to the sick implying frequent visits, taking care of them and emotional support throughout. This norm is compulsory for relatives, friends and even neighbours. Poor diet, everyday distress connected with long-term unemployment, poverty, uncertainty and discrimination all reduce the organism's resistance to virus and bacteria and contribute to longer duration of diseases and greater complications. Also, nearly four fifths of Roma complain that they do not have enough money to buy needed medicines, especially in the case of prolonged diseases. As a result, many diseases that usually do not have dire consequences on the health of Bulgarians in general become chronic for a large number of Roma or have a negative impact on other organs.

According to the data from the comparative survey *Health and the Roma Community* [...], 28% of those surveyed suffered some type of indisposition such as a cold, virus or some other disease forcing them to reduce their main activities in the two weeks preceding the interview. This is a very high number and is just one more indicator of the severe morbidity situation facing the Roma community. The elderly and children were the most vulnerable age groups: 39.6% of Roma over 45 and 38.2% of children aged 0–9 had been sick. Type of housing seems to be a significant factor accounting for higher morbidity: the proportion of people suffering from different symptoms in the two weeks leading up to the interview was highest among those who lived in sub-standard housing (36%) or in shanty towns (32.4%). Children most frequently suffered from the common cold, flu and cough. Adults suffered more symptoms indicative of different diseases: heart disease, bone and joint disease, kidney problems, nervous system disorders or viral diseases.

This survey showed that 12% of the entire Roma population (including children) suffers from some type of disability or from a serious chronic disease. One peculiarity which is characteristic of the Roma community is early disability and widespread chronic disease as early as middle-age. One third of men and two fifths of women age 45–60 have partially or entirely lost their ability to work due to poor health. The proportion of those suffering from chronic disease or disability in the over 65 group rises to 70%. Three fifths of the men and three quarters of the women claimed they have some chronic disease or are disabled.

The survey showed that the size of settlements, the area of residence (integrated or isolated) and housing type are also significant factors leading to higher levels of disability. Some of these factors also entail other significant processes such as poverty, poor education and poor access to medical services. Rural populations face many difficulties in gaining access to medical services and suffer higher levels of long-term unemployment and poverty. The proportion of people who suffer from chronic illness or who are disabled is highest among rural Roma. In contrast, Roma living in Sofia have a better chance to be diagnosed and obtain a disability certificate. That is why the proportion of disabled among this latter group is the highest and the proportion of those who suffer from chronic illness but are not categorized as disabled is lower.

Many different obstacles are faced in obtaining a medical disability certificate. A serious problem is that sick people have to submit to a huge number of medical examinations which are expensive and are not covered by the Public Health Service. This financial problem is particularly critical in the case of the poor who face permanent and high expenses for life-support medicines. Another problem is connected with the administrative organization and bureaucracy surrounding medical services acting as a particular barrier to the illiterate and, once again, the poor. The third problem is that in many places the regional medical centres have closed down and sick people have to use the services of what is known as the Expert Physicians Commission in Sofia or other distant cities. Because of this, the poorest sick people cannot obtain a disability certificate and are therefore deprived of social pensions and a series of other benefits provided for people who cannot ensure their income because of health problems.

Accidents in the Roma community are commonplace. During the 12 months immediately preceding the interview, 12.2% of all those surveyed had suffered an accident. This figure was double (21.3%) in the case of older children (10–15 years of age). Particularly surprising was the fact that more women than men fall victim to accidents. About half of the injured women and children had suffered domestic accidents. This is an indirect indicator of the spread of domestic violence in this community.

One of the most shocking findings made through the survey *Health and the Roma Community* . . . is that a huge amount of the medicines that Roma consume or give to their children are not prescribed by a physician for the health problem in question. Many medicines are bought without a prescription and are given to children and these are not only common medicines such as aspirin, paracetamol and some other widely used painkillers but also antibiotics, allergy medicines, tranquilizers, sleeping pills and others. Over half of the Roma population is inclined to self-medicate with non-prescription medicines on different occasions and women engage in this sort of self-treatment more frequently than men. The proportion of Roma consuming self-prescribed medicines increases with the age. The progression is unmistakable: one third of the young are inclined to take non-prescribed medicines rising to 50% among the 30–44 age group and over three quarters of the Roma population people over 45 consumed at least one of the listed medicines without any prescription in the two weeks preceding the interview. Three quarters of the men who self-medicate take two or more unprescribed medicines as opposed to two thirds of the women.

This practice explains the frequent deterioration of patients' health, the high proportion of people suffering from chronic disease and accounts for part of the high premature death rate in the community. There are no other surveys monitoring self-medication and therefore we cannot compare Roma behaviour with that of other ethnic groups but the results are very disturbing nonetheless. Physicians with many Roma on their patient lists and neighbourhood-based Roma health mediators must immediately be made aware of this practice. Health institutions and the media also need to join forces to inform the society about the problems and dangers connected with the self-treatment.

A new survey covering the entire population should be conducted to monitor the self-medication situation throughout the country and to determine just how much medication is being sold outside of pharmacies. The institutions must take immediate initiatives to keep pharmacies within the legal market and help them from going out of business. The Bulgarian population traditionally trusts the advice received from pharmacists concerning minor ailments mild traumas, typical problems related to menopause or other common conditions. The search for medical advice from pharmacists grew as a result of the bureaucratization of the health system, increase in the compulsory fee for medical examinations and the rising number of people without health insurance over the last several years. This custom is not likely to change quickly and if pharmacists with medical education and a licence for the sale of medication are replaced by uneducated traders the consequences for human health, especially among the poor, will be catastrophical.

According to the data gathered from the *Health and the Roma Community* survey, last year 14% of Roma who were ill, indisposed or pregnant failed to receive the health services they needed. This happened slightly more often with adults than with children. People without health insurance are exposed to greater risk—21% of them did not receive the medical service they needed. Residents of isolated Roma neighbourhoods, especially those with poor hygienic conditions, often failed to receive the medical services they needed. Lack of health insurance was most likely the major obstacle. There are, however, other factors such as poverty, low level of education, lack of communication skills limiting interaction with representatives of different institutions, men's tendency to become verbally aggressive in frustrating situations, etc. In the presence of some (or all) of these conditions, the risk of conflict and refusal of the physician to provide the required services or to forego negative stereotypes, prejudices and discriminating attitudes towards the patient increases.

Data from the present survey show that immunization problems affecting Roma children have not yet been overcome. In almost one third of the households with children the parents declared that their children have some immunizations but they are not sure if they have all of them. Girls are more often left unvaccinated than boys. Children in isolated neighbourhoods are two and a half times as likely to be unvaccinated than those living in integrated neighbourhoods. Young children are more likely than older ones to have gaps in their immunization calendar. According to physicians, this could partly account frequent indispositions observed among the youngest children in the Roma community.

Poor diet, insufficient oral hygiene, lack of prevention and seeing the dentist when it is already too late are the reasons underlying the poor dental condition of Roma children as from a very early age. One fourth of the youngest age group experience many teeth and gum problems. 12.5% of the children up to age 9 and 28% of those between 10 and 15 had at least one permanent tooth extracted. Adult Roma also have very poor dental health despite being a very young population. Two thirds have cavities or pulpitis; three fifths have had at least one tooth extracted; and half have not undergone treatment to replace missing teeth. One out of every three suffers from bleeding gums and one out of every five had a loose tooth/teeth.

According to data obtained, one fifth of those surveyed stayed in hospital at least one day during the year immediately preceding the survey. Small children have the highest hospitalization rate (one third) followed by the over 45 group (one fourth). The proportion of hospitalized women is higher than that of men due to the longer life expectancy of women with health problems. Access to health institutions is more difficult for the poorest Roma. Only 13.5% of those who live in the most dire conditions—shacks constructed of whatever is available—had been hospitalized. A proportion of the sick people from the shanty towns were probably unable to cover private hospitalization expenses.

Roma spend more time in hospital than the rest of the population. Assuming that average hospital stays in 2008 are comparable to those of 2006 (the last year for which we have National Health Centre data), the average duration of hospital stays for Roma was 2.6 days longer than that of the rest of the Bulgarian citizens. Comparison of data for the whole population shows that:

- in the case of surgery, Roma spend more time in hospital than the rest of the population;
- Roma children often enter hospital with multiple symptoms indicative of an advanced stage of different diseases which means that many medical examinations need to be conducted in order to determine the right diagnosis and medication;
- Roma children often need ongoing treatment of already contracted diseases before operation;
- adult Roma often need to stay in hospital longer because of the severity of the many diseases they suffer and/or because of the general poor health condition of the patients who recover slowly.

According to survey data, hospital expenses in the case of 71.5% of hospitalized Roma during the last 12 months were covered completely by the National Health Fund. The Health Fund covered absolutely all expenses of hospitalized Roma related to medical examinations aimed at more precise diagnosis and treatment of the diseases without surgical intervention. The families had to cover all expenditures or to make additional payments for surgical procedures in most of the cases.

The survey data support the conclusion that more Roma use free hospital services compared to the rest of the Bulgarian population. This is easy to explain—a large proportion of the Roma population is included under one or more categories of people whose medical treatment is completely covered by State funds: the number of children in the Roma community is two and a half times higher than that of the Bulgarians; a substantial number of Roma are registered as poor and are therefore exempt from paying consumer fees and out-of-pocket treatment expenses; and disability occurs at a young age in this community. Many Roma without health insurance mainly use emergency room services.

According to survey data, in 2008 16% of the Roma population used emergency room services—one fifth of the children and one seventh of the adults. Roma lacking health insurance frequent emergency room facilities nearly two times more often than those with health insurance. For most of them, especially the poorest, this is the only way to receive qualified medical assistance, three-day hospitalization and even an emergency operation. Last year 22.4% of Roma without health insurance received medical services through emergency rooms compared to 12.5% of those with regular health insurance.

Half of the people that used emergency services during the last year did so only once. One fifth used emergency services twice during the year. One out of every nine women and children received emergency services five or more times.

Roma women in Bulgaria visit the gynaecologist quite regularly. One fourth of them visited this specialist during the last year for reasons other than pregnancy. Young Roma women go for gynaecological check-ups for reasons other than pregnancy three times more often than those over 45. Breast and uterine cancer prevention in the Roma community is insufficient. Women between the ages of 30 and 44 submit to pap smear tests more frequently than younger women—almost half of this age group had this test. Those who live in Sofia and other large cities have an easier time gaining access to this examination (54% underwent the test) but only 25.6% of rural Roma women had a pap smear. One fourth of Roma women examine themselves for breast cancer. Women from the villages had mammographies 2.8 times less frequently than those living in capital cities.

The National Council for Cooperation on Ethnic and Demographic Issues acquired mobile laboratories for uterine and breast cancer screening through a PHARE project in 2008. Tens of thousands of Roma women will be able to undergo these examinations for free if the Ministry of Health provides the required financing to keep the screening program in operation. The amount of money needed is not great at all and it is unacceptable to halt the program at such an early stage. Many physicians working on this project are afraid that it will be shut down and the expensive equipment will be privatized.

One fifth of the Roma population has sight problems (18.6%) and one ninth (12.0%) have auditory difficulties. These are most prevalent among the elderly. There are no statistical data broken down by gender for these health problems.

Poverty and poor living conditions are not the only factors that influence Roma health. Quite a lot of them have an unhealthy lifestyle. Over half of the Roma men and one third of the women smoke on a daily basis. On average, men smoke 24 cigarettes daily while women smoke 17. The highest proportion of heavy smokers is in the 30–44 year old group where 52% smoke on a daily basis.

In 17.4% of households at least one member has a problem with alcohol or drugs. These problems are more frequent in households located in poor, run-down buildings (21%) and in isolated neighbourhoods (22%). The access of addicts to medical care is minimal due to the fact that many of them lack health insurance.

Over four fifths of adult Roma have sedentary lifestyles. This is due to a lack of sport facilities and open spaces for recreation purposes in their neighbourhoods, but also because, in general, sports and keeping in shape are simply not a priority. Roma do not engage in physical activities or sport during free time more frequently than the country's other ethnic groups. Ninety percent of the Roma population over 30 do not practise sport or do any physical exercise. The problem is especially serious for women who spend most of their time engaged in passive activities and whose daily routines are physically less demanding than those of men.

The daily diet of Roma is unbalanced towards bread, starchy foods and sweets. A quarter of the population eats fruit only once or twice a week and one third consumes fruit occasionally or never. Fish is extremely rare in their diet and they do not eat a sufficient quantity of vegetables.

The diet of children and women is even more unbalanced compared to that of adults and men. Children consume fruit, dairy products, pasta, rice and potatoes more often than adults but they also consume many more sweets. Meat, eggs, fish, vegetables and salads are consumed only rarely. The main difference in the diet of men and women is that women eat sweets more often than men and consume less meat, fish and vegetables.

General Recommendations

A combined effort involving many institutions is required (Ministry of Health, Council of Ministers, National Council for Cooperation on Ethnic and Demographic Issues, Ministry of Labour and Social Policies, Ministry of Finance, local authorities and civil society structures) to overcome the negative health trends affecting disadvantaged ethnic minorities.

Government spending on healthcare needs to be increased. In 2005 it totalled only 444 $ PPP per capita. Everything possible should be done so that hundreds of thousands [of] Bulgarian citizens with chronic diseases or who need cancer surgery do not have to discontinue medical treatment due to financial difficulties.

Physicians warn that Public Health funds earmarked for cancer and diabetes medication will only cover half the needs of those suffering from these maladies.

An urgent change is needed to end the established practice of patients having to pay two-fifths of the cost of treatment out-of-pocket which leads to poverty even for families whose incomes are above the national average. The Ministry of Health and the Health Fund should examine the experience of Greece and other countries as concerns institutional and family insurance which takes the burden off the family budget in the event of disease or surgery.

More aggressive measures must be taken to reduce the severity of poverty among Roma. Poverty and limited access to medical services are the major factors underlying poor health.

Roma inclusion in neighbourhoods must be accelerated in the general town planning of all settlements with separate Roma neighbourhoods and comprehensive development plans need to be made to enable the construction of technical infrastructure there, to legalize homes in an acceptable state of repair and to tear down those which are life and health threatening and those which impede the construction of roads, water pipelines, sewerage systems, and electricity and telephone lines in the neighbourhoods.

The construction or renovation of utilities in Roma neighbourhoods needs to be accelerated to rehabilitate a significant number of dwellings and to build new inexpensive municipal housing for the homeless and for those living in very poor conditions and for families whose homes will be demolished for the building of utility infrastructures in the neighbourhoods. Every home must be provided with clean drinking water with a view to improving local hygiene.

The streets and alleyways between houses in Roma neighbourhoods should be cleaned more often. Regular rat extermination, control and disinfection of the dog population in the neighbourhoods and more strict control of the conditions for raising domestic animals in Roma neighbourhoods and villages, are also needed.

More collaboration is needed between the Ministry of Health, the Ministry of Education and Science, the Health Fund and the media (especially the electronic media) to ensure permanent improvements in the health and reproductive culture of the population.

[. . .][iii]

---

iii [Ed. note] Specific recommendations have been omitted.

*Ilona Tomova is a professor at the Institute for Population and Human Studies at the Bulgarian Academy of Sciences and president of its Council of Scientists.

Tomova, Ilona. "Health and the Roma Community: Analysis of the Situation in Bulgaria." In *Health and the Roma Community: Analysis of the Situation in Europe: Bulgaria, Czech Republic, Greece, Portugal, Romania, Slovakia, Spain*, edited by the Fundación Secretariado Gitano, 97–107. Madrid: ROMANI CRISS (Roma Center for Social Interventions and Studies, Romania) and THRPF (Health of Romany People Foundation, Bulgaria), 2009.

QUESTIONS FOR DEBATE

The EU has identified four key target areas where progress is essential for improving Roma inclusion—employment, education, housing, and health.

Employment

Employment of low-skilled Roma with poor educational qualifications and literacy is seen as the most intractable problem in improving Roma inclusion.

- Are antidiscrimination legislation and prosecutions the only way to raise Roma employment levels?
- What other methods might make a difference?

Education

The most successful action to promote Roma inclusion has been the sustained NGO campaign to widen desegregation in Bulgarian schools. Yet even here the evident positive results have not led the government to assume responsibility for school desegregation on a national scale.

- What lessons can be learned from the Bulgarian experience?
- Could these be applied to other target areas for Roma inclusion?

Housing

The example of the city of Avilés in demolishing its shantytowns and rehousing their inhabitants among the wider population without friction can partly be explained by the relatively low number of people to be relocated. Yet, in spite of the severe difficulties currently afflicting the Spanish economy, many other municipalities in Spain are continuing to abolish their shantytowns in a similar way without provoking popular unrest or extremist demonstrations.

- Does this suggest that resolute political will on the part of national and local governments is the key to desegregating of Roma concentrations elsewhere?
- What problems might be involved?
- Do you think that spatial desegregation should always be the goal in improving living conditions for Roma communities?

Health

The overall health situation of Roma in Central and Eastern Europe is deteriorating, partly because of their widespread impoverishment following unemployment but also as a result of damaging effects to the public health services caused by economic problems. This is especially true of Bulgaria—the EU's poorest member state.

- What practical steps would you suggest to improve the health status of Roma—particularly of the young and the elderly?
- Do you think that the problem of the invariably poor health of Roma populations can be tackled in isolation?

Part 4:

Anti-Gypsyism: Options for Roma and Pro-Roma Activists

Killing Time: The Lethal Force of Anti-Roma Racism

*by Bernard Rorke**

In the aftermath of the gun attack on a Roma family in Slovakia on June 17 [2012] by an off-duty policeman which left three dead and two wounded, there followed a surge of online support for the gunman. According to Irena Bihariová, from People against Racism: "public discussions turned into mass glorification of the murderer and hateful responses towards the victims." She warned of heightened inter-ethnic tension where public debate styled the assailant as a hero and the victims as the guilty parties.

Earlier this year in April, in the neighbouring Czech Republic in the town of Chotěbuz, a Roma man was killed, shot in the head with a crossbow. The assailant claimed the victim was one of three men intent on committing a robbery, that he had been aiming at their feet. The victim's cousin alleged that he shouted, "You black whores, I'll kill you," before deliberately taking aim and firing. The attacker later expressed his appreciation for the rally of support by the extremist Workers Social Justice Party, and the 600 signatures on a petition organized by local people in his defence.

Last January, two Roma brothers aged 22 and 24 were shot, the younger killed, by a 63-year-old local retired businessman who happened to be by the railway tracks on the outskirts of the Czech village of Desna at 1:30 a.m. and carrying a firearm. State attorney, Lenka Bradáčová immediately ruled out a racial motive, and on June 18 announced that the man would not be charged as he "used a firearm to prevent an attack on him and not to cause injury or death."

That same week in January, in the Prague 3 district of Jarov, three youths confessed to the brutal murder of a Roma woman, who was beaten, kicked and stabbed to death. According to local residents, the attackers, known for giving Nazi salutes in the streets, had been harassing and assaulting homeless people in the area for weeks prior to the murder. One of the perpetrators was remanded in custody.

In the Czech town of Sokolov after an incident involving police officers, a 33-year-old Roma father of three, died in hospital on May 6. According to eye witness reports, police officers arrested Ludovít Kašpar, handcuffed him and then attacked him, kicking him and beating him. Official sources had no comment to make on the case, as it was under investigation and that any remarks would be purely speculative.

And in Romania, in May two young Roma men aged 24 and 18, were shot dead by police officers in separate incidents. The European Roma Rights Centre and Romani CRISS have demanded an independent and public investigation into the two fatalities, reminded the authorities that under international law the use of lethal force by police officers must be justified and proportionate, and called on them to condemn these deaths.

These latest killings, all occurring in the first half of 2012 cast a grim shadow over the European Union Roma Framework and all its lofty ambitions. Lethal summary justice, vigilante excesses and wanton bloody murder make a mockery of National Roma Integration Strategies. The detail in each of the above cases may differ and the circumstances may be disputed, but the one common denominator is that Roma people continue to die at the hands of state and non-state actors within the European Union.

These killings are not happening in a vacuum. According to Thomas Hammarberg, anti-Roma rhetoric from politicians and media has often preceded acts by vigilantes such as mob violence and pogroms, and "distorted minds" can and do understand such messages as a call "for action": "We see today a growing number of attacks on Roma committed by individuals mobilized by racist anti-Roma ideology. These are premeditated attacks, with the intent to kill, that target random individuals or families because of their ethnicity."

What is especially troubling about the wider phenomenon of anti-Roma violence in recent years is the indifference and ambivalence of the majority towards the victims. Worse still, acts of violence often prompt open support from sections of the wider public for those who would mete out rough and ready "justice" and inflict collective punishment on Roma.

Such violence often occurs where local and national politicians speak openly of the need to deal with "gypsies," and appear to condone violent excesses as "understandable." Perhaps the most notorious example was Italy in 2008. Following arson attacks on Roma camps, then Minister of Interior Roberto Maroni was quoted as having stated, "That is what happens when gypsies steal babies, or when Romanians commit sexual violence," and Umberto Bossi's reported response to the outbreaks of mob violence was that "people do what the state can't manage."

On March 8 2011, a resolution of the European Parliament on Roma called on the European Commission to link social inclusion priorities to a clear set of objectives that included protection of citizens against discrimination in all fields of life; and for the Commission, as guardian of the treaties, to ensure full implementation of relevant legislation and appropriate sanctions against racially motivated crimes. This is all well and good, but the constant clamour for "Brussels" to do something should not obstruct the plain fact that primary responsibility to combat racism, protect citizens, diffuse tension and promote dialogue lies within Member States.

Back in 1993 Václav Havel described the Roma issue as the litmus test for the new democracies. In 2012 it's become a litmus test for democracies across the entire European Union. Today the reality for many Roma citizens remains one of dread and fear. The challenge facing Europe is to banish that fear, guarantee the safety and security of its citizens and ensure that the rule of law prevails without prejudice across all Member States.

*Until December 2013, **Bernard Rorke** was international research and advocacy director for the Open Society Foundations' Roma Initiatives Office.

Rorke, Bernard. "Killing Time: The Lethal Force of Anti-Roma Racism." Open Society Foundations Voices, July 18, 2011. http://www.opensocietyfoundations.org/voices/killing-time-lethal-force-anti-roma-racism.

Dogmatism, Hypocrisy and the Inadequacy of Legal and Social Responses Combating Hate Crimes and Extremism: The CEE Experience

*by András L. Pap**

This paper was written as a response to an unprecedented series of lethal attacks against Roma in 2008 and 2009 in Hungary.[1] The issues raised in the paper, however, touch on a broader set of questions. The following pages convey the frustration of a central eastern European human rights lawyer facing the misdirection and misinterpretation of the constitutional role of certain human rights principles and arguments, which (i) disarm crucial defence mechanisms that constitutional democracies have and need to mobilise countering anti-democratic extremist movements, and (ii) practically prevent efficient legal action against discrimination and obstruct combating hate crimes in particular. I argue that the lack of readjustment of both the legislative formulation and the practical interpretation of a number of classic human rights (such as free speech, freedom of assembly, protection of informational privacy), which were essential tools and both symbolic as well as practical achievements in the process of the political transition, seriously threaten the functioning of the new and fragile liberal democracies in the CEE[i] region.

Inadequate Social Responses

In order to understand the phenomena at hand, we need to dwell shortly on the socio-legal developments of the past two decades. Twenty years ago, in the stormy process of the 'refolution',[ii] the constitutional revolution that enabled the peaceful transition from Communism to constitutional democracy, Hungary—like other, lucky states in the CEE region, which successfully avoided brutal social conflicts or ethnicised civil wars, and where conflicts were diverted to roundtable negotiations with representatives of the retreating regime—was a young champion of human rights and constitutionalism. Even though the textual formulation of constitutional and legislative provisions that concern some of the fundamental rights was, inevitably, rushed and incomplete, this did not cause any disturbance

i [Ed. note] Central and Eastern European.

ii [Ed. note] A term coined by the Oxford historian Timothy Garton Ash to characterize the 1989 regime changes as half evolutionary reform, half revolution.

in the process of democratisation, since these provisions were both the guarantees of and practical means for overcoming the communist dictatorship. Free speech meant freely criticising the oppressive regime and campaigning for candidates at the free elections. Freedom of association and assembly meant forming dissident parties and rallies. Constitutional rights equalled democracy and opposing the exercise of these rights (whether or not such opposition was procedurally or textually justified) meant opposing democracy. Those were times to fight for the enforcement of these rights, not for debates on their content, extension and interpretation. Although there was an absence of popular euphoria about all this, there existed a subconscious common understanding about the profound meaning of these core constitutional principles and, in the following years, the socio-legal dynamics in the region were quite promising. An organic development seemed to take place, even if governments were sometimes slow or reluctant in overcoming certain aspects of post-communist institutional legacies by failing to properly reform, say, the judicial system or combat corruption, or respond to maladministration or maltreatment by law enforcement agencies. Activist constitutional courts and ombudsmen, alongside visible and influential human rights NGOs, were formed and were able to shape the process of building a constitutional state.

Despite facing severe economic problems, the fresh air of constitutionalism seemed to permeate the public sphere, which was also inspired by the perspective of joining the ever-appealing club of western political and economic alliances such as the EU and NATO. In the past few years, however, something has dramatically changed: having achieved all of the goals and dreams that people had during 1989–1990 (market economy and an unlimited selection of consumer goods, EU and NATO membership, etc.), Hungarian and other CEE societies are unable to digest the stress and frustration that emerged as a social cost of all these changes. Instead of appreciation, or even nationalistic pride over the achievements, there is an unprecedented degree of social, political, and ethnic tension, and pessimism.[2] Along the way, the role and image of the CEE region has also changed in the outside world, torn by the economic crisis. After a miraculous birth and a short and shaky childhood, prematurely, but irreversibly, CEE societies stepped into the age of adulthood. In this world they confront other autonomous and self-interest driven grown-ups, and there is little appreciation for their special status and preciousness, which, until then had been taken for granted and formed an important component in their self-identity. This phenomenon of passing adolescence is also mirrored in how fundamental rights are perceived.

Following the exceptional moment of the transition era, these societies entered the stage of normalcy, where all viable liberal democracies reside: where daily, complex and demanding debates take place concerning the desirable and acceptable interpretation of constitutional rights. Fundamental rights are no longer simple, one-dimensional, black or white substances: democracy is specifically known for the fact that there is room and a crucial need for healthy debates on the daily operation of constitutionalism. Constitutional democracy itself is the interaction of a very intricate web of participants—political parties, the parliament, the head of state, the constitutional court, the ombudsmen, the political press, human rights NGOs, the government, etc.—with each and every member having a separate set and degree of responsibility for spelling out the specific and optimal reading of the constitution. There are no given answers and one-size-fits-all models to follow. Due to historical and socio-political givens, in one fully functional constitutional democracy, there is a need for an elaborate and robust self-protection mechanism, and thus there may be a need to prohibit holocaust denial and to criminalise hate speech; in another, the cornerstone of a stable and well-functioning constitutionalism lies in the very fact of basically unlimited speech, be it political or commercial. In one fully functional constitutional democracy, race and ethnicity are used in official state records; in other, also fully functional constitutional democracy, the prohibition on registering people's race, religion, and sexual orientation is a substantial expectation of the electorate. And so on. Constitutional democracies thrive on free debate concerning the proper recipes for constitutionalism. Hungary, like other countries in the CEE region, in my opinion, is facing severe difficulties in meeting the demands of an adult-democracy in this regard. Many of the aforementioned democratic actors are unprepared to face the new, albeit inevitable, and in a sense normal phenomena that non-state agents can use constitutional rights in an unconstitutional manner.

In well-functioning constitutional democracies, questions around fundamental rights do not only arise in the context of the state curtailing the people's freedom. Since these rights themselves may very well be in conflict there are often debates about their relative importance. This should, of course, be familiar to young democracies, too, but it seems as though participants in the democratic process sometimes respond inadequately to the necessary task of balancing properly clashing fundamental rights. Sometimes, even human rights advocates fail to understand that imperfections and certain inherent contradictions within the legal system do not reveal the failure of an interpretation that conforms to the constitution and that classic, traditional dogmas (of say freedom of assembly, unlimited free speech or personal data protection) are not immediately apparent and omnipresent answers in all situations.

Consider this example: in August 2009, international neo-Nazi organisations were planning a demonstration in Budapest to commemorate the death of Hitler's deputy, Rudolf Hess. Although Article 2 of the 1989 Act on Assembly[3] prohibits demonstrations that would violate criminal provisions (the demonstration would clearly fall under this category, violating several provisions within the Criminal Code), Article 8 only allows for the police to prohibit a demonstration if it will obstruct the functioning of crucial state institutions or severely impede traffic. Thus, the demonstration—which obviously carried a foreseeable risk of violence and intimidation of a great number of people—could not legally be banned, only disbanded in the event of disorder. In this case, however, the Hungarian police decided to ban the demonstration in advance. Clearly, human rights NGOs (among them the one I am a member of) had a well-founded rule of law argument in protesting against this prohibition,[4] especially, since a few months earlier the Hungarian police tried to use a textually similarly unfounded argumentation to prevent a Gay Pride March. Nevertheless, as on other occasions what they thereby did—as the neo-Nazis expected and manipulated them to do—was to create sympathy in the media for, maybe not the cause, but the means. It is quite telling that in the midst of this controversy the police, without hesitation, approved the registration of another, purportedly 'unrelated event', a demonstration initiated by Tamás Polgár, a noted rightist radical blogger (writing under the name Tomcat) and Endre János Domkos,[5] a well-known skin-head leader commemorating Walter Rudolf Hess, a Nobel-prize laureate from physiology in 1949,[6] who was, obviously only a namesake for Rudolf Walter Richard Hess, the Nazi.

The case shows the complexity of the issue: an imperfect, twenty-year-old law and a classic liberal dilemma. This sort of problem is a recurrent, indeed ordinary event in constitutional democracies and ought to be resolved in a routine manner. The answer, however difficult this may seem, is obviously not to approach the law in a selective manner, upholding it when we sympathise with the cause and disregarding it when we do not. We have to acknowledge the complexity of solutions a constitutional democracy may offer. One might say that it should fall under the constitutional role of the police to take responsibility for resolving the contradiction between two clauses of the law on the freedom of assembly and come up with an interpretation, tailored to the event in question but in line with the constitution, that favours Article 2. Alternatively, the courts, which have the responsibility of deciding appeals against administrative decisions by the police, might act themselves or they could request a constitutional review by the constitutional court itself. Another possibility would be that the parliamentary legislators could rapidly introduce a bill amending the law. Civil-liberties absolutists may very well decide to argue for the superiority of certain rights, although it is questionable whether there are constitutional super-clauses—like freedom of speech, assembly or data protection—through the lenses of which state actors can afford to and should be obliged unconditionally to see the entire world. This would be particularly dangerous in young, premature democracies like Hungary, because state-actor participants in the constitutional process, who are traditionally conservative and resistant towards the idea of human rights and civil liberties, will most likely use these arguments as an excuse for not protecting other constitutional rights.

Following this long introduction, I turn to a case study of Hungarian law and law enforcement practices because legal issues around extremist movements have been particularly relevant here in the past few years. The Czech Republic has faced similarly unpalatable political forces... but their electoral success is negligible compared to their Hungarian counterparts. And in Bulgaria... the law has barely come into the matter. I consider first the failure to combat and prosecute hate crimes because of misinterpreted data protection, and second controversies around the banning of extremist political organisations. This will allow the reader to see how the general arguments discussed above play out in practice. In particular I will show how the resistance to collecting ethnic data by law enforcement authorities, a resistance that is strongly supported by human rights arguments in Hungary and which seems superficially appealing and constitutionally justified, is in fact neither a constitutional must, nor good policy. Hungary is one of the (many) countries in which extensive legal restrictions on the collection of non-anonymous data concerning ethnic, national or religious identity have prompted law enforcement authorities to simply deny that ethnicity is of significance in their actions—even when these involve the investigation of race crimes. Thus, in the first case study[7] I will argue that surrounded by an omnipresent and legal culture of data protection that claims to trump all other considerations, the authorities refrain from identifying victims' ethnicity. In order to avoid making uncomfortable and—given the prevalent anti-Roma or xenophobic sentiments in these societies—unpopular decisions, law enforcement officials, as well as prosecutors and judges, successfully avoid recognising racial motivation in violent criminal behaviour, even if the existence of racially motivated crimes logically presupposes the notion of membership in a racial or ethno-national community. The outcome is that a narrow and treacherous interpretation of the superficially minority-friendly principles of ethno-racial data protection actually runs contrary to the interests of the victimised groups. The example of race crimes provides a vivid demonstration of the Murphy-law of hate prejudice: notwithstanding the sweetest sounding constitutional and statutory language on equal treatment, free choice of identity and the protection of sensitive data, it is always the discriminatory practice of the majority that actually defines attribution of ethnic affiliation. Thus, when what is at issue is the maltreatment of members of various ethnic groups, no difficulties in definitions arise for the would-be discriminating party, but do arise when state actors are called to defend those discriminated against. In fact, conceptual ambiguities may sometimes worsen the effect of protective measures provided for the victimised group.

The second case study, dealing with the banning of extremist paramilitary organisations, will show that not even the existence of narrowly tailored legislation designed for this sort of case guarantees action if law enforcement operates in a hypocritical and cynical politicised arena.

Inadequate Legal Responses

In Hungary, as in many places across Europe, there are tragic, historical precedents when censuses and other administrative lists have been used to identify people as enemies of the state and discriminate against them. There is, therefore, an understandable shyness towards practices that include collecting ethnic data without the explicit permission of the concerned persons, or policies that would curtail the free choice of (ethnic) identity. However, such a restrictive approach to ethno-national data classification causes severe constitutional problems.

Hungarian law allows for the handling of data on racial and ethnic origin only with the consent of the person concerned.[8] Articles 2(2) and 3(2) of Act No. 63 of 1992 on the protection of personal data and the use of public data prohibit the handling of sensitive data, such as ethnic origin, without the concerned person's explicit permission. In order to stay on the safe, and less labour-intensive, side of the data protection controversy, officials habitually claim that recording the racial status of victims of racial violence would run against statutory provisions, even though the Criminal Code acknowledges certain racially motivated crimes, such as 'violence against members of a community' or 'incitement against a community', all of which presuppose membership in the given (e.g. racially or ethno-nationally defined) community. In general, as Lilla Farkas points out, with Hungarian law allowing for the handling of data on racial and ethnic origin only with the consent of the person concerned, the effect is to severely impede the prospect of litigation against indirect discrimination or institutional racism.[9] The Hungarian Criminal Code (Act IV of 1978) criminalises four types of behaviour that may fall under the racially motivated category. (Racial motivation is implied in the wording of the law.) These are: genocide (Article 155), apartheid (Article 157), violence against members of a community (Article 174/B),[10] and incitement against a community (Article 269).[11] Nevertheless, it is safe to say that the first two have never, and the latter two have only very rarely occurred in the official record.

Let us look at the statistics:[12] the number for reported and investigated cases are follows: for 'violence against members of a community' the numbers of reported cases were as follows: 2005: 15, 2006: 13, 2007: 20, 2008: 13, 2009: 23. Out of this only one case was [indicted] and made it to the court. In regards of 'incitement against a community' the following number of cases were reported: 2005: 27, 2006: 22, 2007: 34, 2008: 24, 2009: 48. This led to only one indictment in the years 2006–2009 and to 2 in 2005. Concerning perpetrators, the number of indictments were as follows: for 'violence against members of a community' 2005: 2, 2006: 2, 2007:3, 2008: 11, 2009: 25; for 'incitement against a community' only one indictment reached courts annually.[13]

This should by no means imply that racial crimes and violence are non-existent in Hungary, but rather, as said above, that law enforcement agents, as well as prosecutors and courts, are very reluctant to recognise racial motivation in violent and non-violent crimes committed against Roma and other minority victims. Officers and officials habitually claim that the lack of clear legislative guidelines for the establishment of racial motivation means that most such instances only qualify as nuisance, assault or mischief. On the other hand, many politicians and experts argue that the criminal legislation in force could easily allow for a less narrow, more minority-friendly interpretation. Although it will always be the prosecutor who will decide on what grounds to indict the defendant, she will usually follow the police's determination on the nature of the criminal offence. As for the police, officers claim that in determining whether an offense is racially motivated they take notice of internal guidance issued by the Attorney General that directs prosecutors when considering and qualifying the indictment. This means that the only legal guidance is an internal policy guide, which, needless to say, would not stand up very well against any constitutional challenge.

Another debate, a technical yet important one, concerns the legal status of perceived ethnicity. One could argue that data relating to one's perceived ethnic origin is not explicitly prohibited by the Data Protection Act. Under the aforementioned Article 2 of the Act, sensitive data is defined to include 'personal data revealing racial, national or ethnic origin [...].'[14] In the approach widely accepted in Hungarian professional literature, the term 'data' must be interpreted extensively to mean any fact, information, or knowledge that can be linked to a person. According to a comprehensive and influential analysis: 'Hungary's information rights regulations do not distinguish between data and information; legal professionals use the two terms interchangeably. Beyond data identifying natural persons, personal data includes everything that can be correlated with a specific person with the help of the identifying data. The information does not necessarily have to be factually true. Indeed, false information could constitute a special case of personal data, as long as it satisfies the rest of the criteria. In this way, data implying Roma origin is regarded as personal data even if the subject in question does not happen to be Roma as well as in cases where he does declare himself to be Roma. Finally, the notion of 'data' also comprises inferences drawn from one or—as is typically the case—several pieces of information. For instance, information must be considered personal (even sensitive) data if it is an inference, whether well-founded or unjustified, from other data (such as a surname more often borne by Roma individuals than by others) that does not in itself necessarily imply minority status.'[15]

Under this approach, absurdly, even the following statements may constitute a violation of data protection laws: 'Nelson Mandela is a black human rights activist'; 'Robert Fico is a Slovak nationalist politician'; 'Ariel Sharon is Jewish'; 'The Pope is Catholic'.

Furthermore, not only inferred data (which is what journalism is built on), but also false data—for example the statement that 'Stevie Wonder is white'—would be illegal under data protection laws. Hungarian practice, due both to the proper and improper interpretation of the data protection law, is absurd in other areas as well: the media would report that officials found illegal, toxin-laced meat products in a supermarket-chain, but due to data protection concerns, would not disclose the name of the company. Even if a nationally known politician were to be arrested for, say, corruption charges, in line with the guidelines, the police would only use initials of the suspect when issuing a press release. Political bodies, like a parliamentary committee or opposition parties, which are constitutionally intended to assist initiatives revealing data on the conduct of daily business by the state and the government choose to ignore or even oppose these claims. For example, the Hungarian Civil Liberties Union (HCLU) once had to sue the Constitutional Court for not disclosing a petition sent by a Member of Parliament seeking the constitutional review of a provision of the Criminal Code. The court, in line with the Constitutional Court (the ultimate guarantor of fundamental rights!) was of the opinion that cases initiated by Members of Parliament amount to private data and are to be exempt from disclosure. The case reached the Supreme Court, with the HCLU's requests denied at all instances.[16]

The aversion to transparency, as well as the political and public responsibility induced by such, is also present in a somewhat unexpected realm: the broad practice adopted, most strikingly, by the media. News reports, televised or printed, habitually refrain from publishing the full names of people featured in reports, and use initials or first names at best—even if those mentioned are politicians or other public figures. For example, following the official press release of the police and MTI, the official Hungarian News Agency, media organs used the label

'György H.' to refer to the mayor of District 7 of Budapest, who was arrested for charges of corruption—despite that fact that the identity of the mayor is known to almost everybody in the country.[17] This sort of absurdity is daily practice: a court in a libel case referred to Imre K., a Hungarian Nobel-prize laureate in literature—the only Hungarian ever to receive such a prize. It is also quite telling that the law transposing the EU's racial and other equality directives, Act 125 of 2003 on Equal Treatment identifies the publication of the names of those found guilty in discrimination as a separate sanction[18] that the Equal Treatment Authority, the equality body established by the law may (!) apply. And the practice of the newly formed organisation reflects the above attitude: concerning its activities in 2009, the Authority proudly reported that following the 1087 complaints they received, 351 cases were processed by the Authority, which led to 48 instances where discrimination was established, of which a mere 33 were actually made public.[19]

Banning the Guard

My second example of inadequate response—an intriguing combination of legal, political and social—concerns the case of the Hungarian Guard ('Magyar Gárda'), a paramilitary organisation closely affiliated to a recently emerged right-wing extremist party, the Movement for a Better Hungary ('Jobbik Magyarországért Mozgalom', or 'Jobbik' in common parlance). In this case, the government has clear and undisputed legal tools for action and, according to political statements and declarations the relevant authorities are instructed to take action against illegal activities. In reality, however, no action is taken by authorities—possibly due to the rather restrained level of protest raised by civil society and opposition political parties—which are aware and conscious of the popularity of anti-Roma political rhetoric. The outcome is the injection of a politico-legal placebo—the introduction of a narrowly tailored, explicitly case-driven piece of legislation to disband the organisation. Despite a binding court order, however, no action is taken to enforce the law and there is no courage to seek a cure for the disease instead of treating the symptoms: seeking to ban the parliamentary and European Parliamentary party, Jobbik. This path of course could be risky, especially if not done in a 'wholehearted' way, as demonstrated by the Czech case,[iii] or if prepared in an unprofessional manner, with, for example, the secret service infiltrating the party, as happened in Germany.

---

iii [Ed. note] An attempt in 2009 to ban the right wing extremist Workers' Party, which failed due to inadequate legal preparation by the Czech government.

In June 2010, the Office for Democratic Institutions and Human Rights (ODIHR) at the Organisation for Security and Co-operation in European (OSCE) published a special report based on a field study carried out in Hungary on the issue of anti-Roma hate crimes.[20] This is how it presents the facts of the Hungarian case in respect of Jobbik (founded in 2002) and its affiliate, the para-military organisation the Hungarian Guard[21] (founded in 2007, with Jobbik's leader serving as its leader):

> A major plank of the party's platform is the need to battle what it refers to as 'Gypsy criminality'.[22] *Jobbik* was able to attract only marginal support in elections prior to those for the European Parliament in June 2009, never having reached 9 per cent support in any electoral district and attracting only 2.2 per cent when running as part of a coalition in the 2006 parliamentary elections. The party then managed to garner 15 per cent of the vote and pick up three seats at the elections to the European Parliament. [...][iv] In the Spring 2010 *Jobbik*, for the first time entered parliament (with skinhead leaders in its grouping), gaining 12.18 % of the seats.[23] Generally, *Jobbik* receives its highest level of support in areas where there was a significant Roma minority...
>
> Since fall 2007, their programme has emphasised battling 'Gypsy criminality', and the organisation's militant attributes have become more pronounced. The Hungarian Guard has organised and led marches and rallies across the country, particularly in places where inter-ethnic conflicts or attacks have occurred or crimes have been committed in which the perpetrators, alleged or otherwise, were Roma. Events at some locations have apparently been held at the request of local non-Roma residents.... The Hungarian Guard has been joined by a number of other ultra-nationalist formations, including the Goy Bikers (*Gój Motorosok*) and the Nationalist Bikers (*Nemzeti Érzelmű Motorosok*) ...
>
> Following anti-Roma speeches made by Hungarian Guard leaders at the 9 December 2007 rally... the Capital Chief Public Prosecutor's Office, in Budapest, filed a motion in the Capital Court calling for the dissolution of the Hungarian Guard Traditional and Cultural Association, arguing that its activities violated the Freedom of Association Act. The motion referred to international human rights norms under the ICCPR [International Covenant on Civil and Political Rights], ICERD [International Convention on the Elimination of All Forms of Racial Discrimination] and ECHR [European Convention on Human Rights]

---

iv [Ed. note] Cuts in the ODIHR report made by Pap.

and the jurisprudence of the Hungarian Constitutional Court regarding the right to human dignity. Prosecutors argued that the Guard's activities violate the human dignity and equality of the Hungarian Roma, thus violating their rights and freedoms under the Freedom of Association Act, and that these are sufficient grounds for the group's dissolution under the Act.

Members of the Hungarian Guard demonstrated near the court building during the trial and the proceedings had to be postponed temporarily when a judge's request to be recused after she received threatening anonymous telephone calls was granted by the President of the Court.

In December 2008, the court of first instance, the Municipal Court of Budapest, ordered the dissolution of the Hungarian Guard Association, ruling that the organization's programme is based on discrimination and that it operates as a 'means to create a climate of fear, while its activities—marches by its members in Roma populated settlements and the speeches of its leaders—constitute a breach of the rights of other citizens by violating their right to dignity and equality'.

The Association appealed the decision, arguing that the Hungarian Guard Association for Protecting Tradition and Culture was not the same as the Hungarian Guard Movement—the actual paramilitary formation, which is not a legal entity—and was thereby unaffected by the ruling. The Guard remained active and continued recruiting members, including adolescents and children. On 2 July 2009, the court of second instance upheld the lower court's ruling, referring to Article 5 of the ECHR and Article 4 (b) of the ICERD in its decision. The Guard remained active and, in response, a 14 July Government decree created the statutory offence of 'participating in the activities of a banned social organisation', effective 17 July. Based on the statute, anyone who conducts activity that has been declared illegal in a court order banning an organisation faces punishment of a fine of up to 100,000 Hungarian forints (about 365 euros). Leading the activities of a banned social organisation had already been covered as a misdemeanour under the Hungarian Criminal Code.

The Guard continued holding events and, on 22 August, the town of Szentendre, to the north of Budapest, saw the swearing in of hundreds of new recruits to the 'New Hungarian Guard Movement'. Some participants in the event, including the head of *Jobbik,* took part dressed in the uniform of the banned Guard. The police brought administrative charges against 176 people for 'participating in the activities of a banned social organisation'. On 18 November, the Government broadened the range of punishable conduct in connection with a banned social organization, introducing a fine of up to 50,000 forints for anyone who participates in the activities in a banned social organization in any way or who wears the uniform thereof or any uniform resembling that of a banned social organization at a public event.[24]

Despite the fact that the Magyar Gárda has been banned by a binding court decision, lacking government action, its members still hold rallies. The Guard keeps reappearing under new names and with slightly changed uniforms. Jobbik's leader, Gábor Vona, wore a Gárda vest to the inauguration session of the Parliament in 2010.[25] Political parties, and governments, including that of the newly elected right-wing coalition, led by Viktor Orbán, which won a sweeping victory in Spring 2010, are unwilling to take straightforward action against the popular far-right, and engage in an ambivalent Janus-faced politics: sometimes issuing minor fines at isolated Gárda events, but allowing the party-leader to wear Gárda uniform in Parliament, and generally showing reluctance to form a uniform front or even to take a firm stance against the anti-democratic Jobbik and its affiliate, the manifestly illegal Guard. What we see instead is the toleration of a proliferating quibbling, where the Guard Movement, a non-legal entity is free to exist, since it is different from the Guard Cultural Association, or a 'New Guard' ('Új Gárda') is seen as untouched by the ban on the 'Magyar Gárda', even though its members, leaders, activities and rhetoric [are] identical, and only its uniform was redesigned slightly.

The Way Out: Proactive Efforts in Line with the Constitution

The question is: how to escape from this trap of quibbling, which seems to be particularly deeply embedded in the post-communist societies, and which in fact ridicules rule-of-law constitutionalism and prevents the protection of citizens' fundamental right not to be violated. In the Guard case the answer seems simple: first, and foremost, enforce the law. Thinking back to Murphy's law of prejudice, the solution to the question is, obviously, in the hands of the legislator. However, the very lesson taught by well-functioning constitutional democracies (and this may apply to a broader range of cases too) is that no other participants of the democratic process are relieved from their constitutional responsibilities if the legislators fail to provide adequate solutions. As mentioned above, another accessible route lies in a constitutionally correct interpretation of the existing laws.

To begin with, we should point out that there is a substantial and constitutionally relevant difference between classifying ethno-racial identity for affirmative action, for positive (individual or collective) minority rights, and for providing protection against discrimination and criminal victimisation. When using preferential treatment, members of the minority group have to declare their membership in a minority group as a precondition for being awarded those additional rights. In addition to such a declaration or statement, it may be reasonable to set certain objective eligibility criteria, such as knowledge of the given minority language or participation in a minority organisation. By contrast, a case of discrimination does not involve the affirmation of ethnic identity or making a declaration to that effect, but rather calls for protection against discrimination based on a personality trait assumed by the external world (because of the victim's physical appearance, for example). In this case, instead of attaching additional rights to the optional declaration of identity, the law should offer protection against discrimination based on the prejudices of the majority. The point in anti-discrimination cases is not to prove affiliation with an ethnic group so much as to decide whether the accused committed the discrimination by identifying the person as belonging to a group based on stereotypes held by the majority—which, of course, would constitute sensitive data. Even under European and, to stick with our case, Hungarian law, routine blindness of investigative and prosecution authorities to recognise the racial motivation behind crimes, implies a misinterpretation of data protection laws. If the Criminal Code explicitly defines racially motivated crimes, this in itself constitutes a sufficient legal mandate for prosecuting such crimes and for processing the ethnic data deemed necessary for their prosecution. Needless to say, what is to be registered is not the fact that the person is, say, of Roma ethnicity but the fact that the discrimination or the attack has been committed on the assumption that she was Roma.

There are few positive examples that prove that a constitution-friendly interpretation can prevent narrow-minded, dogmatic practices that all refer to data-protection issues.

The first good practice example from Hungarian case law came up in a strategic litigation lawsuit brought in 2006, by the Chance for Children Foundation,[26] against the City of Hajdúhadház and two municipal schools on charges of discrimination.[27] In this case, Judge Tamás Endre Tóth appointed an expert to investigate allegations of segregation. Adopting a rather peculiar method, the expert proceeded to ask a committee composed of members of the local Roma government to identify, based on names and home addresses, which of the pupils—all of whom were admittedly personally known to the representatives in question—they recognised and considered as Roma. In the next step, the data were rendered anonymous and used to supply a percentage ratio of Roma and non-Roma pupils among the children attending the schools concerned.

In a statement, which the Court admitted for the most part,[28] counsel for the plaintiff insisted that the sensitive data—that stacked up to prove a practice of segregation—had not been processed unlawfully, considering that the appointed expert and the local elected Roma representatives used the latter's official knowledge to define whom they knew/considered/assumed to be Roma. Moreover, the information was submitted to the court in anonymous form as pure statistical data, and so was unsuited to identify specific natural persons. So, at the stage when the expert report was filed, the ability to identify individuals in a way that could raise concerns over privacy and data protection was out of the question. Beyond any issues raised by the provisions of the Data Protection Act, counsel also underlined the importance of considering the implications of the minority law,[29] which assigns to local minority self-governments the essential task of protecting their communities, as well as vesting them with special rights in minority education. She asked how the duty of protecting interests could possibly be fulfilled if the local minority representatives did not know whether the person on whose behalf they took action was Roma or not. The members of the Roma minority self-government of the City of Hajdúhadház maintained daily contact with the members of the local Roma community, living together with them on or near the settlements and representing them on a daily basis to the staff and teachers of the accused schools. Years of experience in this small town had taught them not only which members of the community professed themselves to be Roma, but also whom the defendants regarded as belonging to that minority. In other words, counsel was of the opinion that, pursuant to the anti-discrimination act, it was not the ethnic background professed by the subject her/himself that had to be demonstrated but the defendant's assumption about the ethnic belonging of the subject. In other words, the Data Protection Act does not regulate the processing of data on perceived ethnicity but those data that derive from self-professed ethnic belonging. Finally, the counsel asked the Court, should the defendant claim that its own assumptions about which of the children were Roma diverged from those formed by the minority representatives, the Court then order the defendant to come out and specifically say which pupils it regarded as Roma and on what grounds. Unsurprisingly the defendants demurred.

A further case in point is a project which was run by the Hungarian Helsinki Committee, in cooperation with the National Police and the Police Academy in the fall of 2007 and the spring of 2008, which examined traffic stop/ID check practices within the force, specifically searching for signs of discrimination based on ethnicity. Through the six months of the project, police officers performing ID checks in the presence of civilian observers filled in a so-called RK form (a standard form provided for ID checks in the Interior Ministry Decree 3/1995

BM), and were also asked to anonymously complete another form, supplying the details of the action (time, place, reason, result), the sex and age of the stopped individual, and stating whether the acting officer deems the individual to be 'Asian', 'Arab', 'white', 'black', 'Roma/gipsy', or 'other'. The purpose of the survey was to identify the groups most often targeted by ID checks and the most frequently cited reasons for those checks, as well as to gauge the efficiency of these operations in terms of law enforcement and the discovery of crimes. In completing the form, then, officers made a record of the checked individuals' perceived ethnicity—and they did so with the advance permission of the Data Protection Commissioner and the Minority Commissioner, both of who had approved the methodology and mechanism of the survey.[30] As for the results, the survey has revealed that a Roma person is three times as likely as a non-Roma person to be stopped by police for an ID check, and that this discriminative treatment cannot be justified citing higher crime rates among the Roma minority, simply because the data do not provide proof for that assumption. In short, on the evidence of the aggregate ethnic data, the researchers found no difference whatsoever in the results brought by respectively checking the IDs of Roma and non-Roma citizens, such as could be used to retroactively justify the police action in terms of a 'reasonable suspicion' or 'objective criteria' underpinning an act of discrimination.

Closing Remarks

To sum up the above, constitutional democracy puts a heavy weight on participants of the democratic process: law makers, government officials, law enforcement officers, judges, prosecutors, media workers and human rights organisations alike. Pointing fingers to the others and evading this responsibility is just as harmful as falling victim to sectarianism and monolithic dogmatism. Instead, responsibility, creativity and courage are what constitutional democracies demand and the people deserve.

This paper has taken the legal case history of one country in order to demonstrate some points that are surely generalisable beyond the borders of modern Hungary. Although the nature and history of the extremist movements in the Czech Republic diverge from their Hungarian comrades, it is striking that the Czech authorities have at times got themselves into a similarly difficult situation to the Hungarians. Attempts to ban movements or suppress demonstrations have been half-hearted and it seems that a similar post-communist unease over dealing with conflicts over fundamental rights (free speech versus protection from violation as an individual or as a member of a community) has arisen there. The initial effort in the Czech Republic by the Topolánek cabinet to ban the extremist

Workers' Party was so sloppy that many observers suspected it of having been essentially 'for show'. After that government lost a confidence vote, the caretaker Fischer cabinet was appointed and succeeded in making the case to the court that the party should be banned. This second effort was met with general public approval, largely due to media reports linking the party to a particularly gruesome arson attack and to the Litvínov riots. Of course, this has not stopped the individual members involved from exercising their right to association in a new party with an almost identical name. Another loose end which Czech authorities have yet to tie up is the fact that those who initiated in the Litvínov riots[v] in 2008 have still not been prosecuted.

And the same story can be repeated elsewhere—in other words: the Hungarian case, for all its local absurdity, speaks to a wider European malaise, at least in the new member states and one that—in the light of increasingly aggressive campaigning statements by parties like Jobbik—needs to be addressed urgently.

ENDNOTES

1. See for example <http://www.monstersandcritics.com/news/europe/news/article_1494257.php/Sixth-Roma-murder-victim-laid-to-rest> or <http://www.time.com/time/world/article/0,8599,1895255,00.html>
2. According to a survey by the pollster institute Századveg-Forsense, published in March 2009, Hungarians are more pessimistic then ever. The value of the 'comfort index' showed an all-time low (of 18). <http://www.szazadveg.hu/kutatas/archivum/kozvelemeny-kutatas-es-partreferencia-elemzes/soha-nem-ereztuk- meg-ennyire-rosszul-magunkat-131.html>. Also see *Eurobarometer 63, Public opinion in the European Union*, p. 11, <http://ec.europa.eu/public_opinion/archives/eb/eb63/eb63_en.pdf>.
3. Act 3 of 1989.
4. See <http://helsinki.hu/Friss_anyagok/htmls/614>.
5. See <http://nol.hu/archivum/archiv-100606>.
6. See, http://hvg.hu/itthon/20090903_walter_rudolf_hess_tomcat> and <http://szentkoronaradio.com/belfold/2009_09_03_tomcat-es-domokos-endre-janos-megemlekezese-walter- rudolf-hessrol>.
7. For a more elaborate analysis, see András László Pap: 'Human Rights and Ethnic Data Collection in Hungary', *Human Rights Review*, Vol. 9, Issue 1, March 2008, pp. 109–122.
8. The law, of course, does not prohibit the anonymous collection of census data and law can, in principle, prescribe other circumstances when ethnic data can be collected.
9. In cases of indirect discrimination not only the ethnicity of the plaintiff(s) but also of the comparator(s) must be established. The latter may prove an insurmountable task. See Lilla Farkas (2004): 'The Monkey That Does Not See', *Roma Rights Quarterly*, 2004/2.
10. Before 1 February 2009, the name of the offence governed by the Article 174/B of the Criminal Code, was 'violence against a member of a national, ethnic, racial or religious group'. As a result of Act No. 79 of 2008 (amending certain acts with a view to protecting order and the operation of justice) Article 174/B of the Criminal Code was extended to cover any group of

v [Ed. Note] A violent 500-strong crowd organized by the extremist Workers' Party battled with police trying to defend the Roma population of Litvínov.

the population; the name of the offence was also modified to 'violence against a member of a community'.

11. In addition, Article 269 of the Criminal Code involves a sub-paragraph on the ban of using totalitarian symbols (269/B—as a result of the amendment in 1993), and a sub-paragraph (269/C) on the ban of denying, doubting, or trivialising genocide or crimes against humanity committed by totalitarian regimes (269/C). The latter sub-paragraph originally dealt only with holocaust denial (it came into force in February 2010). A few months later, as a result of a legislative initiatives of the newly elected Hungarian government, this sub paragraph was amended: from July 2010—in order to cover the 'EU framework decision on combating racism and xenophobia', 2008/913/JHA—269/C is extended to the crimes of both 'national socialist' and 'communist regimes', and the term 'holocaust' is no longer there in the text.
12. Source: Unified Police and Prosecution Statistical Database.
13. For earlier years, the statistics were as follows: incitement against community cases registered: 1999: 3, 2000: 8, 2001: 12, 2002: 5, and 2003: 11. This meant that the following number of offenders had been identified and indicted: 1999: 9, 2000: 12, 2001: 9, 2002: 5, 2003: 9, and in 2004: 11 identified from which 8 indicted. According to official statistics, in 2003 2 people were indicted and two convicted under Article 174/B; in 2004, the numbers were 8 and 6, respectively. So, for example in 2003, 2 people were indicted and two convicted under Article 174/B; in 2004, the numbers were 8 and 6, respectively. In 2007, in cases of 'violence against a member of an ethnic, national etc. group' charges were only filed in 6 cases, and only 9 crimes became known to the public out of the 20 recorded. (In 5 instances, the complaints were turned down, and in 8 cases the investigation was declared closed.) The 34 allegations of 'hate crimes' resulted in only one charge being filed, and 8 acknowledged felonies being added to the record. (In 16 cases the complaints were turned down, and the investigation declared closed in another 16.) In 2008, 'violence against a member of an ethnic, national etc. group' was reported to the authorities in even fewer, only 13, cases of, out of which 8 cases resulted in prosecution; 24 cases of 'incitement against community' were reported, from which only one prosecution resulted. In 2009, the number of reported cases of 'violence against…' increased to 23, out of which 7 cases resulted in prosecution. The number of reported cases of 'incitement against community' doubled to 48 in this year compared to the previous year, from the 48 cases, 3 cases were considered as offences, but only one prosecution emerged.
14. The Data Protection Act differentiates the concept of sensitive data within the category of personal data. These sensitive data constitute a type of personal data referring to an essential trait and thus a vulnerable part of the subject's personal identity, which is therefore given a special degree of protection by law. Of course, not all personal data are sensitive in nature; the notion is restricted to those categories that are expressly listed by the Act. The Act divides sensitive data into two groups depending on the level of special protection accorded to them. On the one hand, we have data pertaining to race, national and ethnic minority background, political opinion or affiliation, religious or other philosophical beliefs, and membership in advocacy organisations; on the other hand, there are those data that are related to health, pathological addiction, sexual orientation, and criminal record. Article 2 clause 2.
15. László Majtényi, Iván Székely and Máté Dániel Szabó (2006): *Roma támogatások és jogosultságok egyéni követésének lehető ségei* (Possibilities for tracing individual Roma subsidies and entitlements), Budapest: Eötvös Károly Institute, p. 10.
16. See, <http://tasz.hu/hu/informacioszabadsag/33> (in Hungarian).
17. See for example, <http://www.hirszerzo.hu/cikk.hunvald-ugy_ki_verte_at_a_kiraly_utca_15_lakoit.97638.html>
18. Article 16.
19. See, <http://egyenlobanasmod.hu/data/2009tevekenyseg_szamok_tukreben.pdf>
20. Organisation for Security and Co-operation in Europe, Office for Democratic Institutions and Human Rights, *Addressing Violence, Promoting Integration. Field Assessment of Violent Incidents against Roma in Hungary: Key Developments, Findings and Recommendations*, June–July

2009. Warsaw: OSCE-ODIHR, 15 June 2010, pp. 32–5, <http://www.osce.org/documents/odihr/2010/06/44569_en.pdf>

21. The full name of the organisation is: Hungarian Guard Association for the Protection of Tradition and Culture ('Magyar Gárda Hagyományőrző és Kulturális Egyesület'). It was registered as a cultural organisation aiming to 'prepare the youth spiritually and physically for extraordinary situations that might require the mobilisation of the people'.

22. One example is the statement by Csanád Szegedi, MEP, Jobbik on 21 November 2009: 'The unfortunate and tragic Gypsy terror in Sajóbábony proved that the parties of the parliament have eroded the police and the law-enforcement bodies to such a degree that they are unable to protect the Hungarian population from Gypsy criminality. Contrary to the information provided by the media, the truth is that Gypsy criminals have attacked peaceful Hungarian citizens yet again. The issue today is not only the isolated actions of Gypsy criminals in different settlements but, unfortunately, we have to say, the fact that the Gypsies and the parliamentary parties are terrorizing the Hungarian population in North-Hungary. The Movement for a Better Hungary calls on the national heads of the police to—even if it means using extraordinary measures—stop the Gypsy terror in Sajóbábony too. If the police that have been waiting for taxpayers' money are unable to carry out its job it has the duty to co-operate with the New Hungarian Guard Movement. The gendarmeries of the New Hungarian Guard are ready—with the necessary legal authorization—to restore public order in Hungary'. 'A *Jobbik* fellép a tomboló a cigányterrorral szemben' (Jobbik Steps Up against the Frantic Gypsy Terror), <http://zuglo.Jobbik.hu/a_Jobbik_fellep_a_tombolo_a_ciganyterrorral_szemben>

23. <http://valasztas.hu/hu/parval2010/index.html>

24. Organisation for Security and Co-operation in Europe, Office for Democratic Institutions and Human Rights, *Addressing Violence, Promoting Integration. Field Assessment of Violent Incidents against Roma in Hungary: Key Developments, Findings and Recommendations*. June–July 2009, Warsaw: OSCE-ODIHR, 15 June 2010, pp. 32–5, <http://www.osce.org/documents/odihr/2010/06/44569_en.pdf>

25. <http://www.economist.com/blogs/easternapproaches/2010/06/hungary_3>

26. 'Esélyt a Hátrányos Helyzetű Gyerekeknek Alapítvány' (CFCF).

27. Judgement No. 6P. 20.341/2006/50.

28. Based on the litigation documents and the kind personal account of Ms. Lilla Farkas, counsel for the plaintiff.

29. Article 5 (2).

30. Ferenc Kőszeg and Lorna Králik, (2008), *Control(led) Group. Final Report on the Strategies for Effective Police Stop and Search (STEPSS) Project*, Budapest: Hungarian Helsinki Committee.

References

Balogh, Lídia (2009), 'Etnikai adatok kezelése a magyarországi sajtóban' (Ethnic Data Processing in the Hungarian Press), *Föld-Rész*, 2, 3–40, pp. 81–91.

Farkas, Lilla (2004),'The Monkey That Does Not See', *Roma Rights Quarterly*, 2.

Kőszeg, Ferenc and Lorna Králik (2008), *Control(led) Group. Final Report on the Strategies for Effective Police Stop and Search (STEPSS) Project*, Budapest: Hungarian Helsinki Committee.

Majtényi, Balázs (2006/2007): 'What Has Happened to Our Model Child? The Creation and Evolution of the Hungarian Minority Act'. In European Yearbook of Minority Issues, Vol. 7.

Majtényi, Balázs and András László Pap (2009), 'Should ethnic data be standardized? Different situations of processing ethnic data', in Máté Dániel Szabó (ed.), *Privacy protection and Minority Rights*, Budapest: Eötvös Károly Policy Institute, pp. 63–88.

Majtényi, László, Iván Székely and Máté Dániel Szabó (2006), *Roma támogatások és jogosultságok egyéni követésének lehető ségei* (Possibilities for tracing individual Roma subsidies and entitlements), Budapest: Eötvös Károly Institute.

Pap, András László (2006), 'Minority Rights and Diaspora Claims: Collision and Interdependence', in Osamu Ieda (ed.), *The Status Law Syndrome: Post-Communist Nation-Building or Post-Modern Citizenship?*, Sapporo: Hungarian Academy of Sciences, Institute for Legal Studies—Hokkaido University.

***András L. Pap** is a senior research fellow at the Hungarian Academy of Sciences Institute for Legal Studies and an associate professor, Eötvös University Faculty of Humanities, Department of Media and Communication, and a recurrent visiting professor at the Central European University Nationalism Studies Program. He is also a member of the Hungarian Helsinki Committee.

Pap, András L. "Dogmatism, Hypocrisy and the Inadequacy of Legal and Social Responses Combating Hate Crimes and Extremism: The CEE Experience." In *The Gypsy 'Menace': Populism and the New Anti-Gypsy Politics*, edited by Michael Stewart, 295–331. London: Hurst & Co., 2012.

The paper was written under the aegis of the Bolyai Research Scholarship of the Hungarian Academy of Sciences as part of the 68361 OTKA Research Grant. It was first published with the support of the Organization for Security and Co-operation in Europe, Office for Democratic Institutions and Human Rights.

Options of Roma Political Participation and Representation

*by Márton Rövid**

This paper[1] seeks to provide a critical overview of the main discourses of Roma and pro-Roma organisations in the last two decades and to develop an analytical framework for studying national and international forms of political participation and representation.

Shifting Discourses

One can observe a shift in the focus of dominant discourses of Roma and pro-Roma organisations. (1) In the 1970s and 1980s claims of self-determination were at the forefront; (2) from the 1990s until the early 2000s the focus shifted to human rights violations; (3) from the late 2000s the social and economic integration of Roma has been the main priority.[2]

(1) The *self-determination* approach underscores the importance of recognising that Roma are different, and advocates a form of autonomy. Roma may enjoy either (i) territorial or (ii) personal autonomy.

(i) Territorial autonomy would imply that a certain territory where Roma form the majority of the population is invested with jurisdiction over a substantial number of minority issues and exercises this jurisdiction in its own responsibility. As far as I am aware, there exists no such territorial form of Roma autonomy. There are several settlements where Roma form the majority of the population (for instance in Gadna in Hungary, or in the Šuto Orizari district of Skopje in Macedonia); however, they do not enjoy special collective rights, and the mayors and local self-governments have the same rights and duties as all the others in that country.

There have also been attempts to create a country for the Roma (*Romanestan*). Such claims have been advanced either by self-appointed "Gypsy kings" or extreme right-wing nationalist politicians/activists who wish to get rid of the Roma living in their country.

(ii) Personal or non-territorial autonomy appears to be more suited for dispersed Romani communities. This form of autonomy is granted on the basis of membership of a minority, not residence. Probably the most well-known functioning non-territorial autonomy is enjoyed by the ethnic and national minorities in Hungary, including the Roma. The real challenge for political theory and institutional design is to determine whether such a non-territorial form of autonomy is desirable and feasible on a transnational level.

(2) The *human rights* approach promotes the civic equality and the protection of the fundamental rights of Roma. Accordingly, Roma are to be fully integrated into mainstream political and social institutions.

The human rights or anti-discrimination approach is appropriate for minorities that were involuntarily excluded from common institutions on the basis of perceived race or ethnicity. However, numerous minorities are in the opposite position: they have been involuntarily assimilated, stripped of their own language, culture and self-governing institutions.[3] These groups need counter-majoritarian protections not solely in the form of anti-discrimination and undifferentiated citizenship, but rather in the form of various group-differentiated minority rights.[4]

On the whole, at the bottom of the hierarchy of minority rights is the principle of non-discrimination and of equal rights. The next step is special, group-differentiated rights, which take into account the differences of minority members, and can be granted as individual or collective rights. If the collective rights amount to some form of essential self-determination (political, cultural, other) they become autonomy. Autonomy can be either territorial or personal.[5]

(3) The focus on the *social inclusion* of Roma has grown out of the critiques of the (i) self-determination and (ii) human rights approaches.

Figure 1. The hierarchy of rights.

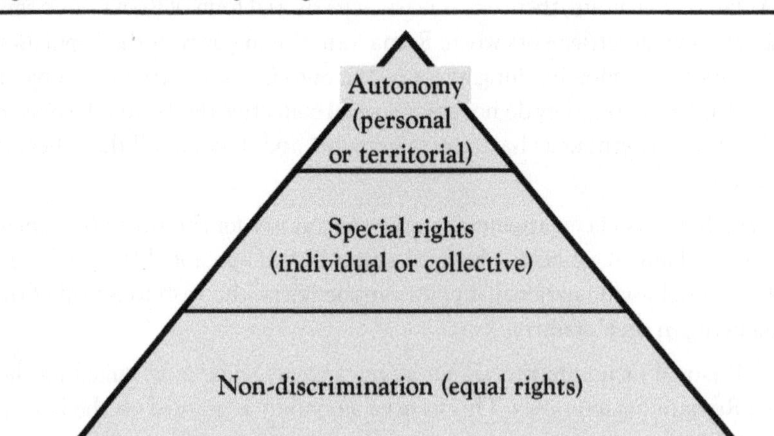

(i) Approaches focusing on self-determination and minority rights have been criticised for downplaying the issues of segregation and exclusion from common institutions, such as schools, workplaces, hospitals, etc. Having the right to establish Roma schools does not facilitate overcoming the exclusion of those Roma students who would like to attend mainstream mixed schools and/or classes.

Furthermore, the discourse of self-determination may be easily interpreted as contributing to the ethnicisation of social problems, thus undermining inter-ethnic solidarity.

> The promotion of some essential "difference" between "Roma" people and everyone else in society exploits traditional prejudices and low expectations. "Difference" is used to explain Roma impoverishment, social tension and conflicts, migration, and the failure of "integration" initiatives. It conserves the political isolation of "Roma" people and supports the ideology of segregation.[6]

Moreover, it is cheaper to promote the ethnic difference of Roma than to improve the living conditions of the masses of Roma who have lost their jobs and to provide access to decent education, housing and health care.

(ii) In return, it is common to criticise the human rights/anti-discrimination discourse for neglecting economic and social processes other than discrimination that contribute to the marginalisation of Roma. Focusing exclusively on discrimination forces a very simplistic vision of social relations, blaming only the prejudiced majority. Such an approach is insensitive to the diversity of local inter-ethnic relations, as well as human rights violations within Romani communities: for instance, domestic violence, human trafficking and usury.[7]

Furthermore, extreme (and even moderate) right-wing political forces may exploit such simplifying approaches, turn them inside-out, and blame the Roma for increasing crime, aggression and other social ills. Attributing social disadvantages to racism also diminishes the elite's responsibility, by blaming popular prejudices for their failure to act.[8]

National and European policy-makers gradually realised that the misery of huge proportions of Roma cannot entirely be explained by racism. Following the collapse of communism and the restructuring of national economies, most Eastern European Roma suddenly fell out of the legal labour market and started gradually sliding out of society. The neo-liberal transition led to the formation of an underclass, i.e. both economically and socially excluded populations being locked outside civil society and class structure.[9]

(iii) Each of the three waves of Roma strategies (EU pre-accession, Decade of Roma Inclusion, EU Framework Strategy) has aimed at the social and economic inclusion of Roma. Each initiative has attempted to improve the coordination, monitoring and financing of national strategies.[10]

Concentrating on "the poverty of [the] geographically concentrated post-transitional rural and suburban underclass [to] which the majority of EU's Roma population is directly subject to or indirectly threatened by"[11] is a legitimate and vital policy focus. Developing the isolated and extremely poor micro-regions in Eastern Europe is a crucial policy objective and will hopefully improve the living conditions of many Roma.

However, not all the difficulties faced by Romani communities throughout Europe are related to the post-communist transition. The recent EU Framework Strategy explicitly excludes "the complex phenomena of ethnicity-based discrimination [and] issues of migration"[12] and implicitly excludes the social difficulties of all other "Roma" groups, those who do not live in impoverished post-communist regions, such as itinerant groups struggling for adequate stopping places or Ashkali immigrants forced into concentration camps such as the *campi nomadi* in Italy—to mention only two blind spots.

Furthermore, aiming for common European objectives may result only in attaining the lowest common denominator. For instance, the EU Framework Strategy aims to ensure that all Roma finish primary school, a very modest objective, which most EU countries have already accomplished, and should rather aim at increasing the number of Roma students in secondary and tertiary education.[13]

Moreover, identifying Roma with misery and social exclusion reproduces precisely those stereotypes that contribute to the exclusion of Roma. Associating Roma with unemployment and calling for their social assistance stigmatises the whole group as a "social burden" and may lead to dangerous policies aiming at disciplining "workshy" Roma.[14]

Options of National-Level Political Participation and Representation

The pyramid of rights can be translated into options of political participation. (i) At a fundamental level, Roma participate in any given political community on the basis of their formal political equality. Such a colour-blind approach relegates ethnic differences to the private sphere and advocates the individual equality of each citizen.

Accordingly, Romani citizens participate in the *demos* on the same footing as any other citizen. They have supposedly the same claim in the distribution, control and exercise of political power as any other member of the political community. As equal citizens, they participate in elections, and can also be elected as representatives.

However, in practice, such a citizenship regime does not seem to provide for the political participation and representation of Roma. Studies suggest that Roma are largely underrepresented on local, national and European levels.[15] Considering their proportion in the general population, there should be dozens of Romani MPs across Eastern Europe. Instead, in 1999 Bárány counted five MPs of Roma origin in the whole of Eastern Europe who were elected on their own or on the lists of mainstream parties.[16] For instance, in Slovakia (where Roma are estimated to make up 9–10 % of the population) no Romani candidate was elected to the parliament till 2012.

Colour-blind citizenship regimes may allow ethnic/minority organisations to participate in local and national elections either as political parties or as associations. For instance, in Bulgaria parties based on ethnic identity are constitutionally forbidden to register; nonetheless, it is possible to register as a political party if the organisation does not explicitly disclose its ethnic focus (as in the case of *Free Bulgaria* and the *Democratic Congress Party*, both having a predominantly Romani membership).[17]

Only those Romani parties managed to secure seats in the national legislatures that allied themselves with mainstream parties and risked becoming their satellites. Overall, the number of Roma elected to national parliaments either on mainstream or on Roma party tickets has been minimal, far below their demographic proportion.

While there is no visible progress in terms of parliamentary representation, the situation is more encouraging on the local level, as there are now Romani mayors and councillors in all the Central European countries except Poland. In Romania, for example, the number of elected Romani members of local councils grew from 106 in 1992 to 136 in 1996 and 160 in 2000.[18]

Romani citizens may also further their interest in non-electoral forms such as private bodies (associations, foundations, charities)[19] and public bodies (consultative and expert bodies, governmental agencies, etc.), and via so-called traditional leaders. As for private bodies, Klímová identified 120 registered Romani associations and foundations in the Czech Republic, 280 in Hungary, six to ten in Poland, 150 in Romania, and almost fifty in Slovakia.[20] Romani citizens may also engage in informal activism, and take part in demonstrations, social movements and online political organising.

Most Eastern European states have established public bodies to deal with the "Roma issue". These Roma-specific organisations include inter-ministerial commissions and committees, a plenipotentiary or secretary of state, personal advisors to the prime minister or president, ministerial coordinators, etc. All these Roma-specific institutions have only advisory and consultative functions.

Both Roma and non-Roma may work in such public bodies. Although they are typically appointed as civil servants, they are also supposed to represent Roma and give voice to their interests. The non-electoral and electoral fields may also be linked. In the 2000 Romanian elections, a Romani MP from the Roma Party gained a seat (in addition to the reserved one) through a coalition agreement with the Social Democratic Party, which also guaranteed the Roma Party the posts of Adviser on National Minorities Issues in the Presidency Office and the Head of the Office for Roma Issues, with the title of Under-Secretary of State at the Ministry of Public Information.[21]

As for traditional Roma leaders (such as *vajda and bulibasha*), they were historically appointed by local authorities to take charge of keeping order and collecting taxes in Romani communities. There still exist such traditional leaders, whose status is usually dependent on charisma and wealth and passes from father to son. In addition to local leaders, one can find in Romania the self-appointed King (Florin Cioabă), Emperor (Iulian Rădulescu) and President (Bercea Mondialu) "of all Roma". Such leaders are recognised only by a handful of followers, although some authorities still see them as negotiating partners, thus giving them an aura of legitimacy.

Some of the traditional leaders find their way into electoral politics and become members of local governments or fill positions in national or supranational bodies. Cioabă, for instance, formed the Christian Centre of Roma party, and ran—unsuccessfully—in the 2000 national elections for the Chamber of Deputies, but was elected as a representative on the Sibiu City Council and is also the President of the Plenary Assembly of the European Roma and Travellers Forum. It is important to emphasise the fact that most Roma regard such leaders, even if elected, with aversion and find their actions detrimental to Roma.[22]

(ii) Some countries accord special rights to minorities, to facilitate their political participation and representation. In Romania a seat in the lower chamber of the parliament has, since 1990, been reserved for a Romani representative. Each representative occupying the reserved seat has come from the Roma Party (now officially called Roma Party Pro-Europe, Partida Romilor Pro-Europea).

The system of reserved seats for Roma representatives in national or local assemblies has been tried in Bosnia and Herzegovina, Croatia and Slovenia. However, the system does not preclude the election of more than one MP. In the 2008 Romanian parliamentary elections two Roma were elected for the first time: one was elected for the reserved seat, and another was elected on the list of a mainstream party.[23]

Other electoral techniques intended to improve the political representation of minorities include exemption from certain electoral rules (such as the minimum threshold), the over-representation of defined ethnic/national regions, race-conscious districting, and quotas for party lists.[24]

(iii) Roma enjoying a form of autonomy have an additional sphere of political participation and representation. In particular, in Hungary minorities enjoy collective rights in the fields of education, media, culture and the use of minority languages. The bearers of collective rights are minority self-governments on the local and national level, which are intended to be partners to local self-governments and the national government respectively.

The powers of local minority self-governments include the right to ask for information, make a proposal, initiate measures and object to a practice or decision related to the operation of institutions that violate the rights of the minority; such a self-government can define within its authority the circle of protected monuments and memorial sites, its own name, medals and decorations, and the holidays and festivities of the minority; it can establish institutions, companies, schools, media, or scholarships; most importantly, it must give its consent to any act of the local government affecting the minority population in their capacity as such.

Each minority group can establish one national minority self-government or national assembly. These represent the interests of the local minority self-governments on the national level. The local is not subordinated to the national level, and nor are local minority self-governments obliged to report to the national one. The national assemblies have similar powers to the local minority self-governments, but with a national scope.

The following table recapitulates the options of state-bounded political participation of Roma in both electoral and non-electoral arenas.

Options of Transnational Political Participation[i]

The "Roma issue" has also emerged in the international, above all European, political arena. Citizens of Romani origin have a range of options for participating in international/European politics that may fit into the above tripartite scheme.

i [Ed. Note] See table 2 and List of Abbreviations after bibliography for acronyms.

<table>
<caption>Table 1. Options of state-bounded political participation and representation.</caption>
<tr><th rowspan="2"></th><th rowspan="2">electoral</th><th colspan="3">non-electoral</th></tr>
<tr><th>private body</th><th>public body</th><th>traditional</th></tr>
<tr><td>autonomy</td><td>minority self-government</td><td rowspan="8">associations, foundations, activism</td><td rowspan="8">consultative and expert bodies, governmental agencies, Ombudsman</td><td rowspan="8">traditional leader (vajda, bulibasha, etc.)</td></tr>
<tr><td rowspan="5">special rights</td><td>communal reserved seats</td></tr>
<tr><td>exemption from rules (e.g. lower threshold for ethnic parties)</td></tr>
<tr><td>over-representation of minority territories</td></tr>
<tr><td>race-conscious districting</td></tr>
<tr><td>quotas of mainstream parties</td></tr>
<tr><td rowspan="2">formal political equality</td><td>Romani political party</td></tr>
<tr><td>Romani MP of mainstream political party</td></tr>
</table>

(i) Similarly to any other members of democratic polities, citizens of Romani origin are supposed to be represented in international politics principally by their own state. Bilateral and multilateral agreements are drafted, agreed upon, ratified and implemented by bodies of participating states. International organisations have also been founded by and are primarily composed of states.

Ram—based on her empirical study—found that, indeed, most Romani activists and leaders had little interest in gaining international attention or in lobbying on the international level for improving their rights. Some Romani activists explicitly told her that it is not civic associations that should speak with the EU, but that it is the role of their government.[25]

However, as demonstrated above, Roma are not adequately represented on the national level, and so their respective states are not likely to represent their interests in the international arena. Romani citizens may seek non-electoral forms of transnational political participation or engage in the only existing form of international electoral politics, the European Parliament.

The European Parliament has been actively involved in the struggle against the discrimination and social exclusion of Roma. The first MEP of Romani origin was Juan de Dios Ramírez Heredia, who was elected three times on the party list of the Spanish Socialist Workers' Party in 1987, 1989 and 1994. From Eastern Europe, Viktória Mohácsi was elected in 2004 on the list of the Hungarian Alliance of Free Democrats, and Lívia Járóka was elected in 2004 and 2009 on the list of the Fidesz-Hungarian Civic Union.

The Romani MEPs have played a vital role in putting the plight of Roma on the EU's agenda, as well as in the drafting and adoption of various EU level resolutions and recommendations,[26] including the recent EU Framework Strategy for Roma Inclusion.

It is to be noted that EU citizens can only vote for national party lists; therefore citizens of Romani origin cannot vote for individual Romani candidates. However, the underrepresentation of Roma in the European Parliament appears to be even more severe than in most national legislative bodies, as currently only one out of 736 members is of Romani origin.

(ii) Granting special political rights to Roma on a transnational level appears to be a utopia at the moment. However, there are several plans for reforming the European electoral system. Introducing a Roma quota on national party lists of Member States with a significant Romani population is one option to improve the representation of Romani citizens. It is theoretically also possible to have reserved seats for stateless minorities/nations in the European Parliament. Furthermore, if European political parties were allowed to form and their candidates were allowed to run in elections, Romani candidates might also consider forming their own European party.

(iii) Having a transnational form of autonomy would imply that Romani citizens living in various states could have jurisdiction over a substantial range of issues pertaining to them. This would essentially entail a form of self-determination and self-governance of dispersed stateless groups.[27]

Meyer argues that Roma have a legitimate claim to transnational autonomy, being a transnational non-territorial minority that has been persecuted for centuries.[28] A special status of transnational minority may provide protection from the discriminatory treatment by national states under which they have suffered for so long, as well as *de jure* statelessness resulting from the disintegration of multi-ethnic Eastern European countries.[29] As for the institutional setting of transnational autonomy, Meyer remains vague:

> Although it is not easy to see how the special status of being a transnational minority could be incorporated into the existing present-day legal frameworks, there can be no doubt that the efforts of the Roma to gain trans-national cultural and political autonomy is a legitimate

aspiration. In the light of the Saami experience, gaining such autonomy is best seen as a long-term goal whose realization presupposes, *inter alia*, the success of the Roma in establishing democratically legitimate elected bodies of representation.[30]

Klímová, relying on the national-cultural autonomy concept of Karl Renner and Otto Bauer and the agonistic patriotism of Ephraim Nimni, argues for transnational cultural autonomy for indigenous and Romani communities.[31] She notes that the two groups have three characteristics in common: (1) they have a strong sense of feeling different or even separate from the majority societies that surround them, and—unlike national minorities—they still operate under their own laws and customs outside those of the majority society; (2) they have dispersed settlement patterns; (3) they are severely alienated, due to the treatment from majority societies.

Referring to the deep mistrust between majority societies and Roma, Klímová argues that "internal citizenship-based solutions" are not feasible. "The citizenship rights fail to do justice because they emanate from a state that has subordinated the Romani and indigenous laws, autonomy and forms of political organization. They are merely an instrument of absorption and assimilation."[32] As an alternative, Klímová embraces the radical vision of deterritorialisation of all nations promoted by Nimni:

> If the roof that each nation seeks becomes non-territorial, if each nation can be sovereign without claiming exclusive territorial control, the infusion of politics with culture and nationalism on its own is not dangerous. If territory cannot become an exclusive property of a particular ethnonational group, we do not need to fight over it. If we have no minorities and majorities, we do not need minority protection.[33]

<table>
<tr><th colspan="4">Table 2. Options of transnational political participation for Roma.</th></tr>
<tr><th rowspan="2"></th><th rowspan="2">electoral</th><th colspan="2">non-electoral</th></tr>
<tr><th>private body</th><th>public body</th></tr>
<tr><td>autonomy</td><td>transnational (cultural) autonomy?</td><td rowspan="5">IRU, RNC, ERTF, OSF, ERRC, ERIO, informal activism</td><td rowspan="5">EU Platform, CPRSI, MG-S-ROM</td></tr>
<tr><td rowspan="2">special rights</td><td>reserved seat in the European Parliament?</td></tr>
<tr><td>quotas of mainstream/European parties?</td></tr>
<tr><td rowspan="2">formal political equality</td><td>global: via states</td></tr>
<tr><td>EU: Romani MEP; European Romani political party?</td></tr>
</table>

It appears that the drive for trans-state forms of autonomy—of both scholars and activists—is largely driven by mistrust towards state legislation and policies based on negative experiences. Minority rights are granted by, dependent on, and often misused by state authorities. As a consequence, several Romani activists are seeking a form of self-determination and self-government outside the mechanisms of state.

Conclusions

This paper has analysed three discourses that have been embraced by Roma and pro-Roma organisations and initiatives in the last two decades focusing on human rights, self-determination (minority rights) and social inclusion. The article also presented an analytical framework for analysing electoral and non-electoral forms of political participation on national and international levels.

The minority rights (and cultural autonomy) approach is clearly inadequate to promote the social inclusion of Roma. In a similar manner, Roma-specific policies or strategies without effective education, employment and social policies, providing tangible and equal social rights for every citizen, are bound to remain hollow.

The recognition of Romani culture and identity, as well as the historical disenfranchisement of Romani populations, is no less urgent. However, given the prejudice and discrimination that Romani citizens face in various spheres of life, the Romani recognition struggle should aim for *both* (legal, political and social) equality *and* the *freedom* to identify oneself and live as Roma. As long as non-Romani citizens can overwrite one's choice of identity (i.e. stigmatise someone as "gypsy"), the struggles for democratic equality and recognition cannot and should not be disentangled.

The *idea* of Romani self-determination has been debated on the grounds of either questioning the social reality of the Roma nation or emphasising its reactive character. Acknowledging the dangers of developing a homogenising and reactive national identity, the struggle for the recognition of the Roma nation should not be dismissed altogether; rather, a dynamic and open conception of the Roma nation should be embraced, one that allows for multiple identities, experimentation and voluntary assimilation. Romani citizens should have the opportunity to recollect, negotiate, develop and reaffirm their own identity and culture.

Romani cosmopolitan claims originate from experiences of exclusion and hostility either in their "home country" or as immigrants and asylum seekers in a "receiving country". It implies the rejection of the universal nationalist programme (according to which each individual belongs to one homogenous nation that is to be protected by a nation-state) and the demand for a global or European legal order guaranteeing the liberty, self-determination and fundamental rights of Romani citizens throughout the world without the mediation of states.

However, offering the example of a stateless Roma nation to the rest of humanity may be interpreted as replacing the *demos* with *ethnos*, thus promoting a non-territorial version of universal nationalism. The general vision of deterritorialisation of *all* political communities is neither feasible nor desirable. On the other hand, dispersed nations and diasporas, such as the Roma, could enjoy supplementary non-territorial cultural autonomy, similar to the Hungarian model, but on the European level. Accordingly, the EU could provide the legal framework for transforming the European Roma and Travellers Forum into a genuine European Roma Parliament, with sufficient power and resources to effectively exercise trans-state non-territorial cultural autonomy.

The allegedly most advanced existing form of transnational democracy, the European Union, remains underdeveloped. Its complex deliberative, decision-making and governance structures are dominated by Member States. The rights of EU citizens remain obscure and fragile, and their direct access to EU bodies is very limited. The targeted expulsion of Romani immigrants from France in the summer of 2010 tragically demonstrated the limitations of European rights. Moreover, the European electoral system does not allow for counterbalancing the political marginalisation of Romani citizens. On the contrary, it further reduces the political weight of the Roma, since only one or two MEPs are supposed to represent the largest "European minority", comprising 10–12 million European citizens.

Endnotes

1. In 2012 Márton Rövid earned a PhD in political science at Central European University [...].
2. Márton Rövid, "One-Size-Fits-All Roma? On the Normative Dilemmas of the Emerging European Roma Policy", *Romani Studies* 21 (2011) 1: 1-22.
3. Often-cited examples are the Catalans, or the Hungarian communities living in Hungary's neighbouring countries.
4. Will Kymlicka, *Multicultural Odysseys: Navigating the New International Politics of Diversity* (Oxford; New York: Oxford University Press, 2007), 90.
5. Georg Brunner and Herbert Küpper. "European Options of Autonomy: A Typology of Autonomy Models of Minority Self-Governance", in Kinga Gál, ed., *Minority Governance in Europe* (Budapest: Open Society Institute, 2002), 17.
6. Martin Kovats, *The Politics of Roma Identity: between Nationalism and Destitution* 2003 [cited 2 October 2011].
7. Márton Rövid and Angéla Kóczé, "Pro-Roma Global Civil Society: Acting for, with or instead of Roma?", in Mary Kaldor, Henrietta L. Moore and Sabine Selchow, eds., *Global Civil Society 2012: Ten Years of Critical Reflection* (Basingstoke: Palgrave Macmillan, 2012).

8. Kovats, *The Politics of Roma Identity*.
9. Iván Szelényi and János Ladányi. *Patterns of Exclusion: Constructing Gypsy Ethnicity and the Making of an Underclass in Transitional Societies of Europe* (New York: Columbia University Press, 2006).
10. Rövid and Kóczé, "Pro-Roma Global Civil Society".
11. Working Document on the EU strategy on the social inclusion of Roma, Committee on Civil Liberties, Justice and Home Affairs, Rapporteur: Lívia Járóka, 28. 9. 2010.
12. *Ibid*.
13. For an overview of the limits and potentials of the EU Framework for Roma Integration, see Bernard Rorke, *Beyond First Steps. What Next for the EU Framework for Roma Integration?* (Budapest: Open Society Foundation, Roma Initiatives Office, 2013).
14. Júlia Szalai, "Az elismerés politikája és a cigánykérdés", in Ágota Horváth, Edit Landau and Júlia Szalai, eds., *Cigánynak születni* (Budapest: Aktív Társadalom Alapítvány—Új Mandátum Könyvkiadó, 2000).
15. Zoltán Bárány, *The East European Gypsies: Regime Change, Marginality and Ethnopolitics* (Cambridge: Cambridge University Press, 2002), Ilona Klímová, "Romani Political Representation in Central Europe. An Historical Survey", Romani Studies 12 (2002) 5, Peter Vermeersch, *The Romani Movement: Minority Politics and Ethnic Mobilization in Contemporary Central Europe* (Oxford and New York: Berghahn Books, 2006), and Aidan McGarry, "Ambiguous Nationalism? Explaining the Parliamentary Under-Representation of Roma in Hungary and Romania", *Romani Studies* 19 (2009) 2: 103–124.
16. Zoltán Bárány, "Ethnic Mobilization without Prerequisites: The East European Gypsies", *World Politics* 54 (2002) 3: 277–307.
17. Bárány, *The East European Gypsies*, 213.
18. Klímová, "Romani Political Representation in Central Europe", 119.
19. For a critical overview of civil society involvement in the social inclusion of Roma, see Angéla Kóczé, "Civil Society, Civil Involvement, and Social Inclusion of the Roma", *Roma Inclusion Working Papers* (Bratislava: UNDP Europe and the CIS Bratislava Regional Centre, 2012).
20. Klímová, "Romani Political Representation in Central Europe".
21. Klímová, "Romani Political Representation in Central Europe", 117.
22. For instance, the biggest Romanian Romani party (Partida Romilor Pro-Europea) refuses to take part in the work of the European Roma and Travellers Forum as long as Florin Cioabă chairs its Plenary Assembly <http://www.ertf.ro/viz/About%20ERTF/10-0/en>.
23. Aidan McGarry, *Who Speaks for Roma?: Political Representation of a Transnational Minority Community* (New York: Continuum, 2010), 91.
24. Andrew Reynolds, "Electoral Systems and the Protection and Participation of Minorities", Minority Rights Group International, 2006.
25. Melanie H. Ram, "Interests, Norms and Advocacy: Explaining the Emergence of the Roma onto the EU's Agenda". *Ethnopolitics: Formerly Global Review of Ethnopolitics* 9 (2010) 2: 201.
26. For a detailed overview of all Roma-related international documents, see Balázs Majtényi and Balázs Vizi, eds., *A Minority in Europe. Selected International Documents Regarding the Roma* (Budapest: Gondolat Kiadó, 2006).
27. Márton Rövid, "Solidarity, Citizenship, Democracy: The Lessons of Romani Activism", in Dieter Halwachs, ed., *European Yearbook of Minority Issues* (Leiden and Boston: Martinus Nijhoff Publishers, 2012).
28. Lukas H. Meyer, "Transnational Autonomy: Responding to Historical Injustice in the Case of the Saami and Roma Peoples", *International Journal on Minority and Group Rights* 8 (2001) 2–3.
29. *Ibid*., 300: the breakup of Yugoslavia and Czechoslovakia left thousands of Roma stateless, as the citizenship laws of the new countries discriminated against them.

30. *Ibid.*, 301.

31. Ilona Klímová-Alexander, "Transnational Romani and Indigenous Non-Territorial Self-Determination Claims", *Ethnopolitics* 6 (2007) 3.

32. *Ibid.*, 399.

33. *Ibid.*, 411.

Bibliography

Bárány, Zoltan. "Ethnic Mobilization without Prerequisites: The East European Gypsies". *World Politics* 54 (2002) 3: 277–307.

Bárány, Zoltán. *The East European Gypsies: Regime Change, Marginality and Ethnopolitics*. Cambridge: Cambridge University Press, 2002.

Brunner, Georg, and Herbert Küpper. "European Options of Autonomy: A Typology of Autonomy Models of Minority Self-Governance", in Kinga Gál, ed., *Minority Governance in Europe*. Budapest: Open Society Institute, 2002.

Klímová, Ilona. "Romani Political Representation in Central Europe. An Historical Survey". *Romani Studies* 12 (2002): 5.

Klímová-Alexander, Ilona. "Transnational Romani and Indigenous Non-Territorial Self-Determination Claims". *Ethnopolitics* 6 (2007) 3: 395–416.

Kóczé, Angéla. "Civil Society, Civil Involvement, and Social Inclusion of the Roma". *Roma Inclusion Working Papers*. Bratislava: UNDP Europe and the CIS Bratislava Regional Centre, 2012.

Kovats, Martin. *The Politics of Roma Identity: between Nationalism and Destitution* 2003 [cited 2 October 2011].

Kymlicka, Will. *Multicultural Odysseys: Navigating the New International Politics of Diversity*. Oxford; New York: Oxford University Press, 2007.

Majtényi, Balázs, and Balázs Vizi, eds. *A Minority in Europe. Selected International Documents Regarding the Roma*. Budapest: Gondolat Kiadó, 2006.

McGarry, Aidan. "Ambiguous Nationalism? Explaining the Parliamentary Under-Representation of Roma in Hungary and Romania". *Romani Studies* 19 (2009) 2: 103–124.

McGarry, Aidan. *Who Speaks for Roma?: Political Representation of a Transnational Minority Community*. New York: Continuum, 2010.

Meyer, Lukas H. "Transnational Autonomy: Responding to Historical Injustice in the Case of the Saami and Roma Peoples". *International Journal on Minority and Group Rights* 8 (2001): 2–3.

Ram, Melanie H. "Interests, Norms and Advocacy: Explaining the Emergence of the Roma onto the EU's Agenda". *Ethnopolitics: Formerly Global Review of Ethnopolitics* 9 (2010) 2: 197–217.

Reynolds, Andrew. "Electoral Systems and the Protection and Participation of Minorities". Minority Rights Group International, 2006.

Rorke, Bernard. *Beyond First Steps. What Next for the EU Framework for Roma Integration?* Budapest: Open Society Foundation, Roma Initiatives Office, 2013.

Rövid, Márton. "One-Size-Fits-All Roma? On the Normative Dilemmas of the Emerging European Roma Policy". *Romani Studies* 21 (2011) 1: 1–22.

Rövid, Márton. "Solidarity, Citizenship, Democracy: The Lessons of Romani Activism", in Dieter Halwachs, ed., *European Yearbook of Minority Issues*. Leiden and Boston: Martinus Nijhoff Publishers, 2012.

Rövid, Márton, and Angéla Kóczé. "Pro-Roma Global Civil Society: Acting for, with or instead of Roma?", in Mary Kaldor, Henrietta L. Moore and Sabine Selchow, eds., *Global Civil Society 2012: Ten Years of Critical Reflection*. Basingstoke: Palgrave Macmillan, 2012.

Szalai, Júlia. "Az elismerés politikája és a cigánykérdés", in Ágota Horváth, Edit Landau and Júlia Szalai, eds., *Cigánynak születni*. Budapest: Aktív Társadalom Alapítvány—Új Mandátum Könyvkiadó, 2000.

Szelényi, Iván, and János Ladányi. *Patterns of Exclusion: Constructing Gypsy Ethnicity and the Making of an Underclass in Transitional Societies of Europe*. New York: Columbia University Press, 2006.

Vermeersch, Peter. *The Romani Movement: Minority Politics and Ethnic Mobilization in Contemporary Central Europe*. Oxford and New York: Berghahn Books, 2006.

List of Abbreviations

CPRSI	Contact Point for Roma and Sinti Issues within the Organization for Security and Cooperation in Europe
EP	European Parliament
ERIO	European Roma Information Office
ERPC	European Roma Policy Coalition
ERRC	European Roma Rights Centre
ERTF	European Roma and Travellers Forum
EU	European Union
IRU	International Romani Union
MG-S-ROM	Committee of Experts on Roma and Travellers within the Council of Europe
MEP	Member of the European Parliament
MP	Member of Parliament
NGO	Non-governmental organisation
OSF	Open Society Foundations
PER	Project on Ethnic Relations
RNC	Roma National Congress

***Márton Rövid** is a research and advocacy officer at the Decade of Roma Inclusion Secretariat Foundation.

Rövid, Márton. "Options of Roma Political Participation and Representation." In *Roma Rights 2012: Challenges of Representation: Voice on Roma Politics, Power and Participation*. Budapest: ERRC, 2013. http://www.errc.org/article/roma-rights-2012-challenges-of-representation-voice-on-roma-politics-power-and-participation/4174/1.

Choices to Be Made and Prices to Be Paid: Potential Roles and Consequences in Roma Activism and Policy-Making[i]

by Nicolae Gheorghe (in collaboration with Gergő Pulay)*[1]

[...]

[T]he common aim of the Roma movement should be clear: the organisation, mobilisation and eventual re-mobilisation of Roma, based on pursuing the struggle against racism and discrimination. Part of this process is to unite the various often competing groups in the Roma movement in flexible but effective ways. This will enable Roma groups to collaborate and work together with local authorities, civic associations, churches and political parties. Agreement on common interests is a prerequisite for Roma at local and higher levels to define a coherent policy agenda. In other words, Roma themselves should take increased responsibility for initiatives to improve the situation of their people. It would be hard to overestimate the importance of activists, economic entrepreneurs and intellectual and moral Roma elites in this process. Poverty and exclusion are usually presented as insurmountable barriers to social mobility or political mobilisation. Activists tend to think decision makers can only be made aware of the situation and stirred by dramatic images of Roma as victims of their societies. I also played a part in backing these ideas, especially during the 1990s. But we seem to forget that some of our people have already achieved economic and educational success. Like us, they are part of an emerging middle-class, both amongst the Roma and in mainstream society. Our common projects, self-funded initiatives and voluntary associations have a crucial role in identifying future prospects for Roma civil society.

Most of us working in this field are Roma through our discourse; because we *talk* about being Roma and not because we *live* as many Roma do. We often have to describe the Roma way of life and culture to others. So, for many of us, discourse and language are basic assets for legitimising our positions and building our careers. At the same time we feel a sense of urgency, created by the need to provide evidence of action in promoting 'good causes'. We should be aware that

---

i [Ed. note] Nicolae Gheorghe's article is a response to an earlier one "The Price of Roma Integration" by the Hungarian activist András Bíró. Both articles were edited by Will Guy and published in *From Victimhood to Citizenship: The Path of Roma Integration* (Budapest: Kossuth Publishing Corp., 2013).

the language we use touches other people's sensitivities and has actual consequences for their lives. However appreciating possible consequences should not prevent us from speaking frankly and admitting our failures while explaining the context. Tackling controversial issues in order to renew the vocabulary of human rights is part of *the price* we have to pay.

Recent political developments—particularly the re-emergence of nationalism and populism after EU-accession—suggest that the liberal, human rights-oriented approach to Roma integration failed to achieve many of its expected goals. The rise of anti-Gypsyism and violent attacks on Roma in the Czech Republic, Hungary and Romania are evident signs of crisis. Re-examination of the origins of these tensions is needed to prevent further exploitation of the 'Gypsy question' by right wing extremism and populist leaders in their quest for electoral majorities. . . . This would benefit not only Roma but our democracies too. One source of contemporary anti-Gypsyism and hostility towards Roma has been our own unwillingness to mention certain issues. This has allowed them to become the exclusive domain of extremist politicians, the police, populist justice and mob-violence. Putting them on our agenda is a step towards resolving them. The language we are searching for should not arouse hostility to Roma but instead should provide alternative frames. This allows thoughtful treatment of controversial issues, which would otherwise be labelled 'Gypsy crime' or attributed to the 'genetic force of Gypsy nomadism'.[2] Certain statements in this paper might be criticised as reinforcing stereotypes although my intention is quite the opposite. I want to start developing appropriate language for tackling previous taboos or *open secrets*.

It is hard to take this step because going beyond the limits of political correctness requires a considerable effort. It might be argued that this endeavour is doomed to failure from the start, since no alternatives yet exist to already established discursive frames. Renouncing certain basic elements of the human rights approach to Roma appears dangerous, since it could lead to unpredictable consequences both for how we speak and in practice. The natural assumption is that this discursive change opens Pandora's Box, leaving Roma defenceless against racism where the victim is blamed or subsequent pogroms legitimised. This is why many Roma activists and engaged experts fail to acknowledge or even mention these issues. Instead of seeking viable solutions, we restrict our role to *policing thinking*. In cases where certain Roma deserve blame, we intervene and demand that racist statements should be condemned. This strategy can be seen as reducing freedom of speech, since it conveys the message that Roma cannot be criticised. Many core concepts of our anti-racist vocabulary are eroded in the process—including the very notions of 'racist' or 'racism'—since these are often used without any proper definition of their meaning or scope. Such confusion results from a lack of reflection and critical analysis of previous or continuing anti-racist initiatives. This is one reason why no public agreement could be reached on identifying principal forces behind contemporary forms of racism. As is often seen, public figures—including representatives of the extreme right—can easily reject the racist label by pointing at someone else as 'the racist'. Now we are witnessing an apparent resurgence of tensions and hatred directed at Roma and other European minorities without knowing what exactly should be categorised as 'racist'.

Roma activists, policy-makers and other engaged experts are often haunted by visions of holocaust, ethnic cleansing or genocide. Discussions are constrained by fear that certain ways of speaking can make the recurrence of such tragedies more likely. Liberating ourselves from these fears does not mean denying the Holocaust or treating it differently. The idea of holocaust is familiar to all, regardless of ethnic identity or particular historical and political contexts. Holocaust as an operator allows an immediate switch from local experiences to the disturbing spectre of concentration camps and allows us to portray the plight of Roma communities as part of a greater historical narrative. Nevertheless, actions to raise public awareness about the social and historical implications of the Holocaust are not equivalent to reducing the whole Roma issue to the tragic experience of World War Two. Racist discrimination has been decisive throughout Roma history but it does not exhaust its entirety. Such a reduction runs the risk of losing sight of the internal dynamics and particularities of different Roma communities in their own social contexts.

Shared Responsibilities

The way out of the vicious circle of blaming an undifferentiated racist 'other' and making claims merely on the grounds of eternal Roma victimhood is to take into account our *shared responsibilities*. These are not limited to the general and frequently oversimplified categories—'Roma' and 'non-Roma'; local communities and the authorities; the media and NGOs and activists—but they have implications for each and every one of them. Even if these responsibilities are always unequal, asymmetrical and often even hierarchical, taking them all into consideration is one step towards confidence-building and the renewal of the social contract amongst all actors. One part of this process is to acknowledge controversies *within* Roma communities which are part of their dynamism but also threaten to undermine relations with their external environment. What I mean by responsibility is related to the way we think about common concerns. For instance, I am personally not a police officer nor a member of an agency opposing the trafficking of children. Nevertheless, I consider it my task to examine the processes leading children to beg at Italian churches or railway stations and—with supporters—to raise this as an important issue for public debate by creating a language based on solidarity and desire for change.

Racist ideologies suggest that crime is not a matter of exclusion, deprivation and poverty but of ethnicity or genes, implying that Roma are hereditary criminals. People forget that the primary victims of such crimes are members of the very same communities: relatively wealthy Roma robbed by other Roma; wives beaten by alcoholic husbands; the weak exploited by stronger people—such as those in debt to local money-lenders demanding exorbitant interest rates. On the other hand middle-men in human trafficking networks are not all Roma, which means that these issues cannot be dealt with simply as ethnic problems specific to 'Roma'. In general the framework of shared responsibilities is not diametrically opposed to the liberal human rights discourse. Rather it is meant to overcome the pitfalls apparent in many of the anti-racist projects since 1989, including those initiated and coordinated by myself.

Associating Roma with criminality has a long social history in Europe. In the Third Reich it underpinned a racial ideology that Roma were biologically inferior, parasitic and asocial by nature.[3] These deviant characteristics were often attributed to *nomadism* as a cause of their detachment from wider society and petty criminality. The Communist regimes of Central and Eastern Europe tried to eradicate this supposed heritage—sometimes by force—by turning Roma into regular workers and sending their children to school. But after 1989 the dominant discourse regarded the Communist approach as completely mistaken. Nevertheless, this view conflicts with the nostalgia for those times of many former industrial and agricultural workers and public service employees—with their memories of full employment and accessible social housing. During post-socialist transition Roma started to make claims for their emancipation. They were soon granted various rights—firstly as citizens; secondly as acknowledged national, ethnic or cultural minorities of their respective states; and thirdly as victims of previous persecution for which they were compensated.

Criminality was attributed to social causes and any supposed link with ethnicity was rejected. If Roma, by definition, are victims of society and its institutions, they are not to blame for being poor, or for the fact that some of them make their children beg. However, excusing them can prevent us appreciating that criminality, exploitation or human trafficking is inevitable in conditions of long-term unemployment and structural exclusion. Social excluded communities are largely perceived by outsiders as Gypsy and so it is natural that popular 'folk-theories' will assume a link between exclusion and Gypsiness. But what actually is the nature of this relationship and what is the legitimate—and not only the *correct*—way of speaking about it?

Roma activists and experts sometimes appear to be hesitant about the prospect of this discursive shift. Some think that our language and epistemology is not yet capable of dealing with an intermediate level between individualisation and generalisation. Although we might sense these distinctions and frequently discuss them in private, we are not yet sufficiently confident to express them openly. My view is that, even if we still lack a sufficient vocabulary for public debate, we have to start searching for its elements. One condition for discursive change is to avoid victimising the entire Roma population but this is what we are seemingly afraid to risk. Among themselves human rights activists and other experts might agree that it is unacceptable to defend human traffickers or those exploiting other Roma. But then they retreat to safer ground, maintaining that criminality is primarily a police domain and any discussion should remain 'colour-blind', leaving ethnicity aside. My suggestion is that, as civic activists or social workers, development of our language and practice are equally important aspects of crime prevention. Do I betray my people if I say so?

The rigid stance of many activists, clinging to their politically correct discourse, has historical origins. After 1989 the principal task of human rights organisations had been to dismantle the institutional frameworks of Communist regimes and control the emerging practices of new post-socialist governments.[4] However, in my opinion, their activities contributed to the persistence of a cold war-like mentality within civil society. Being in action is always a powerful motivating force but simply to oppose governments and public authorities is to ignore the fact that although we have competing concerns, we may also have shared interests.

Entering into debate with racists is not the same as justifying or supporting them. Paying attention to what they say is legitimate in order to develop an alternative account. It is not the same as a public official taking discriminatory action against someone or using discriminatory language. Bear in mind that *discrimination* by the human mind is necessary in the sense of differentiating or distinguishing, for example between colours, smells and sounds. Discrimination turns into something to be opposed once it disadvantages a group of people because of their age, ethnicity, race, gender or social origin. Sometimes those who aim to represent and defend the Roma give the impression that each and every act of discrimination—including all differentiations and distinctions—is necessarily negative.

I might try to express this in other words but I cannot avoid discrimination once I realise that my own self-presentation as Rom requires others to differentiate and acknowledge me in this identity. A first step in effective self-affirmation by Roma is for them to be recognised by others as someone different. As a second step we have to be careful that this act of self-identification and its acknowledgement by others is not going to bring disadvantages. This explains the need for affirmative action—another aspect of discrimination—in particular initiatives to compensate for a legacy of group disadvantages by ensuring that individuals have equal opportunities. Affirmative action is part of a negotiation process that needs to be monitored in order to protect the interests of those who were initially targeted by such a policy. Today human rights work concerning Roma has to target the vulnerable and to be reoriented towards the rights of children, women, the disabled, the elderly and victims of drug abuse. The problem is that these rights are not yet codified and monitored as strongly as civil and political rights such as the freedom of association or the freedom of speech.

Imagined Cosmopolitanisms—Some Biographical Remarks

As mentioned, instead of a systematic theory this paper consists of a collection of personal reflections. Throughout my life I have been trying to explain myself, my own subjectivity and the experience of being different from others—even if I did not exactly know the roots of this difference. Maybe I am not a 'true' Rom because I have been assimilated through my education and occupational trajectory, because I do not live in keeping with Roma values and I also had a non-Roma wife. I grew up as part of a group in which Romani was not spoken as a first language, my relatives did not live in extended families and my parents did not follow traditional occupations. Previous generations in my family were already integrated into the social life and economy of their villages as blacksmiths and musicians (*lăutari*). My first cousins, sisters and their in-laws took their first upward steps on the ladder of social mobility as industrial and construction-site labourers, cleaners and handicraft workers. Our identity and memories of being *ţigan* were based more on the experience of discrimination and external stereotypes, less on commonly shared meanings of being Roma in a vernacular, ethnic sense. Why am I different then as a Rom or *Ţsigan* if I feel in many other ways similar and equal to others? This is an enduring dilemma for me and for many of my kin and fellow Roma, even if we live with this difference day by day.

Sometimes it is an obligation imposed from the outside and not necessarily a personal choice. It might be perceived as a cultural deficit that is damaging for the individual or the group. Some might try to find an escape by hiding it or striving to assimilate to mainstream society. Others try to explore it, speak openly about it and eventually legitimise it. To solve this dilemma I decided at a certain moment of my life that I am a Rom, although I was not necessarily obliged to be. Activism meant an opportunity to come into terms with the meaning and heritage of being *ţigan*. To relieve the tensions that went along with using this category, I affirmed my social and cultural background and projected it onto Roma social history and culture.

I was educated in an era when Romania was following the Soviet model—before the emergence of Ceausescu's national Communism. I believed the Communists had the means to create equality, to improve the lot of the poor and to support people with disadvantaged backgrounds, including the Roma. I internalised the dogmatism of the official ideology with the international proletariat as its core. Alongside this, I also embraced the internationalism—or cosmopolitanism—and anti-nationalism of those times. This ideology was obviously aimed at legitimising the imperial structures of the Soviet Union but as a teenager I saw it rather as an entry point towards a kind of universalism which embraces the ideas of revolution and humanism, the renaissance and the French era of encyclopedism. In the late 1970s and then during the 1980s I established contact with experts on Roma culture, including sociologists and activists in the International Romani Union. I learnt to consider the Roma as people who form a genuinely world-wide diaspora. After the fall of Communism, I started to argue for a cosmopolitan—or at least European—perspective in Roma activism on these grounds. Following the international proletariat, my self-portrayal as part of this widespread Roma diaspora was another form of imagined cosmopolitanism. My mobility between international organisations and the various places I have been has been part of this. I thought: I have my own adaptive techniques as I know several languages; I have people to meet in many places in the world and I know how to manage my life while living out of a suitcase. However, I never intended to represent the Roma as nomadic people. After two decades of mobility, working with international organisations, I am back in Romania. Yet throughout my life I have maintained my genuine allegiance to my Romanian citizenship, to my home and family in this country.

My life story is hardly unique. In countries such as Romania, Hungary, Slovakia and Serbia—but also in Spain and France—many Roma are familiar with the historical experience of co-habitation and co-existence with others—even if it was full of ambiguities most of the time. The same peasant might drink together with you in the local bar today but tomorrow he might say that you are just a bloody *ţigan*. Racial differentiations cannot be fully eliminated by law or state policies; to a certain extent we have to live with them. As long as someone accepts the fact of being Rom, *Ţsigan* or Gypsy, it also involves an expectation of being treated as different by others—with all of its advantages and disadvantages. As long as you want to be a Rom, *Ţsigan* or Gypsy, you must know that it entails a cost. This cost was paid by common people such as the Roma victims of murders in Hungary or the riots in the Czech Republic, in Slovakia and Romania. Our goal should be to diminish these costs as much as possible, to keep them to acceptable limits and eventually eradicate them. Nevertheless, being Rom or *Ţsigan* or Gypsy is not solely a destructive or damaging experience. It also brings advantages and resources, such as being more flexible than others or knowing how to use one's brain instead of pure force alone. At the same time these features do not provide any grounds for claiming some unlimited forms of freedom: the rule of law applies to everybody and being someone who travels around or claiming to be an 'eternal nomad' is no excuse for neglecting this fact.

On Roma Experts

Since I gave up my posts, the organisers of international meetings have adopted different strategies to include me in their programmes although I have no institution, organisation or association to legitimise me. At the 2008 European Roma Summit in Brussels I appeared in the programme identified simply by my name, without any further title or status. It might sound narcissistic but I considered it a challenge to appear without anything placed after my name. At the 2010 European Roma Summit in Córdoba the organisers felt uncomfortable with this, so they listed me in the programme as a 'Roma expert'. I think it was a rather worse solution than the previous one: 'Roma expert' is one of the titles to use if there is nothing else to say about a person.

The concept of 'Roma expert' can easily take on pejorative overtones. Sometimes this notion refers to a kind of '*gadjo*'[ii] figure who only pretends to be Roma in order to take advantage of this label while building a personal career. These 'experts' could always be criticised for not being familiar with the life and culture of Roma in a more genuine sense—no matter how smart and effective they are or how many relatives they mobilise in their projects. On the other hand they tend to feel more comfortable in the middle-class environment of NGOs and

ii [Ed. note] In the Romani language *gadjo* is the term for a non-Roma person, *gadje* in the plural.

policy-related meetings. In these contexts their belonging is taken for granted as they can rightfully claim to be Roma since they came from Roma organisations. Meanwhile their identity and position are often contested by those Roma—including some leaders—who base their legitimacy on their origins from ethnically 'unambiguous' and more traditional family backgrounds. These are the forces at play which explain the split between Roma activists—or the elite—and the very communities they are supposed to represent. We are not yet in the position of possessing a *functional elite,* as our ability to mobilise effectively is limited. Our parents moved upwards from the lowest strata of society as service providers or members of the working class. As a continuation of the same trajectory we moved one step further by becoming part of the non-Roma middle class as bureaucrats, intermediaries or middle-men. Advancing further on this social ladder is part of a historical trend and, as such, is not a negative development in itself. However, these trajectories are highly divergent from the lives of many people we aim to represent.

In spite of their identification and their efforts to create links that bridge differences, the lives of Roma intermediaries belong more to mainstream society—even if they claim that they do their work in a more considerate, friendlier or more effective way than others. In spite of this in most cases they are as remote from other Roma as any other social worker. At the same time in their dealings with non-Roma they have to conform to the role designated by their ethnicity and are often questioned by others as to whether they share the cultural characteristics or behaviour regarded as 'traditional' for this ethnicity. If they are honest, they acknowledge that they don't share most of these features. Another way of dealing with the dilemmas of this schizoid situation is to start dressing or behaving in a way that is assumed to be 'traditional'. The apparent risk of this attempt at 'authenticity' is that in the end it turns into play-acting where 'Roma identity' is constructed by means of imitating stereotypical aspects of an ethnic culture. Representations of Roma culture are often simply responses to other people's expectations of the performance of otherness. Conjuring up such exotic or folkloric images—including making a joke of oneself—can be detrimental for the Roma, precisely because it is done in order to satisfy the expectations of others and serve them as customers. Many of these cultural representations have no connection with the people at grass-roots level, since usually they are neither the main audience nor the primary market for them. My own answer to these dilemmas is that Roma intermediaries can perform occupational roles and achieve personal fulfilment, primarily at an individual level, if they are able to articulate a coherent set of values and principles. These values do not imply any strict adherence to mutually exclusive concepts of being Roma, Romanian or Hungarian, since they can be defined in more universalistic terms such as respect and the creation of bridges between different cultures.[5] However, even in such a dialogue, it is necessary to clarify the potential contribution, specific markers and 'uniqueness' of Roma. Various attempts have been made throughout history to specify these ethnic markers. The concepts that have been used most frequently to resolve this dilemma are *nomadism* and the *relationship of Roma to land and territory*.

Slavery, Nomadism and Territory—Reflections on the Romanian Case

In his essay, [András] Bíró suggests that the uniqueness of Roma is related to their status as 'eternal nomads' and to their lack of a relationship with land, both in a spiritual and economic sense.... As he understands it, the relationship to land has to be a productive one, which rules out selling one's labour and remaining a service provider instead of becoming an owner, farmer or manager. Roma are considered to be attached to land, a country or a state only in superficial ways and this disconnectedness gives them the potential for various kinds of mobility—as is happening nowadays when they migrate to Western European countries or Canada. Since Roma are constantly liable to move around, in this sense they correspond to the stereotype of the nomad.

I must admit that when I first read this argument of Bíró, I reacted emotionally and rejected it. I still feel this opposition while seeking plausible alternatives, although I acknowledge the consistency of his approach. At the same time I also recognise the limits of my own argument, especially in terms of its emotional or identity-related aspects. To summarise the main point of this section in advance: Roma in the Romanian principalities had been slaves, which means that they had been collectively bound to land—even if this link appeared rather indirect, making it easier for them to leave a specific place and move elsewhere. Roma *are* connected to territory—and not only in the Romanian case—so the concept of nomadism is not the key to their specificity.[6] Instead of denying this link, I argue that different kinds of relationship to land and territory should be taken into consideration. Consequently large segments of the Roma population can be regarded as settled, without them having been farmers or landowners. In this context I take into account several historical regimes—the two Romanian principalities of Wallachia and Moldavia, the Habsburg and the Ottoman Empires and the Western world. Here the connection to land is articulated mainly in juridical terms rather than the organic terms used by Bíró.

Roma Slavery in the Romanian Principalities

I grew up as a descendent of *ţigani vatraşi* (settled Gypsies) in Romania. The history of these people cannot be understood without taking into account *robia* (slavery), both as an institution and as experienced in these Romanian principalities. I discuss *robia* not to complain about it, or denounce it or even to claim to be a victim, but simply as a matter of fact. *Robia* was an economic and social institution which produced the group of people to which I belong. These *ţigani* had long-term connections with local territories and the associated social history, precisely because of their position as settled *robi* (slaves).[7] From the end of the fourteenth century until the mid-nineteenth century they were tied to land owned by *boiars* (lords) and monasteries, while working as servants in the courts of the lords, blacksmiths and field hands, etc. Enslavement produced *ţigani* as *robi* by historical and social categorisation, and not as a category containing 'ethnic stuff'. The process reached its apogee in the period between the end of the eighteenth century and the mid-nineteenth century.[8] In those times the terms *ţigan* and *robi* became equivalent, referring to the Roma and their socially subordinate status. It was a period when these principalities entered the European capitalist wheat and cattle markets and larger landowners were looking for a labour force to exploit in an overwhelmingly agricultural market economy.

The institution of *robia ţiganilor* (Gypsy slavery)was an important element of the feudal class structure in Wallachia and Moldavia. These principalities had a unique position since they had not been occupied by the Ottoman Empire like Bulgarian territories or what is present-day Dobrudja. Their relative autonomy generated massive additional labour requirements, which could only be met by the intensive exploitation of the local population by the Vlach and Moldavian princes. Similarly, in the Habsburg Empire during the era of Maria Teresa, agriculture and local industries also needed far more workers and supposedly unproductive Roma were forcibly settled to provide additional labour. To mark this change in status, they were renamed in German as *neu bauer* and in Romanian as *neo-rustic* (new peasant) or in Hungarian *új magyar* (new Hungarian). As in the Romanian principalities Roma were tied to land owners. Meanwhile the more technologically advanced and less labour-intensive economies of Western Europe allowed more opportunities for small groups to continue following a travelling way of life. However these mobile bands were far less numerous than the Roma populations of Central and Eastern Europe[9] and the basis of their nomadic life style was that they were peripheral, if not redundant, to the wider economy. In Western Europe they were tolerated as people who were often on the move and they are the ancestors of today's *Gens du voyage*, *nomadi* and *Travellers*. However the travelling populations in these countries also have non-Roma groups....

Connection to Land as Compulsory Integration

Many examples from the times of *robia* and the deportation form part of a history of victimisation. A neglected aspect of such a history is that Roma actually managed to survive such experiences and this gave them a distinctive sense of identity. Therefore, if we characterise Roma solely by the image of a nomadic life, the experience of *robia*—which lasted for centuries—was quite the opposite. For generations these people worked as agricultural labourers, just like ordinary peasants. Their social and economic integration was derived from their social status *as* slaves. Through this institution, Roma became part and parcel of their local societies and economies, even if only in a marginal and inferior position. After the abolition of slavery they continued living in their local communities but as inhabitants, which was a step towards becoming citizens of modern Romania—even without owning land. Not all Roma groups were involved in agricultural work and some were traders. However, they retained cultural, economic and religious links to their local societies. Roma fought in both world wars—as did my grandfather in the first and my father in the second—and some were even given land in the post-war land reforms. In this way Roma were gradually integrated as part of Romanian society and in many cases eventually assimilated into today's Romanian nation.

The trajectory of the social status of these Roma could be understood as a process that developed from a necessary connection to land, as *compulsory integration*. They did not lack a relationship to land, as such—as suggested in the concept of nomads—but rather a relationship to land as *patrimony* that can be owned and inherited over generations. In this sense there are long-settled Roma communities all over the Balkans, in Central and Eastern Europe and in Spain. However, this relationship is hardly unique to Roma since it is the common condition of the agricultural proletariat throughout Europe and beyond. These people were selling their labour wherever it was needed, while still experiencing emotional attachment to their land and territory. I share this sense of belonging with many other Roma in Europe. My argument is that one consequence of Roma subordination is that we have a level of integration and assimilation which has made us part of our societies, justifying our claim for full rights as citizens in the contemporary sense of the word.

The experience of those generations of Roma who worked during and after slavery and later throughout the twentieth century—including the decades of Communism—is proof that they, like other people, can be factory or agricultural workers and not just service providers. Their history demonstrates that Roma can be productive in economic terms. However their fate depends largely on the state of economy and contemporary social structures, as well as their ability to integrate as citizens. Instead of labelling Roma as 'eternal nomads', it is more accurate to say that they have the capacity to be flexible workers. Whether their way of life is nomadic or settled largely depends on economic, social and historical circumstances. The same people who were regular workers during the Communist era often became migrants after 1989, simply because altered economic conditions in Eastern Europe had made them redundant. Indeed such people were just as likely to travel abroad as their non-Roma fellow citizens, who also migrated to Western Europe for employment.[10] The concept of nomadism as an explanatory factor has been used mainly to refer to some tens of thousands of Roma in France and Italy, often living in squalor. However, such insanitary conditions have nothing to do with 'nomadism' but, as with many non-Roma migrants, are the inevitable outcome of being forced to live in severely overcrowded accommodation or densely packed camp sites.

[...]

Endnotes

1. The content of this text had been worked out in the interviews and discussions I had with Nicolae Gheorghe in Bucharest and Salerno during 2009–2010. It also includes certain fragments from his previous writings, notes and speeches that he delivered to various audiences. Throughout the process of editing I was following his suggestions regarding the structure of the argument. (Gergő Pulay)
2. As could be seen, criminality amongst some groups of Roma was often a topic of extended political discussions in countries such as Hungary, particularly during local or national electoral campaigns.
3. Uses of this ideology were not limited to Fascist Germany since it also provided conceptual grounds for action by the Vichy-government in France and wartime deportations in Romania.
4. Organisations such as Helsinki Watch and other US NGOs, among others, were some of the main players in this field.
5. See: Acton, Thomas & Gheorghe, Nicolae (1999): Dealing with Multiculturality: Minority, Ethnic, National and Human Rights, In *The Patrin Web Journal*,... <http://reocities.com/Paris/5121/multiculturality.htm>
6. I regard this as valid for both the direct and metaphorical senses of the concept 'nomad'.
7. The historical account presented here is based on the following paper: Gheorghe, Nicolae (1983): The origin of Roma's slavery in the Romanian principalities, In *Roma*, 7 (1): 12–27.
8. The institution of slavery did not exist anywhere else in nineteenth century Europe; slavery was practiced only in times of war and on an individual basis, even in the Ottoman Empire.
9. Although in Romania a significant part of the Roma population maintained a travelling life style up till the 1950s and 60s.
10. In recent years an estimated 3–4 million Romanians sought work in Western European countries. However distinctive characteristics make Roma migrants more visible than others, such as whole families with children travelling together.

***Nicolae Gheorghe** was a leading advocate for Roma issues—before and after 1989—up until his death on August 8, 2013. He sought to base Roma identity on a public praxis, rooted in human and civic rights, as well as on a reshaped Romani cultural code. In 1993 he founded the influential Romani CRISS NGO in Romania and from 1999 was the first contact point and subsequently, until 2006, the first adviser for Roma and Sinti Issues at the OSCE Office for Democratic Institutions and Human Rights (ODIHR).

Gheorghe, Nicolae (in collaboration with Gergő Pulay). "Choices to Be Made and Prices to Be Paid: Potential Roles and Consequences in Roma Activism and Policy-Making" (extract). In *From Victimhood to Citizenship: The Path of Roma Integration—a Debate*, edited by Will Guy, 43–58. Budapest: Kossuth Publishing Corp./Pakiv European Roma Fund, 2013.

The publication was supported by the Open Society Foundations and the Freudenberg Stiftung.

Used by permission.

Is There Any Point in Dialogue with Extremists?

*by Gwendolyn Albert**

Nicolae Gheorghe argued in his paper[1] that controversial or criminal(ised) enterprises such as begging, forced marriage, and human trafficking have become grist to ultra-right mills because of Romani silence on these issues. I applaud all efforts to eradicate all practices that violate human rights; however, I dispute the notion that Romani silence is to blame for these issues being exploited by the ultra-right. The ultra-right in Europe is not interested in dialogue with the objects of their contempt, and operates on a level that is 99% fantasy. In the Czech Republic, for example, completely groundless rumors are regularly spread at local and national level of Roma receiving some sort of special advantages, usually financial, that simply do not exist. Granted, begging, forced marriage, and human trafficking are not myths, but the ultra-right would never be interested in what Romani people have to say about these topics or anything else—and they are not serious interlocutors on any topic to do with human rights in any event, by virtue of their own inhumane and racist politics.

***Gwendolyn Albert** is a non-Roma Romani rights advocate who has been writing and translating articles for the past seventeen years for the Czech Roma media and educational nongovernmental organization ROMEA. She is currently coauthoring a book on Roma issues with Jack Greenberg (see Part 5: Postscript).

Albert, Gwendolyn. "Is There Any Point in Dialogue with Extremists?" In *From Victimhood to Citizenship: The Path of Roma Integration—A Debate*, edited by Will Guy, 169. Budapest: Kossuth Publishing Corp./Pakiv European Roma Fund, 2013.

1 Gheorghe, Nicolae, "Choices to Be Made and Prices to Be Paid: Potential Roles and Consequences in Roma Activism and Policy-Making" [see extract in this volume], in *From Victimhood to Citizenship: The Path of Roma Integration—A Debate*, ed. Will Guy, 41–99 (Budapest: Kossuth Publishing, 2013).

Open Letter to the Non-Extremist Anti-Romani Demonstrators in the Czech Republic

*by the ROMEA Association**

To Whom It May Concern:

We are turning to you with questions to which we ourselves do not know the answers. We hope to be able to reflect on these questions together with you, without mutual recriminations and constructively, if possible, in the interest of understanding one another and helping to resolve these matters without maligning one another.

In the discussions posted beneath our articles about the anti-Romani demonstrations in Rumburk and Varnsdorf in the fall of 2011, as well as our articles about such events this year in České Budějovice and Duchcov, the opinion has been expressed that news server Romea.cz tars all anti-Roma demonstrators with the same brush and labels them either neo-Nazis or racists. This is, of course, a mistaken impression. We do not believe any such thing and we have always been careful to distinguish in our reporting between the various kinds of people who are demonstrating.

We condemn the generalizations that are made about Romani people from all corners of this society, and that is why we do our best to avoid generalizing ourselves. That does not mean we are always successful, at least from the perspective of others, but we are holding a discussion inside the ROMEA association about this and are really, honestly trying to do our best.

We have spoken with many of you who have demonstrated against Romani people in various towns around the country, and we have learned that among you are people who are friends with (some) Roma in your daily lives. We have also learned that some of you are frustrated by the deteriorating social situation in the country—for example, you may have been without work yourselves for some time. Of course, we have also run into the racists and xenophobes who have led these protests of hate against the Romani ethnicity as a whole.

There is a difference between how people behave in their everyday lives and how they behave during these demonstrations. In Břeclav, České Budějovice, Duchcov, Krupka, Nový Bydžov, Rumburk and Varnsdorf (or at least during one demonstration there), some of you have marched side by side with extremists—nationalist chauvinists, Nazis, racists and xenophobes.

In Varnsdorf, you marched on the Sport residential hotel, where the extremists kicked off a street conflict and then retreated while the rest of you bore the brunt of the police intervention. Maybe you learned from that and refused to allow extremists on the podium at your subsequent protests.

In other places, of course, it's been different—not only were you not ashamed to participate in an action together with extremists, some of you even accommodated them, whether you were aware of it or not. These are people who are known for the ideological motivation of their primitive behavior and violence, and many are recidivists (and not just of this kind of crime).

A large number of these extremists do not work, they are often less educated, and their behavior shows signs of aggression and sociopathological tendencies. They criticize minorities and Romani people for being what they are themselves, to a large degree: Troubled, uneducated, and unemployed.

These people are exploiting you for their own aims and purposes. They are manipulating your dissatisfaction with what is going on in our country. They are manipulating you also because everything to do with coexistence—ghettos, social housing, unemployment, etc.—has long gone unresolved here.

The extremists do not offer any solutions. They offer conflict, hatred that leads to brutal aggression against anyone and everyone (e.g., against police officers).

In the final analysis, the police interventions in these places cost an immense amount of money which the police could be using instead to beef up everyday patrols to keep citizens safe. The municipalities could be using that money to finance platforms where all citizens could meet, irrespective of their differences, to talk with one another and enjoy some shared experiences. Maybe you have the feeling that no one but the extremists is interested in your problems, but do you realize where this all might lead?

In Rumburk and other places, you have shouted racist slogans together with the extremists and heard them call for violence against other people. The same thing played itself out in Duchcov, where two neo-Nazis organized an anti-Romani action that subsequently openly praised the murder of Romani people.

In České Budějovice, you chanted the racist cry of "black swine" on the square against Romani people. Then you marched with the neo-Nazis who were giving the Nazi salute along the way (shouting "Heil Hitler" and raising their right arms in the Nazi salute), and you shouted other racist slogans.

In all of these cases, the situation risked growing into physical violence against Romani people. It was aimed at all Romani people, because the collective blame you are ascribing to them, in combination with the psychosis of the mob, commands you to make no distinctions among those you have chosen as your target.

We want to ask the following questions and attempt a constructive dialogue with you. We will be very glad to hear your responses:

We understand that you are bothered by problems with some people, some of whom are Romani. What can we do together to get those responsible for resolving these problems to take real action?

What exactly is bothering you, and where, specifically? Please describe your specific problems—we won't get anywhere by making generalizations and we will only be playing into the hands of extremists by making them.

Do you believe it is possible to prevent individuals—any individual, whether from the majority society or the minority—from committing violence against others? Can any man, for example, the President of the Czech Republic, prevent another man from brutally beating and raping a woman? Can any woman, for example, Mother Teresa, keep a woman from murdering her own child? Most Romani people do not approve of the actions of specific wrong-doers who share their nationality, but are unable to stop them.

We can discuss whether and why impoverished Romani people from the ghettos are, to a greater degree than is customary in society, uneducated, unemployed, and unqualified. We can also discuss how these people have to square up to the problems that a culture of poverty causes. We can seek solutions together, but not hatred or revenge against an entire minority.

We are forgetting our history. What do the horrors of Nazism and World War II, which the Nazis unleashed, mean to you today?

Are these "problems with the Roma" that are causing you to demonstrate less acceptable to you than the methods the Nazis once used against members of the Czech nation?

Some of you say you have had bad personal experiences with Romani people. Were those experiences with all Romani people, or just with some of them? Are you really only protesting about your own bad experiences? Do the fabrications, lies, prejudices and stereotypes making the rounds on the internet play any role in your decision?

Wouldn't it be more reasonable to do your best to resolve these problems with coexistence peacefully, for example, by patiently negotiating with local Romani authorities, through community work, by helping to tutor children, etc.?

In your view, is it better to resolve coexistence problems through street protests? What result are you expecting? Do you believe the Romani people will pack up and move away? If you approve of expelling other people this way, do you call that a method for "resolving problems"? How else will these street protests contribute to genuinely resolving coexistence problems, can you describe how?

Are you willing to use violence against your Roman neighbors? Imagine the following situation, please: You and some extremists break into your neighbors' apartment and a frightened family is crouching in the corner. What will you do, will you participate in mistreating those people?

Do you believe the extremists would not have attacked some Romani people recently even if the police had not blocked your marches? Do you believe the Roma would not have attempted to defend their families against attack?

Do you realize that it was by proclaiming the principle of collective blame that the Nazis *de facto* began the Holocaust?

You are marching with extremists, and very often you are shouting racist slogans with them.

You are marching with extremists, and it doesn't bother you that they are calling for violence, committing violence against police officers, or that violence against Romani people might result. You are not bothered by Nazi salutes or any other manifestations of extremism... Or are you? Why haven't you distanced yourselves from the extremists?

You are not extremists, but have you thought about what you are endorsing and what you really want in this context? Can you achieve it by marching with the extremists?

We are interested in your constructive proposals for resolving these situations. We will try to review them and find an answer or a partner in your particular area to discuss these matters with you.

František Kostlán
Jarmila Balážová
Zdeněk Ryšavý
František Bikár
Renáta Berkyová
Jitka Votavová
Jana Baudyšová
Petra Zahradníková

the ROMEA civic association

*The **ROMEA Association** is a Roma media and educational nongovernmental organization based in the Czech Republic.

"Open Letter to the Non-Extremist Anti-Romani Demonstrators in the Czech Republic."

Translated by Gwendolyn Albert. From the ROMEA website, July 9, 2013. http://www.romea.cz/en/news/czech/romea-association-s-open-letter-to-the-non-extremist-anti-romani-demonstrators-in-the-czech-republic.

Used by permission.

Why I Quit

*by Valeriu Nicolae**

Systemic Reasons

The main focus of most of the important donors, governments and intergovernmental organisations when it comes to the Roma inclusion field is to find positive practices and replicate such positive practices.

Although at first glance finding positive practices seems like a good idea, looking for such positive practices is actually a poor idea considering the systemic failure at all levels to properly address Roma inclusion. This approach does nothing but halt or slow the much needed reform that every single expert with hands-on or academic experience in Roma issues agrees is needed. It provides reasons to continue feeding a profoundly delusional concept of progress, encourages sugarcoating and keeps happy incompetent and clueless people in high-level positions that will continue to take absurd decisions regarding Roma social inclusion.

The successful implementation of a Roma social inclusion project is more likely to be a fairy-tale based on a fake report than a real success. Success does happen, but it is exceptional/accidental, and occurs far more often in spite of existing policies and lines of funding, than because of them.

Overall, EU funding for Roma social inclusion is a failure. There is no disagreement about the failure, the only discussion is about how big the failure is. Opinions of practitioners in the field range from catastrophic to limited.

Funders need to focus on examining the mistakes and reforming the systems in such a way that real success, and not rationalized or imagined achievements are the main results.

The situation of small Roma NGOs that work at the grassroots level, and should be at the core of reform in the Roma communities, needs to become a serious reason of concern. Here are some of the reasons why.

Begging is tiresome and degrading, as work. Sometimes it is an elaborate and grotesque con that involves important amounts of money. More often it is a sad but logical choice for people with no other alternatives or skills to scrape up enough money to survive.

We feel disgusted, ashamed, sometimes guilty, and rarely positively impressed by beggars. Their begging lines are often crude and their servility is off-putting.

We are educated to believe that there are criminal gangs behind beggars that make huge money out of it. Most of the time this is not the case.

Begging is also the way most NGOs survive. The process is more elaborate than begging on the street, but the principles are the same. It is terribly degrading for those who have to do it due to their convictions and honesty, and rather productive for those who cheat.

For NGOs, some obvious reasons make begging the rational choice: unequal relations, a widespread practice of rewarding lip-service, insufficient and poorly designed funding, and corruption.

NGO–donor relationships are in the overwhelming majority of cases unequal, as donors have the resources that NGOs want and need. I am not aware of any major donor in Roma inclusion that tries to identify grassroots NGOs that have had an impact within the communities, or have developed some innovative and successful practices, and offer these NGOs funds. The overwhelming majority of the donors behave arrogantly in their relationships with NGOs: the NGOs have to come to the donors with their requests and do their utmost to please them.

Donors can very easily impose their agendas; very few NGOs will dare to openly criticize wrong funding policies of the donors. Submissiveness towards the donor is a much more pragmatic approach than criticism.

From the lowest rank to the highest official of the donor institution, criticism is a problem. It looks bad and could negatively reflect on the careers of the bureaucrats dealing with funding NGOs.

For an NGO, taking a critical view towards the policies of the donors is more of a suicidal than a smart approach. Donor institutions have a defensive reaction when dealing with critical organisations, even if the criticism is one hundred per cent justified. Medium and deep hierarchies, as are the main donors in Europe, will prefer to protect their employees and their image, and most often will end up deciding to choose a "nicer" organisation for the funding.

People in decision-making positions prefer friendly organisations to efficient but critical organisations. The competition for funding is tough; many organisations apply for the same line of funding. Those responsible for selecting the winning bids are more influenced by their personal likes or dislikes, rather than the quality of the proposed project.

As project-writing for EU-funded projects is nowadays a major business, most of the projects look more or less the same and in many cases have a rather remote connection with the capacities of the implementing NGO. Decisions made by bureaucrats in Brussels—who have no clue about what those organisations really do aside from reports (usually heavily embellished)—are as good as a lottery.

The North-American and Western-European ideas about the functions and responsibilities of civil society organisations are great, but simply inaccurate in the case of Eastern Europe, and almost ridiculous in the case of Roma civil society.

Incentives for cheating are much stronger than incentives for complying to rules that make little sense anyway. Corruption is rampant, as is fake reporting. There are not many choices available out there. The EU funds are badly designed and rather dangerous for any NGO that chooses honesty against pragmatism. Most of the other funding available is short-term projects. Most available projects do not include institutional support, or require a serious co-funding component (20%). There are many costs that are impossible to cover from the lines of the financed projects, and legislation regulating employment and activities of NGOs is still changing constantly. All lead to extra costs for the NGOs.

The way to cover these costs is either through shameless cheating, "creative accounting," or by trying to find other private financial resources. For most NGOs, but in particular for Roma NGOs, this is an almost impossible feat.

In the case of the organisation I led, the way I covered our needs, and the unavoidable mistakes made during the last five years, was through investing a significant amount of my own money, and constant begging (from private businesses).

I was fortunate to be able to do this, but this is not a sustainable model. In most other NGOs, costs are covered illegally (multiple reporting) or at the edge of legality (see previous articles I published on funding).[i]

Abysmal Image and Quality of Roma Leadership

Roma leaders are perceived as corrupt and overwhelmingly inept. Sometimes this is the truth. Exceptions do exist, but those people are almost never as visible as the others. Nepotism is rampant and conflicts of interests are more the rule than the exception when it comes to most of the existing Roma political or civil society organisations. Examples of Roma NGOs that do not employ the near relatives of key staff members are exceptional. Most of the small Roma NGOs that work at the grassroots level are in fact small and unsustainable family businesses.

The European Structural Funds have made an important contribution to the worsening of this situation. The huge amounts of money available through the Structural Funds has led to a profoundly corrupt political elite at the national and local level, creating an almost perfect situation for criminals and crooks

i [Ed. Note] For example, *Manufacturing Realities*, January 2013, http://valeriucnicolae.wordpress.com/2013/01/28/manufacturing-realities/.

to be very much involved in the EU funded projects. In the case of EU funded projects for Roma communities the situation is worse due to the already strong stereotypes associating Roma identity with criminality.

Roma communities expect either to be bribed (for political gains) or to receive all kinds of free services from what they perceive to be very rich NGOs using money given by the European Union for Roma. Cases where Roma communities accuse NGOs of stealing "their money" (money communities believe should have been given directly to them) are not exceptional.

There are situations where very poor and very traditional Roma communities (the target, at least on paper, of many EU projects) are controlled or led by criminals. Those leaders will not hesitate to threaten Roma NGOs and try to extort money from them. Sometimes successfully.

Personal Reasons

For the last five years I led (arguably) one of the most successful small Roma NGOs in Romania. We work in a ghetto in Ferentari. We won some very important prizes in 2012 as recognition for our work—including the 2012 UNICEF award for best Sports and Education project. Close to half a thousand officials from all over Europe have visited our centre and congratulated us for what we have done. We have met with Tony Blair, the UN High Commissioner for Human Rights, OSCE High Commissioner for Minorities, Human Rights Commissioner of the Council of Europe, Prime Ministers, Commissioners, the Romanian President, Ministers of Foreign Affairs, Ambassadors, and world-known personalities. We managed to get private money from non-Roma businesses that helped hundreds of children in one of the most despised areas of Bucharest. Most of those children are Roma. UEFA, Unicredit, Metro, the Romanian Football Federation, and Brentag are just some of those businesses. There are also tens of individuals who fund us and volunteer their time as they believe in what we do. It sounds like one of the miraculous stories the donors should love. We are proud of our achievements in the last years. For two years in a row, I have been nominated among the top 100 Romanians by Foreign Policy Romania for my work with this NGO. A life of honours is much better than one of cattle would be the Aristotelian way to look at it.

But there is also another part.

Constant and humiliating begging for funds, significant amounts of money coming from my own pocket (more than half my household income) in order to bridge the gaps that funding can not cover, including many mistakes. Dealing with threats from drug dealers and other criminals, the impossibility to attract well-qualified staff and to financially motivate existing staff (nobody in the organisation has a salary over 500 EUR per month at this moment), dealing with dramatic changes in the policies of donors and in legislation, extremely stressful situations involving abandoned and abused children, lice, drug addictions, theft, child prostitution, police abuses, children hungry, hugely underdeveloped with HIV or at huge risks of HIV, incompetent or indifferent local authorities.

Having the tires of my car slashed, windshield smashed, having to deal with aggressive alcoholic or addicted parents who couldn't care less about their children or what we do, dealing with emergency rooms and racist doctors, under pressure to shut up and not talk about what goes wrong within the Roma civil society or with the EU funds. Thousands of hate mails for my stands against racism in the stadiums in Romania, constant idiotic rumours about my origins, motivations and private life. Having to listen to people that have no experience whatsoever on the matter about how we should do things and pretend to agree in order to be able to move a tiny bit forward.

Knowing the solutions and being unable to find the ways to persuade people in decision-making positions to listen or to care to change their comfortable but delusional view of the problems in the ghetto. Dealing with the pressure of having to bail-out the organisation with my own savings over and over again due to all kind of bureaucratic delays. Sometimes we received the grants with a delay of over 6 months. Having to deal with the whims and moods of too many people, careful not to burn bridges. Constantly having my skills doubted or being perceived as too emotional or exceptional because of being a Roma. Being too cold and calculated for not being Roma enough. Pretending not to see the institutional racism all around in order to get enough support within those institutions and change things on long term.

Realization that in the large picture what we do is irrelevant as long as we can not change policies, that we are used for image purposes, and some of the professional donors that financed us could not care less what we do with their money as long as the reports look fancy and their name is on the posters; that hard-work and passion is not going to put us in the position to influence anything, and that corruption, lip-service and criminality are much more effective ways to move things.

Tell me I am wrong. Tell me that in fact it is good to lead an NGO in an honest way with all the risks involved. Tell me that there are good reasons why I should carry on. And then think if you would do it.

There are many other frustrations—so many that despite the fact that I abhor quitting, I took the decision to step out from leading the executive position in the NGO I created.

This does not mean I am quitting the ghetto—I still think I can change things there.

*__Valeriu Nicolae__ is a Romanian Roma activist and is a cofounder of the nongovernmental organization the European Roma Policy Coalition. He has worked as a senior consultant for the Open Society Institute and is advocacy adviser for the European Roma Grassroots Organization.

Nicolae, Valeriu. "Why I Quit." *wordpress.com*, February 12, 2013. http://valeriucnicolae.wordpress.com/2013/02/12/why-i-quit/12.

QUESTIONS FOR DEBATE

Almost one in five Roma throughout the EU consider themselves to have been a victim of a "racially motivated" hate crime (assault or threat, or serious harassment) over a twelve-month period. In the Czech Republic this figure was almost one in three. Many crimes are unreported and unprosecuted and, therefore, remain invisible.

- How can hate crimes be made more visible? What difficulties are involved?
- Why are many reported crimes not prosecuted? What can be done about this?

Some activists believe granting minority rights to Roma would improve their situation. Others disagree arguing instead that their rights as citizens should be strengthened.

- Does non-territorial autonomy as in Hungary strengthen the position of Roma?
- Should projects be aimed specifically at Roma communities or is it preferable to target impoverished areas including non-Roma among the beneficiaries?

Many Roma are proud of their distinct culture but others claim that some "traditional" customs (e.g., early marriage and child labour) clash with basic human rights.

- How might such disagreements be resolved?
- Can public discussion of problematic customs provoke a backlash?
- Is it worth the risk? Is it morally defensible to ignore such 'traditions'?

According to remarkably consistent opinion polls a majority of the general public seem to have passively sympathised with anti-Roma attacks.

- How can such people be reached and persuaded?
- Are there better ways than appealing for public debate?
- In what ways can extremist parties be countered most effectively?

Roma NGOs often last for only a relatively short period. In any case they are rarely consulted about policies and projects intended to benefit Roma. Many that survive have been transformed from advocates into service providers delivering social and other assistance to Roma communities.

- Why are many Roma organisations short-lived? How might this be altered?
- How can Roma representation in decision-making bodies be increased? Quotas?
- Need becoming service providers always be a change for the worse?

Part 5:

Postscript

What Is to Be Done?

*by Jack Greenberg**

The European Union must take seriously the importance of swiftly bringing an end to Roma school segregation. It has exacted promises from newly-admitted members of its community, pledging that they will prohibit segregation. To fulfill such pledges will require energetic, proactive, unambiguous insistence on newly admitted nations fulfilling their obligations. Some steps may be easy; others difficult. Enforcement may require tough, controversial political measures. But, it should be clear that nations which continue to operate segregated schools cannot fulfill their treaty obligation to desegregate simply by passing authority on to municipalities and washing their hands of it, perhaps following up with only conferences and rhetoric.[1] If the nations of the Union fail to act, the results will be the continuation of a slow squandering of Roma lives and loss of treasure and humanity for all who live in Eastern Europe.

School segregation is but one factor which maintains Roma in their diminished status. Roma must achieve parity with non-Roma in employment, housing, health, and civil rights generally. But education is the most important of these, particularly because it can lead to the others.

To act effectively, Europe first needs information: Where do Roma live, where do they go to school, what is the ethnicity of students in their schools and nearby schools, how are they and non-Roma distributed among classrooms? Because lack of information about ethnicity, which is concealed from view by national laws and practices, is an impediment to protecting Roma effectively, the European Union should establish an Inspectorate General charged with the task of identifying and describing discrimination and segregation as well as where it exists. This Inspectorate General should be adequately staffed and funded and given the charge of identifying segregation across nations and within schools. National laws which prohibit gathering such information, which were adopted for good reason long ago, should be ignored or overridden by higher European law.

Where segregation exists, it should cease immediately. Municipalities must furnish transportation to facilitate desegregation and supply funds to make it possible. That should not be the obligation of NGOs which often pay for it. For as long as necessary, schools must supply mentors or other aides to assist children and their families during the transition. Desegregation must be treated systemically, not school by school. Desegregation may not be thwarted by white flight. Therefore, orders may also be entered to prevent schools from taking in non-Roma who flee desegregation. This would include not only public schools, but private and religious schools.

National chief law enforcement officers should treat segregation as a grave violation of law and give priority to proceedings aimed at ending it. While it has been debated whether any agency or court, including the European Court of Human Rights, now has power to issue an order (comparable to an injunction) that would require officials in charge of a public school to end segregation, no such order ever has been issued. The European Union should take steps, legislatively or otherwise, to make possible issuance of enforceable orders to make meaningful Article 13 of the European Convention of Human Rights which assures that "[e]veryone whose rights and freedoms as set forth in this Convention are violated shall have an effective remedy before a national authority."

Private litigation to require desegregation should be encouraged and government funding made available to facilitate it. While official enforcement is often preferable, private litigation is not so susceptible to political manipulation or frustration. Most of the school segregation litigation in Eastern Europe so far has been privately funded and directed. While litigation has not yet produced enforced court orders, it does focus public attention. Nathan Margold, who wrote the planning paper that suggested the litigation campaign which led to *Brown v. Board of Education* perceived that "[its] psychological effect upon Negroes themselves will be that of stirring the spirit of revolt among them."[2] That might be true in Europe. One of the most important lessons for the Roma in the American civil rights movement is that a vibrant civil rights movement would be a highly important addition to the quest for Roma rights.

There must be preschool available for all Roma children, and all Roma children should enroll. Children who do not attend preschool start primary grades at a disadvantage and cluster among the least accomplished children in their classes—a form of de facto intraschool segregation, which continues through their school years. A World Bank program designed to promote preschool among all children in Bulgaria is in the offing. If it does not materialize, the same end must be advanced some other way throughout Eastern Europe. Such a program should alleviate financial obstacles (for transportation, meals, school-suitable clothing, and the like), the greatest deterrent to Roma enrollment. Recognizing that some Roma families resist sending their children to school at a very early age, there must be an outreach program to impress upon them the importance of preschool. It should allay Roma concerns about loss of cultural identity.

One final step is vital, something that the Roma themselves, and not the European community, must do. The Roma must make clear, and do so forcefully, that they cannot continue to tolerate subordination. After centuries of subjugation, including slavery, second-class citizenship, ethnic cleansing, oppression under communism, and stigmatization in the modern world, the Roma must launch a movement to claim their freedom. The Roma must take steps to cast off their shackles.

These are stern demands, but Europe has dithered long enough with one of the gravest humanitarian and economic crises of our time.

Endnotes

(Notes have been renumbered for this edition.)

1. Particular thanks to Lilla Farkas concerning the crucial role of municipalities.
2. Mark V. Tushnet, NAACP's Strategy Against Segregated Education 1925–1950, at 15 (1987) (citing Committee Report, May 28, 1930, NAACP Papers, I-C-196).

*__Jack Greenberg__ is the former director-counsel of the NAACP Legal Defense and Educational Fund, who for more than thirty-five years there helped litigate some of the most important cases of the civil rights struggle, including *Brown v. Board of Education*, the landmark school integration case in the United States. He is currently coauthoring a book on Roma issues with Gwendolyn Albert (see Part 4: Anti-Gypsyism).

Greenberg, Jack. "Report on Roma Education Today: From Slavery to Segregation and Beyond" (extract). *Columbia Law Review* 110, no. 4 (May 2010): 999–1001.

QUESTIONS FOR DEBATE

The combination of sustained activism and challenges in the courts was eventually successful in making educational segregation illegal in the United States. In practice, de facto residential segregation still exists in many places. Also life chances, as measured in terms of employment levels, educational qualifications, housing conditions, and health indicators, are significantly worse for many black, Hispanic, and immigrant communities.

- Is legal action against discrimination sufficient in itself?
- What other steps can be taken to combat educational and residential segregation?

Appendixes

Appendix 1: The 10 Common Basic Principles on Roma Inclusion[i]

Principle no 1: Constructive, pragmatic and non-discriminatory policies

Policies aiming at the inclusion of Roma people respect and realise the core values of the European Union, which include human rights and dignity, non-discrimination and equality of opportunity as well as economic development. Roma inclusion policies are integrated with mainstream policies, particularly in the fields of education, employment, social affairs, housing, health and security. The aim of these policies is to provide the Roma with effective access to equal opportunities in Member State societies.

Principle no 2: Explicit but not exclusive targeting

Explicit but not exclusive targeting of the Roma is essential for inclusion policy initiatives It implies focusing on Roma people as a target group but not to the exclusion of other people who share similar socio-economic circumstances. This approach does not separate Roma focused interventions from broader policy initiatives. In addition, where relevant, consideration must be given to the likely impact of broader policies and decisions on the social inclusion of Roma people.

Principle no 3: Inter-cultural approach

There is a need for an inter-cultural approach which involves Roma people together with people from different ethnic backgrounds. Essential for effective communication and policy, inter-cultural learning and skills deserve to be promoted alongside combating prejudices and stereotypes.

Principle no 4: Aiming for the mainstream

All inclusion policies aim to insert the Roma in the mainstream of society (mainstream educational institutions, mainstream jobs, and mainstream housing). Where partially or entirely segregated education or housing still exist, Roma inclusion policies must aim to overcome this legacy. The development of artificial and separate "Roma" labour markets is to be avoided.

i [Ed. note] The Ten Common Basic Principles for Roma Inclusion are still the cornerstone of European initiatives in this area and are intended as guidance for both policymakers and practitioners. They were produced by the European Commission in 2009 with the help of Martin Kovats and Valeriu Nicolae, both contributors to this volume.

Principle no 5: Awareness of the gender dimension

Roma inclusion policy initiatives need to take account of the needs and circumstances of Roma women. They address issues such as multiple discrimination and problems of access to health care and child support, but also domestic violence and exploitation.

Principle no 6: Transfer of evidence-based policies

It is essential that Member States learn from their own experiences of developing Roma inclusion initiatives and share their experiences with other Member States. It is recognized that the development, implementation and monitoring of Roma inclusion policies requires a good base of regularly collected socio-economic data. Where relevant, the examples and experiences of social inclusion policies concerning other vulnerable groups, both from inside and from outside the EU, are also taken into account.

Principle no 7: Use of Community instruments

In the development and implementation of their policies aiming at Roma inclusion, it is crucial that the Member States make full use of Community instruments, including legal instruments (Race Equality Directive, Framework Decision on Racism and Xenophobia), financial instruments (European Social Fund, European Regional Development Fund, European Agricultural Fund for Rural Development, Instrument for Pre-Accession Assistance) and coordination instruments (Open Methods of Coordination). Member States must ensure that use of financial instruments accords with these Common Basic Principles, and make use of the expertise within the European Commission, in respect of the evaluation of policies and projects. Peer review and the transfer of good practices are also facilitated on the expert level by EURoma (European Network on Social Inclusion and Roma under the Structural Funds).

Principle no 8: Involvement of regional and local authorities

Member States need to design, develop, implement and evaluate Roma inclusion policy initiatives in close cooperation with regional and local authorities. These authorities play a key role in the practical implementation of policies.

Principle no 9: Involvement of civil society

Member States also need to design, develop, implement and evaluate Roma inclusion policy initiatives in close cooperation with civil society actors such as non-governmental organisations, social partners and academics/researchers. The involvement of civil society is recognised as vital both for the mobilisation of expertise and the dissemination of knowledge required to develop public debate and accountability throughout the policy process.

Principle no 10: Active participation of the Roma

The effectiveness of policies is enhanced with the involvement of Roma people at every stage of the process. Roma involvement must take place at both national and European levels through the input of expertise from Roma experts and civil servants, as well as by consultation with a range of Roma stakeholders in the design, implementation and evaluation of policy initiatives. It is of vital importance that inclusion policies are based on openness and transparency and tackle difficult or taboo subjects in an appropriate and effective manner. Support for the full participation of Roma people in public life, stimulation of their active citizenship and development of their human resources are also essential.

European Commission. *What Works for Roma Inclusion in the EU: Policies and Model Approaches* (Luxembourg: European Commission, 2012), annex 1, 56–57. http://ec.europa.eu/justice/discrimination/files/whatworksfor_romainclusion_en.pdf.

This republication of the Ten Common Basic Principles is by permission.

Appendix 2: Anti-Discrimination and Equal Opportunities

Anti-discrimination alone is insufficient a means for achieving substantial equality. While legislation is necessary, it is not sufficient. Therefore, it should be complemented by equal opportunity policies. The new EU legislation[i] does not address this specific need, but is certainly no objection to it. It will be in the last instance to each European country according to its specific tradition to develop equality of opportunities policies. Although there clearly is a mutual necessity of anti-discrimination and equal opportunity policy, it is important to stress their distinctiveness. *Anti-discrimination* aims to prohibit certain behaviours directly or indirectly generating discrimination, whereas *equal opportunities* is aimed at facilitating increased involvement of vulnerable groups by removing obstacles to the rewarding of merit.

Generally speaking, equal opportunities policies are implemented on a voluntary basis. There are only few countries in Europe (includes the UK since recently) where public authorities have imposed a positive duty to implement aspects of equal opportunity policies. There is a very broad range of policies falling under the heading of equal opportunities. These include policies aimed at improving the employability of vulnerable groups, policies aimed at increasing their representation within the workforce of private companies and public organisations by setting targets, or policies aimed at imposing non-discrimination indirectly through contract compliance.

[...]

Bousetta, Hassan, and Tariq Modood, eds. *Anti-Discrimination Good Practice Guide* (extract). Bristol, UK: Eurocities Anti-discrimination Exchange (EADE), 2001: 20. http://www.tariqmodood.com/uploads/1/2/3/9/12392325/anti_discrimination.pdf.

i [Ed. note] Article 13 of the 1997 Amsterdam Treaty authorized the European Council "to take appropriate action to combat discrimination based on sex, racial or ethnic origin, religion or belief, disability, age or sexual orientation."